Beyond the Century of the Child

Beyond the Century of the Child

Cultural History and Developmental Psychology

EDITED BY WILLEM KOOPS
AND MICHAEL ZUCKERMAN

PENN

University of Pennsylvania Press

Philadelphia

10 9 8 7 6 5 4 3 2 1

Published by
University of Pennsylvania Press
Philadelphia, Pennsylvania 19104-4011

Library of Congress Cataloging-in-Publication Data
Beyond the century of the child : cultural history and developmental psychology /
edited by Willem Koops and Michael Zuckerman.
     p. cm.
   Includes bibliographical references and index.
   ISBN 0-8122-3704-8 (cloth : alk. paper)
   1. Children—History. 2. Child development—History. 3. Developmental
psychology. I. Koops, W. (Willem) II. Zuckerman, Michael, 1939–
HQ767.87 .B49   2003
305.23'09—dc21   2002075057

Contents

The Child in Developmental Psychology and Pedagogy

Preface

William James tried unavailingly to warn them. From the modern birth of their discipline in the last decades of the nineteenth century, psychologists have aspired to study human behavior according to the norms of science. Most took physics for their model. Some, such as the developmental psychologists, took biology. But even the developmental psychologists idealized the quest for universal laws and aimed to devise theories as timeless as possible.

Classic studies in developmental psychology, such as Lewis Terman's *Study of Gifted Californians* (1925; Oden 1968) and August Hollingshead's *Elmtown's Youth* (1949), did not even collect, let alone take into account, data linked to experiences of war or economic collapse. Neither did the well-known trio of longitudinal studies: the Berkeley Growth Study, Berkeley Guidance Study, and Oakland Growth Study (Eichorn et al. 1981; Elder, Modell, and Park 1993). Neither did the investigations of the next generation, which were predicated on the same scientistic premises and the same disdain for the historical dimension.

It was not until Glen Elder's brilliant *Children of the Great Depression* (1974) that the crucial impact of economic hardship and military mobilization received its first theoretical elaboration. But in recent years he and an increasing contingent of his followers have produced a succession of revelatory studies of the connections between large historical developments and the development of individuals across the life course. The most influential of their works may be their 1993 collection, *Children in Time and Place* (Elder, Modell, and Park 1993).

That collection demonstrated convincingly that cooperation between historians and developmental psychologists was not only possible but also productive. It addressed old problems in new ways, posed new problems, and advanced innovative solutions to both the old problems and the new ones. Mike Zuckerman participated in the conference that produced the collection and wrote the historians' concluding chapter for it. His position was a bit more radical than that of the other participants. As Willem Koops pointed out in a review of the book (Koops 1996), the agreements achieved by the historians and developmental psychologists in *Children in Time and Place* were facilitated by the confinement of their collaboration to subjects and issues of the twentieth century for which there was abundant evidence and a fair continuity of conditions between the scholars and their subjects.

What would happen, Koops wondered, if historians and developmentalists attempted to examine worlds for which we did not have such extensive empirical evidence? What would happen if they tried to study worlds very different from their own? It was precisely these questions on which Zuckerman had insisted in his concluding essay, arguing that "if the historical contribution were authentic, it would endanger the analytic assumptions of the other disciplines and lead to questions and conclusions none had foreseen or even suspected" (Zuckerman 1993b, 232). History, he had said, allows us "an intimation of worlds unlike our own," whereas developmental psychology presumed "that social relations today may be safely projected onto the past." If that presumption could not be sustained, the very foundations of developmental psychology would be imperiled, as Bill Kessen, who wrote the psychologists' concluding chapter for the collection, had already suggested. In an earlier work Kessen had proposed that the modern child and the very idea of child development are cultural constructions and that developmental psychology itself is "a peculiar invention that moves with the tidal sweeps of the larger culture" (Kessen 1979, 262).

In 1996 Koops was invited by the Netherlands Institute for Advanced Study in the Humanities and Social Sciences (NIAS), an institute of the Royal Netherlands Academy of Arts and Sciences, to form an international group of scholars to spend a year in the interdisciplinary study of the history of childhood. Koops immediately discussed the project with Zuckerman, and they agreed to devote the academic year 1997–98 to the project, with a distinguished international team of colleagues: Gerrit Breeuwsma (developmental psychologist at Groningen University), Els Kloek (social historian at Utrecht University), Hideo Kojima (developmental psychologist and educationalist at Nagoya University), and Micha de Winter (pedagogue and educationalist at Utrecht University). All these men and women managed to free themselves for a full academic year to cooperate with us at NIAS in Wassenaar. Together they formed the NIAS research theme group in Historical Developmental Psychology, a dynamic group that found high intellectual excitement—and a lot of fun—in each other's company.

One of the goals of the group was the composition of a book on the history of the changing relationships between children and adults in the twentieth century. Koops proposed that we take for our title for the project "Are We at the End of the Century of the Child?" His idea was to take up where *Children in Time and Place* left off, by going back to much earlier periods of time and indeed to worlds very much "unlike our own." We would have studies of the Western Middle Ages and Renaissance, the Dutch Golden Age, colonial America, and Victorian England. More even than that, we would have studies—studies sweeping over many centuries—of China and Japan.

At least at the outset, the issues that concerned us were very much those we took from the source of the modern history of childhood: Philippe Ariès's *Centuries of Childhood* (1960, 1962). And the most tantalizing of those issues danced around Ariès's idea of the infantilization of the child.

The concept of infantilization embodied the transformation that *Centuries of Childhood* traced. It epitomized the process by which children in early modern Europe began to be set apart from adults and set symbolically—and in some measure actually—in a world of their own. It specified that world as one of spontaneity and irresponsibility in which children were at once protected and permitted liberty to gratify their youthful desires (as adults understood those desires). The imagination and establishment of that special world for children is at the heart of Ariès's "historical change hypothesis" (Koops and Elder 1996; Koops 1996), that since the late Middle Ages there has been a continuous increase in childishness in the cultural representation of children.

Few would deny that the infantilization Ariès described has had a host of beneficial consequences for children. It brought an end to the worst abuses of child labor in the West. It promoted a multitude of other measures to protect the young from exploitation, abuse, and neglect. Its ramifications have grown so extensive that we have come to call the twentieth century "the century of the child," implicitly or explicitly referring to the book of that title written by Ellen Key in 1900 (Key 1900, 1909).

But careful study of Key's work—and of the work of the contemporaneous Child Study Movement—suggests that our improved understanding of the needs of the child has not been wholly beneficial to children or to society. Children have been pushed so far away from the adult world that it has become difficult for them to find the way back. On the inspiration of Rousseau, of Piaget, and of modern developmental psychology itself, children have been understood as developing nonadults. Their sentimental value has grown to unprecedented heights (Zelizer 1981). And we who have accorded them such sentimental value have become convinced that we should not disturb their "natural" development too much. We even incline toward foisting a culture of their own on children and adolescents and allowing commerce to exploit this culture.

The principal question that this book addresses is the question whether we have exaggerated the childishness of our children and thereby infantilized them excessively. Careful analyses of evidence for and against the historical change hypothesis from several places and periods from the fifteenth to the twentieth centuries are put forward by specialists in social history. Consequences for and linkages with child development, pedagogy, and policy are treated by developmental psychologists, pedagogues, and historians. And on the basis of these investigations, balanced conclusions are drawn to the new question that has evolved among us: Are we *beyond* the century of the child?

To begin the work of this book in earnest, we convened a conference at NIAS, in Wassenaar, the Netherlands, in February 1998. We invited more than a dozen distinguished scholars from Europe and America to join the members of the research theme group for what turned out to be an occasion of extraordinary interdisciplinary exchange. Our authors presented drafts for discussion, the rest of us responded, and through it all we found our way to a common frame of reference. After the conference, the authors very carefully accommodated the suggestions that emerged from those remarkable conversations.

We, as organizers of the conference and editors of the book, are most grateful for the cooperation we have enjoyed from every one of our authors. We are no less grateful for the cooperation we enjoyed from every other participant in the conference at NIAS. Their contributions do not appear directly in this book, but they were of foundational value for us all. These treasured colleagues are Urie Bronfenbrenner, developmental psychologist at Cornell University; Judith Semon Dubas, developmental psychologist at the Catholic University, Nijmegen; Paul Jungbluth, educationalist at the Catholic University, Nijmegen; Joseph Kett, historian at the University of Virginia; Christelle Miller, developmental psychologist at the University of Minnesota; Anne Petersen, Senior Vice President for Programs at the W. K. Kellogg Foundation; and Maris Vinovskis, historian at the University of Michigan.[1]

The conference and the book would not have been possible without the support of the Rector of NIAS, Henk Wesseling, Executive Director Wouter Hugenholtz, Secretary Jos Hooghuis, and their staff. The conference and the book would not have been as satisfying to us as they turned out to be without the sage advice of Glen H. Elder, Jr., Howard W. Odum Distinguished Professor of Sociology and professor of psychology at the University of North Carolina, and John Modell, educator, developmental psychologist, and sociologist at Brown University.

We are also most grateful for financial support from the following institutions: the Netherlands Institute for Advanced Study in the Humanities and Social Sciences (NIAS); the Royal Netherlands Academy of Arts and Sciences; the Institute for the Study of Education and Development (ISED), Leiden; the United States Information Service (USIS); and the Barra Foundation.

Finally, we are delighted to acknowledge our gratitude to Eric Halpern, director of the University of Pennsylvania Press, for his expert and supportive editing, and to Alison Anderson, managing editor, for her astute handling of the manuscript. We couldn't have asked for more.

Chapter 1
Imaging Childhood

Willem Koops

The issues that arise concerning children, in both daily life and in a number of scientific disciplines, are characterized by an overwhelming multiplicity. Children, their behaviors, their experiences, and their relationships to other people do not comprise easy-to-identify empirical realities that quickly reveal their structures and functions or their regularities and laws. Children are rather what we adults choose to see and what we have made of them in our cultural history and society. The child seems to be primarily a product of our imagination. This is what Kessen (1979) meant with his critical essay "The American Child and Other Cultural Inventions." We are imaging childhood.

I will illustrate this statement with a short cultural history of the child. My exercise will, I hope, leave the reader with the firm impression that our image of childhood varies throughout history. My historical outing will bring a problem to light, one that comes down to the fact that we have based our upbringing and schooling on an image of childhood that is no longer appropriate. And this is why the demand for normative guidelines for upbringing and education, and the uncertainty about them, are greater than ever. And thus the need for scientific research on children is greater than ever.

In the universities, appreciation, funding, and administrative power lie more on the side of empirical science than on the side traditionally known as humanities. Perhaps partly because of this emphasis, many people currently tend to think that empirical knowledge can resolve our normative issues. Thus it is, I think, that many expect that empirical developmental psychology, my own field of expertise, with its description and explanation of the development of children and adolescents, can offer an orientation as to where we should direct upbringing and development. After my historical excursion, I will show that this is true to only a very limited extent. Normative issues cannot be solved empirically. Knowledge about the development of children does not automatically lead to determining the aim of the upbringing. Perhaps even worse, what we can discover empirically about children's development is not unrelated to what we, in a cultural historical sense, have decided to do with our children. To quote Kessen (1979, 262), "child psychology is itself a peculiar invention that moves with the tidal sweeps of the larger culture." On the other hand, we will only have a chance of liberation from the cultural constructions and imaginations through empirical-analytical knowledge. It is this complex interweaving of facts and norms, of givens and desires, that is the outstanding feature of child studies.

The Origin of the Modern Child

No image is so pliable as that of the child. Since the beginning of the 1960s there has been a separate academic subdiscipline concerned with the history of these pliable images, called the history of childhood. This subdiscipline is primarily inspired by the work of Philippe Ariès (1960, 1962) on the social history of the school and the family. His main work is today still driving academic historical research on ideas *about* children and their upbringing and development. Here I must resist the temptation to expand on Ariès's work and suffice with a brief summary with respect to what I consider his two main hypotheses: the discontinuity hypothesis and the change hypothesis (Koops 1996b, c).

The discontinuity hypothesis assumes that the child did not exist until after the Middle Ages. In medieval civilization there was a negligible difference between the worlds of children and of adults; as soon as the child was weaned, it was seen as the natural companion of the adult. Other historians have found little or no evidence to support this hypothesis. An important book in this connection is that of Hanawalt (1993), which shows that children in London in the fourteenth and fifteenth centuries did in many respects inhabit a world that was specifically for children, not adults. They played more than adults and in separate, safe places; they were part of age groups and had their own age-related social environment (Corsaro 1997). Even Ariès himself has admitted that his discontinuity hypothesis requires far-reaching modifications (Koops 1998).

The change hypothesis states that, from about the thirteenth century, there was a continuous increase in childishness in the cultural representations of children. For this continuous increase in childishness I will use the term "infantilization," that is, the increasing duration of the childhood stage (Van Dale 1995), which is necessarily accompanied by an increasing distance between the worlds of children and adults (Elias 1939; Plessner 1946; Koops 1998).[1] Much empirical historical support has been gathered for the change hypothesis (Koops

1998). Instead of going into the abundant and complex literature, I will illustrate Ariès's notion of the historical changes by referring to a series of paintings. Here you should know that, although Ariès did indeed use many types of historical material to support his change hypothesis, it is his interpretation of the child in the world of art that is most controversial. In the following I will briefly illustrate Ariès's interpretation of children in paintings and refute some of the most persistent academic arguments which so seriously criticize him precisely on this point.

The cultural historical process pointed to by Ariès in the change hypothesis can be illustrated well with the help of works of art. If we follow Ariès, we first see that in the tenth and eleventh centuries children were represented by painters only as miniature adults. Up to the end of the thirteenth century there are no depictions of children characterized by a special artistic representation, only images of men and women on a reduced scale. From the thirteenth century onward the Christ child is portrayed as increasingly childish, in combination with an increasingly motherly Mary. In the fifteenth and sixteenth centuries the genre paintings gradually arose, in which the child was apparently depicted because of his or her graceful or picturesque qualities. In the seventeenth century the modern child was, at last, fully represented in paintings. For the first time there were portraits of children on their own, an intense interest was shown in typical childish scenes (pictures of the reading room, the music lesson, the little child at play), and even family portraits were completely planned around the child.

Probably the most dramatic change in the attitude toward children occurred in the eighteenth century. Jean-Jacques Rousseau (1712–78) is generally seen as the troubadour of the new stance (Rousseau 1763). He encouraged mothers once again to care for their children instead of giving them to wetnurses, and there was a renewed appreciation of the value of breastfeeding. Perhaps we may even say that he instigated the fashion of tenderness toward children. This new Rousseauan attitude can be traced in many paintings on both sides of the English Channel. Beautiful examples are Jean-Baptiste Greuze's *La mère Bien-Aimée*, dating from 1769, and Sir Joshua Reynolds's *Lady Cockburn and Her Children* from 1773, two paintings with a striking abundance of motherliness (see Rosenblum 1988).

Several years ago I made the effort to study the empirical tenability of Ariès's assertions on children in paintings (see Koops 1996b). This was primarily to investigate the tenability of the most important argument *against* Ariès's proposed state of affairs, that his discussion of some tens of paintings (chosen from a population of millions of paintings) certainly cannot be called representative for Western paintings in general (as Ariès claims), and that for this reason alone it deserves to be designated as subjective and thus unscientific. Thanks to a careful as well as time-consuming inventory of Dutch and Flemish paintings that portray children, and thanks also to a careful sampling, we were able to have random samples of paintings rated by adult subjects.[2] For the methodology of our research I refer to the original paper (Koops 1996b). In essence we compared the painted images of children with the characteristics of "childish" mammals, as once described by the ethologist Konrad Lorenz (1971). We operationalized Ariès's change hypothesis so that the infantilization intended by him would mean that images of children in paintings became increasingly childish (according to the features in Lorenz's "Kindchenschema") from the thirteenth to the twentieth century. We simply calculated the correlation between the historic dates and the childishness-scores. The result supported the change hypothesis, which we had *not* expected. The correlation was 0.60, which indicates that paintings in the past emphasized childishness less than did modern paintings. This is a surprising and, I feel, important result, precisely because, contrary to all reasonable expectations, it does *not* refute Ariès's interpretation of the paintings. Even so, objections to this conclusion have been raised from three quarters.

1. In the earliest centuries it was mainly the Christ child who was painted, and that can be misleading on many counts.
2. Perhaps people started painting increasingly younger children in the course of the centuries and the determined correlation coefficient may therefore be biased.
3. Perhaps the result found has nothing to do with changing cultural representations of children but only with a changing painting technique, implying that artists were increasingly successful in reproducing childishness technically in an increasing realistic way.

The nice thing about empirical research is that one can now remove such opposition from the realm of "yes, it is / no, it isn't." In this case, we were able to demonstrate that:

1. If all the portraits of the Christ child are removed from the random samples, the recalculated correlation is *not* noticeably lower.
2. In the course of the centuries it appears, in fact, that *older* children were painted, so the reverse argument is in order: in later centuries increasingly older children were painted in an increasingly childish way, even more childish than younger children (by calendar age) of previous centuries.

3. Our data do not agree with the realism argument, that in the fifteenth and sixteenth centuries children were portrayed as more adultlike than was realistic, in the seventeenth and eighteenth centuries they were more realistically represented, and in the nineteenth and twentieth centuries children's images become exaggeratedly childish. In fact, in this last century one can say that there are what ethologists call "supernormal models"—completely unrealistic, exaggerated images of the original.

The only argument against our research is that it was a small-scale study that requires replication. I readily admit that. But no other empirical research into Ariès's hypothesis has ever been published, indicating that the usual arguments put forward against Ariès's analysis of paintings can be considered of little validity for the moment (see Koops 1996b).

This little exercise concerning the most controversial part of Ariès's influential original study shows that we certainly cannot discard his view on the infantilization of children as a fable.[3] I therefore consider it as important to study the history of pedagogy and developmental psychology, themselves cultural historical phenomena, from an Arièsian perspective, rather than from a naive Progressive view as has been the case for too long.[4] Instead of a gradual progression in our attitude toward children, supported by science, from this perspective there are culturally and historically changing images of children, of which scientific study is rather the result than the cause (see also Koops 1990b, 1992, 1996a, b, c, 1998).

The Oscillations in Pedagogy

Three important phases can be distinguished in the history of Western pedagogy: the source of modern thinking about children in the trio Montaigne, Locke, and Rousseau; the further development by the Philanthropists Johan Bernard Basedow (1723–90), C. G. Salzmann (1744–1811), and Johan Heinrich Campe (1746–1818), with the famous Johann Heinrich Pestalozzi (1746–1827) and Friedrich Froebel (1782–1852) as followers, as well as the disputed Johann Friedrich Herbart (1776–1841); and the "Vom Kinde aus" movement, which as "reform pedagogics" responded to Herbart and the Herbartians and thus recalled Rousseau and the Philanthropists. Representatives of this movement are Ellen Key (1849–1926) and school innovators like Georg Kerschensteiner (1854–1932), John Dewey (1859–1952), Ovide Decroly (1871–1932), and Edouard Claparède (1873–1940).

Michel de Montaigne (1533–92) is normally presented as the first thinker after the Middle Ages who proposed a "natural pedagogy." Under the influence of humanism he broke away from the classic intellectualism (Boyd 1968, 222ff). Children should not be filled with book wisdom but be able to form their own opinions (Pols 1997, 264). John Locke (1632–1704) with his too-well-known "tabula rasa" idea offered the appropriate epistemological background: the blank slate with which the child is born is filled with the impressions he or she acquires, which can be guided by the pedagogue (Locke 1693). Rousseau comes as the culmination of the Enlightened treatment of the child: he thought that natural, age-related development determined *how* the impressions of Locke were received by the child, which forced the pedagogue to show even more humility with respect to nature than Montaigne and Locke realized.[5] Rousseau proposed that pedagogy should be child-directed and that there are age-related phases to which pedagogy should be attuned (Rousseau 1763). Rousseau's ideas were adopted wholeheartedly by the German pedagogical movement known as the Philanthropists.

The word "Philanthropists" in the history of pedagogy refers to a group of German pedagogues which in some way or another were allied to a model school set up by Basedow in Dessau, which was also a teacher training college called the Philanthropinum. Philanthropists combined the spirit of the Enlightenment with the pedagogic influence of Rousseau. Basedow wanted literally to reform education and upbringing according to his reading of Rousseau's *Emile*. According to him, it was important that everything take place at the right time: "zur rechten Zeit, nicht zu spät und nicht zu früh für die Bildung des Verstandes und des Herzens"("at the right time, not too late and not too early for the formation of the intellect and the heart"; quoted by van der Velde 1974). In addition, the Philanthropists encouraged pupils' self-activity and paid much attention to the motivational side of learning. In this respect there was the typical saying of the Philanthropists: "Nicht viel, aber mit Lust" ("Not much, but with pleasure").

The Philanthropists smoothed the way for the influential pedagogue Pestalozzi and for what in the historical pedagogical literature was called the "Vom Kinde aus" movement ("from the child itself"; Gläser 1920). In Pestalozzi's pedagogy the core of this Rousseauan view can easily be traced: "the view that the child is by nature good and that its creative power can be put to improving the world" (Imelman and Meijer 1986, 32). The Vom Kinde aus is expressed succinctly in the following citation from Pestalozzi: "Alles was du bist, alles was du willst, alles was du sollst, geht von dir selber aus" ("Everything you are, everything you want, everything you should, comes from yourself"; van der Velde 1967, 39).

The pedagogical optimism of the "Kindergarten Saint" Froebel (this typing comes from Ligthart; see Prins 1963, 203) was expressed in his ideas on the "nachgehende Erziehung" (the "following" pedagogy). Froebel thought that upbringing should limit itself to "actions which are aimed at guiding (spontaneous) psychological developments as appropriately as possible" (Imelman and Meijer 1986, 264). This all took place in the schools for small children specially founded by Froebel, the so-called *Kindergarten* ("children's garden"), a name that was adopted by the Americans and is still in use today.

One of the most influential pupils of Pestalozzi was Herbart. The scientific study of pedagogy gained its shape in the nineteenth century particularly through his work. It was he who linked practical philosophy—that is, ethics, which was what constituted pedagogy up to that time—with empirical psychology (Depaepe 1998, 121ff). As never before, pedagogy acquired its form as means-goal doctrine, as had been outlined by Immanuel Kant (1724–1804), the great Enlightenment philosopher and admirer of Rousseau. Kant wanted, with the help of ethics, to gain insight into the finality of human development, and the means to reach that goal had to be found in the empirical sciences (see Depaepe 1998). For this means Herbart filled in psychology, and we can say that it has remained so since then, although modern psychology is not exactly the same psychology that Herbart had in mind, of course.

The core of Herbart's scientific pedagogy is summarized in the following statement: "Pedagogy as a science depends on ethics and psychology. The first provides the aim of pedagogy; the latter shows us the way, the means and the obstacles."[6] He wanted the pedagogue to have *empirical* knowledge of people, based on "quiet, unprejudiced observations which should be complemented with self-observation (*Selbstbeobachtung*)" (Strasser and Monshouwer 1967, 71). Herbart, for the first time in the history of pedagogy, clearly described how the normative (ethical, moral, and theological) view could be intertwined with data from experience (psychology, possibly also sociology, pediatric medicine, child psychiatry, anthropology, and history) (Strasser and Monshouwer 1967, 78).

What particularly occupied Herbart with regard to educational practice, and what he did successfully, was develop didactics based on developmental psychological theory. Taking into account the state of insight into cognitive development at his time, Herbart developed didactic strategies with great energy and creativity. He laid the foundation of what in our time has been called instruction technology. He developed a system of steps according to which the child must acquire and master knowledge. According to this technique of formal learning steps, a lesson proceeds following "the classic scheme of motivation, creating clarity, association with the known, synthesis and application" (Depaepe 1998, 123). Even without going into the details, we can see that this scheme is modern in several ways. Herbart thought he could generalize such a system over all learning content, and that makes him the first real didactician. Once again, modern instruction technology has its roots in Herbart's work.

Unfortunately Herbart's followers managed his legacy with less successful results. They reduced his good intentions to "docile, patriotic character formation through scholastic curricula" (Depaepe 1998, 122).[7] They took the flexibility of his concepts and thinking schemes to deform his "theory" in such a way that the concepts "could function as justification for the increasingly scholastic attitudes in public life." And in the history of pedagogy it became common to use the concept of Herbartianism to condemn Herbart as "the founder of the passive intellectualistic listening school" (123). Herbart himself was very unjustly treated by this condemnation. Take, for example, Herbart's concept *Reproduktion*, which in his psychology meant nothing more nor less than reproducing a previously formed representation. In the didactics of his followers this concept was trivialized to reproduction by the pupil of what the teacher taught, simplistic repetition of what had been done already. Second, the account Herbart took of the empirical differences between age groups (see Strasser and Monshouwer 1967, 76, 100) was largely ignored by the later Herbartians. Finally, although many passages worthy of consideration about motivation could be found in Herbart's work, his followers had no appreciation for the didactic and educational importance of motivation. And thus by 1900 Herbart's legacy had indeed become one of "docile, patriotic character formation through scholastic curricula."

It was this end result that provoked the antithetic reaction of the reform pedagogics. The term "reform pedagogics" refers to many progressive educational movements from educational thinkers like Kerschensteiner, Dewey, Decroly, and Claparède and well-known promoters of sectarian school innovative movements like Rudolf Steiner (1861–1925) of the so-called Steiner Waldorf school, Maria Montessori (1870–1952) of the Montessori school, Peter Petersen (1884–1952) of the Jena Plan school, and Helen Parkhurst (1887–1973) of the Dalton school (for an overview, see Imelman and Meijer 1986). It is remarkable that this reform pedagogics, which created the impression of implementing a *reform*, in fact simply continued the Rousseau-Pestalozzi tradition. I thus firmly agree with Jürgen Oelkers's (1996) analysis, which showed that the reform pedagogics is characterized by *conti-*

nuity, not *dis*continuity.[8] Oelkers determined that the reform pedagogics movement simply continued making society increasingly scholastic, that its program was derived from the Enlightenment, and that its so-called innovative "child-directedness" could be simply traced to Montaigne, Rousseau, the Philanthropists, and Pestalozzi (see Depaepe 1988, 134). I would only add that it could also be traced to Herbart, although the reform pedagogues would not acknowledge this because the Herbartians were useful as starting blocks.[9]

In summary, we can state that the history of pedagogy itself is an aspect of infantilization, as it has taken shape since Ariès inspired the historical description of childhood.[10] Perhaps we should also state that pedagogy has played a *prominent* role in this development. Since Rousseau, the child has come to be seen as a developing creature, that in profound respects is completely different from an adult and that must therefore undergo a long developmental process before it can be equated with adults. Under the influence of the shaping and institutionalizing of upbringing and education by the Philanthropists and Pestalozzi respectively, children were put into a separate children's world on an increasingly large scale (public education!), indeed, into a protected world, a kindergarten as Fröbel would have said, in which their spontaneous development could be given optimal opportunities. Is all this now Progress, a continuing Progress supported by sciences such as pedagogy and developmental psychology, that helps bridge the gulf between children and adults?

In my opinion the history of infantilization is much more complicated than a process of unidimensional Progress. In this respect the remarkable development in the nineteenth century that I have just sketched is interesting. It began with Pestalozzi's Rousseauan influence, which emphatically and explicitly wanted to take into consideration the spontaneous development of the child. One wanted to emancipate the child, liberate it from a far too adultomorphic intellectualistic upbringing. But after Pestalozzi's ideas were institutionalized in public education, particularly in Prussia, education became increasingly formalized and ritualized, especially due to Herbart's followers, the fiercely criticized Herbartians. The careful tuning to what one thought one knew about children's developing competencies was, as it were, done too carefully and in too much detail, and was therefore criticized as restricting spontaneity, as limiting the spontaneously developing opportunities of the child, as infantilization. And in the "Vom Kinde aus" movement and the reform pedagogy at the end of the nineteenth century there was a renewed call for following natural development, a call to emancipation. It is my opinion that such a swing—from emancipation to infantilization and back—is perhaps necessarily doomed to continuous repetition.[11] And where is the swing now, in our times?

The Disappearing Child

According to Jan Hendrik van den Berg (1977) children participated in daily life up to about 1700 and between 1700 and1900 were increasingly separated from it. In the twentieth century children slowly but surely returned to the adult world. This movement came from two sides, according to van den Berg. On the one hand adults themselves have become "victims of the process that infantilized the child" (van den Berg 1971), because technology has "removed adults' responsibility" and because "the belief in Progress has vanished" (1977, 167). Adults have "abolished the establishment and thus also the distance between child and adult." On the other hand, children are more important than ever, as important as reform pedagogue Ellen Key was longing for in her bestselling book *The Century of the Child*, where she wrote:

Fathers and mothers must bow their heads in the dust before the exalted nature of the child. Until they see that the word "child" is only another expression for the conception of majesty; until they feel that it is the future which in the form of a child sleeps in their arms, and history which plays at their feet, they will not understand that they have as little power or right to prescribe laws for this new being as they possess the power or right to lay down paths for the stars." (Key 1909, 181)

This call for emancipation left its traces in the twentieth century.[12]

One finds the same approach to adults and children in the twentieth century described by the pedagogue Lea Dasberg, who is much quoted in the Netherlands.[13] Adulthood is no longer attractive since the belief in progress has disappeared. Instead of the longing "When I grow up . . ." there is now a kind of "youth-sentiment," that is, "the nostalgic reminiscing at a young age about the just finished period of puberty and adolescence" (Dasberg 1975, 16).

As a consequence of the new conciliation between adults and children, classic adolescence, as a turbulent transition period between childhood and adulthood, largely disappeared in the second half of the twentieth century. Thus van den Berg came to see the noisy adolescence of the 1950s and 1960s (mods and rockers, the "beat generation," "counter-culture," pop culture; see van den Berg 1977, 160ff) as the last spasms of adolescence, which has since been disappearing rapidly as there is no longer any gulf to cross into adulthood. Ariès made the interesting observation that in our time everyone tries to remain in adolescence as long as possible. "Thus our society has passed from a period which was ignorant of adolescence to a period in which adolescence is the favorite age. We now want to come to it early and linger in it as long as possible" (Ariès 1962, 30). I too have brought regular attention to the fact that the classic image of adolescence as a period of "Sturm und Drang" (as the German Romantics would have it"), or of "normative turmoil" and "oscillations and oppositions" (as developmental psychology and pedagogy would have it since the publication of Hall's classic book (1904) about adolescence) has had its day (Koops 1996a).[14] Today's adolescents have little need to claim an adult position by rebellious behavior; therefore empirically there has been little or nothing left of the traditional generation gap. The classic features of adolescence, such as being unmarried, experimenting with intimate relationships, and being a subject of education, belong just as much to adulthood (Koops, 1990a, c). Most authors put a positive value on this new reconciliation between adults and children. However, Gielis (1995) has shown that there also are certainly negative symptoms. He makes a link between the new "respect for authority vacuum" in the family and the phenomenon he calls "home terrorism" as seen in the form of "battered parents, a new syndrome" (Harbin and Madden 1979). It is estimated that 10–15 percent of adolescents in the United States behave violently toward their parents (Gielis 1995, 96).

The situation now looks rather uneasy. Historically we have set children increasingly further apart from adults; now traditional adulthood is disappearing and it is no longer easy to imagine how children can be drawn into adulthood. There is an excess of "spontaneous development" but a poverty of pedagogic measures to attract children into the adult world. Perhaps the trend will automatically reverse itself, but such optimism could be misplaced. A developmental jump has taken place that is entirely new: the accessibility in every way of everyone, including children, to the fully adult-like mass media.

The first author to identify a fundamental link between the concept of childhood and the mass media was Neil Postman (1992). Following closely on Ariès he pointed out that in a nonliterate world it is not necessary to make a sharp distinction between children and adults. "The concept of 'childhood' had not been required, for everyone shared the same information environment. It was in fact the art of printing books which created a new world of symbols, which in turn required a new concept of 'adulthood.' Adulthood had to be learned. It became a symbolic, not a biological, achievement" (Postman 1992, 36). "School was an institution which had to ensure that children became literate adults. John Locke's metaphor of the mind as 'tabula' depicts precisely the connection between childhood and print: the child as an inadequately written book, advancing toward maturity as the pages are filled "(60). The concept of the child enjoyed its finest hour, in fact its finest century, between 1850 and 1950. A maximal infantilization took place in this period. From then on, since the childless period began, the concept of the child has gone downhill. According to Postman, telegraphy started a process that made information uncontrollable and freed it from parental control. And this development was reinforced "by an uninterrupted flow of invention: the rotary press, the camera, the telephone, the phonograph, the movies, the radio, television" (72). Postman felt that television in particular destroyed the boundary between children and adults: supported by other electronic media that do not depend on the written word, television recreates the conditions of communication of the fourteenth and fifteenth centuries. In the new media climate everything is accessible to everyone at the same time: "electric media find it impossible to withhold any secrets" and "without secrets, of course, there can be no such thing as childhood" (80).[15] Postman's book can be summarized succinctly with the help of the cover text: "The basic line of this book—that our electronic level of information is causing the child to disappear—can also be rephrased as follows: an electronic level of information is causing adults to disappear." And thus this analysis progresses in a natural sequence from those of Ariès, van den Berg, and Dasberg.

In the meantime, we have some real problems. We are no longer concerned with swings between infantilization and emancipation, children in the classic sense of the word do not seem to exist any more, and adulthood has become unclear. This a new and very problematic situation. The title of Stephen Kline's (1995) book, *Out of the Garden: Toys, TV, and Children's Culture in the Age of Marketing*, summarizes this nicely. Our children have been taken out of the garden of innocence, as it were, and transferred to "game-, television-, and computer rooms, in which they can amuse themselves with video games and the Internet" (Depaepe 1998, 226). The problem is that we have developed no pedagogy other than that dating from the time of Froebel, when a separate niche was created for children ("Kindergarten" has a symbolic value here) and it was thought children could only be brought up by keeping them small, as powerfully expressed by Dasberg (1975) in the title of her book (*Grootbrengen door kleinhouden*; "Upbringing by Keeping Down"). We put children in a physically and morally safe environment, and by a multitude of protective measures we tried to channel and to optimize their spontaneous development. But the abrupt delivery of the child to the uncensored mass media with their accompanying coarseness, pornography, murders, and killings ended the world of children unnoticed and ensured that adults lost control of their children's upbringing. Children who are traditionally protected from the world of adult responsibilities but have uncontrolled and unlimited access to the mass media are no longer children but valueless pocket-size adults.

The Contribution of Developmental Psychology

How can we bring up modern children to adulthood? What way do we have to travel to reach it? How much infantilization do we want for the over-emancipated twenty-first-century child? In the first instance, one would think that developmental psychology has much to offer concerning insights into adulthood and the developmental processes leading to adulthood. The empirical analytical character of developmental psychology means, however, that it must limit itself to description rather than prescription. The empirically based description of development offers insight and footholds, but cannot determine what is desirable, what we ought to do with our children. Empirical developmental psychology can, mainly thanks to clever experiments, discover possibilities but not desirabilities, what can be but not what ought to be. Empirical research can reveal pointers as to what we can do with our children, but what we *want* to do with our children and what we want for them is determined by our vision of the future, our vision of the ideal society and ideal relationships between people, our utopia. The child represents an intersection of tradition and the future and is thus a product of our imagination. But of course empirical reality imposes restraints on the imaginable, and these can be determined by empirical analytical scientific study.

Developmental psychology owes a lot to the work of Jean Piaget (1896–1980), the world-famous Swiss academic who was director of the Jean-Jacques Rousseau Institute for pedagogy and developmental psychology in Geneva. Piaget's influence on developmental psychology is comparable to that of founders of other professional fields such as Lorenz in ethology, Ariès in the history of children and the family, and—until recently—Freud in psychiatry. Such founders have introduced a theoretical view and related research methodology that have subsequently determined the core of a scientific (sub)discipline. That does not mean to say that everyone within the discipline follows the founder—just as many will be extremely critical—but nonetheless they will all owe him much.

Piaget drew up a theory of development that was in essence similar to that of Rousseau. The issues he raised, nearly 200 years after Rousseau, based on empirical analytical study of cognitive development in children, were in fact not much more than an expansion of what Rousseau had postulated about children while sitting in his armchair. But note: Rousseau based his theoretical conceptions on artistic-literary imagination that had nothing to do with empirical-analytical research in the modern sense of the word. Neither were they based on everyday observations of children, since in his personal life children hardly appeared other than in the form of unwanted babies. How is it possible that the famous Piaget, with the help of a lifetime of scientific study, identified a course of development that was in principle already seen by Rousseau, who was ignorant of modern research tools? I suspect that the answer is simple and lies in what I have written above about the history of pedagogy. Rousseau's new, revolutionary, and emancipated view of children was realized, culturally constructed, by generations of pedagogues, educators, and parents. And Piaget, with the aid of empirical analytical tools, described and explained children's development in the form it had acquired in history. I am tempted to view this as a fine example of something Einstein is supposed to have said: "Imagination is more important than knowledge."

But if I should leave the matter here I would be doing an injustice to Piaget and to developmental psychology. The power of empirical analytical research methodology, if sufficiently radically pursued, exists in the power of yielding counterintuitive insights. A few remarks on the discoveries made in a hundred years of developmental psychological research will clarify what I mean.

Since Rousseau's *Emile* (1762) and Piaget's later work it has been normal to think that young children, when compared to adults, show many psychological shortcomings: "they cannot, for example, think in a formal operational way; they have their own way of thinking and experiencing things that is difficult for adults to access. It is therefore meaningless to consider them as equals when communicating" (Koops and Meerum Terwogt 1994, 27). And so classic developmental psychology, known as the Rousseau-Piaget tradition, is a theory of shortages: it indicates what children *cannot yet do* when contrasted with adults. Similarly to Rousseau, Piaget distinguished developmental phases with age-specific cognitive structures. Each structure is characterized by a specific idiosyncratic logic, or better pseudo-logic or pre-logic.

Piaget's "structural cognitive theory," which states that children in the subsequent phases have an essentially *different* cognitive structure (from beforehand or thereafter), was denounced as very problematic in the 1970s. This was because many researchers allowed themselves to be guided by a computer model proceeding from what was called an "information processing approach." Critical experimental research at that time clearly showed that children's mistakes in solving logical problems depend not on structural cognitive features as Piaget claimed, but on task features with which children have relatively little experience. Classic research by Peter Bryant (1974), for example, demonstrated this clearly for conservation, that is, children's lack of insight into the conservation of amounts under different display conditions. Research by Tom Trabasso (1977) showed it for transitive inference, which is a form of logical, syllogistic reasoning (see Koops and Hamel 1986; Verwey, Sijtsma, and Koops 1999). With Piaget's structural cognitive interpretations being discredited, many researchers competed to show that children are able to solve Piaget tasks at a much younger age than Piaget thought possible.[16] Eventually it was discovered that even very young children (babies) have at their disposal cognitive operations, symbolic representations, and complex motor patterns (see Koops 1992). This was all totally unsuspected since it did not fit with the Rousseau-Piaget tradition; it did not fit with the common imagination of childhood in our culture.

Thanks to this critical experimental research, which put Piaget's theoretical framework in a vulnerable or at least disputable position, the tacit consensus that in the Rousseau-Piaget tradition a thing like "natural development" has been described, or even determined empirically, could no longer be maintained. From current, what I would like to call neo-Piagetian,[17] research into the so-called "Child's Theory of Mind," which is the child's insight into the folk psychology of fellowmen, it has become clear that young children in principle have a naive psychological theory, with which they can understand fellow people's behavior and which makes them accessible, full partners in communication.[18] Children's structure of thinking about the behavior of fellow people is, from the outset, in essence not different from that of adults. Earlier I concluded that

the classic Rousseauian assumption that young children differ fundamentally from adults and that a natural course of development of about twelve years is needed for them to reach adulthood, is presently, more than ever, based on crumbling ground. Just as ethnologists came to see that primitive tribes were not simply reflecting "primitive" early phases of Western culture, it now appears that psychologists must conclude that young children have far more humanity in common with Western adults than has been assumed in the past two hundred years. (Koops 1992, 273)

The foregoing implies that descriptive research, such as Piaget's, runs the risk of providing a description of development as we have created it in our culture, or rather as we have "imagined" it, which is then interpreted as a necessary, "natural" course of development. The pedagogue Martinus Langeveld's (1950a, b, c) criticism of fifty years ago would seem justified. He called traditional developmental psychology, in which he was mainly referring to Piaget, "retrospective" and not "prospective" (1950c, 50). He wrote that the greatest danger of developmental psychology was "the tendency, a certain world conception, which must be considered as the developmental product of a long cultural historical production process, to assume it to be an end product of nature, resulting from a spontaneous psychological development" (1950a, 11). Thus psychological development acquired the character of "a mechanical dawning from the West European, natural scientific and naturalistic philosophical determined world-picture" (12). More recently this criticism was repeated, without explicitly referring to Langeveld, in a thesis by Gerrit Breeuwsma. Breeuwsma speaks of a retrospective conceptualizing by Piaget that he calls a "tamed" conceptualizing of development. It is "tamed" because the direction and goal of the progress are set (Breeuwsma 1993, 19).

I would like to state firmly that it is exactly this danger of the description of development which makes it unable to construct a goal for children's upbringing, as always so forcefully argued by Langeveld. The choice of an endpoint for development (the rational thinking of adults) led Piaget, as it were necessarily, to a phase theory, in which the child approached the rational thinking of adults in steps. And thus Piaget had to concentrate solely on what Breeuwsma called "rational functioning." The children's author Guus Kuijer has expressed this well: "The phases are a sort of series of locks that ensure that no drop of childishness by accident flows into adulthood" (Kuijer 1980, 15). The child can thus not become anything but a failing adult. It is deceptive that all this appears as "natural development" when it is actually based on a choice made by the researcher without further justification.

Second, it can be concluded from this little exercise that critical experimental research is apparently able to determine unsuspected and unimagined possibilities in children. Despite the Rousseau-Piaget tradition being strongly anchored in our culture, an amazing series of cognitive, social, and emotional skills have now been determined in often very young children, and the possibilities to influence development very early on have multiplied enormously. This is a reason for optimism but also a reason to think more than ever about what we want to do—what we should do—with our children. I emphasize once again that no empirical research at all, however clever and advanced, however well supported by modern information technology, can ever offer norms and values with respect to what we should want to do with our children.

Third, I would like to state, partly to put it into perspective, that it was in the 1970s in developmental psychology that the critical anti-Piaget experiments took place, and that this is also exactly the period in which children's access to the mass media (television) began to get out of control and in which the disappearance of traditional childhood was discussed in the more popular literature (see note 15). Although, out of love for my profession and from common optimism, I am tempted to believe in the radical, critical capacity of scientific experiment, it seems that some doubt about the autonomous power of science should also be mentioned. It cannot be entirely ruled out that the new view on the child that resulted from the research so critical of Piaget came about because our imagination of childishness in daily life was already changing in some respects, so that scientific researchers also started observing and searching with new eyes.

Conclusion

We can summarize the foregoing as follows. First, it was shown that, unlike the discontinuity hypothesis (in the Middle Ages children did not exist, thereafter they did), Ariès's change hypothesis *cannot* be refuted in the light of historical data; information from children portrayed in paintings was presented to support Ariès's hypothesis. The history of pedagogy, but also that of related scientific fields such as the relatively young developmental psychology and the even younger child psychiatry should also be studied in close connection to the cultural historical infantilization. Second, there seems to have been a swing evident in history: infantilization led in the second half of the nineteenth century to a rigid and scholastic approach to children, after which a reform movement arose in which the original starting points that provoked the infantilization were reinstated for the emancipation of the child. Finally, the fear was discussed that the modern child, mainly because of unlimited access to the mass media, can no longer be enticed away from its own infantilized world, since, on the one hand, access to the mass media leads to pseudo-adulthood and, on the other, adults too no longer accept the establishment and would rather identify with children than bring them up. There is thus a huge pedagogical problem: traditionally we allow children to grow up by putting them in a separate niche, a Kindergarten, but at the same time we no longer have any control over children's unlimited access to the stream of adult information from the mass media.

For a while there was hope that empirical developmental psychology would help us out of this impasse: empirical description of development would offer footholds for the desired direction for upbringing and development. But after further consideration we must conclude that traditional developmental psychology, with a prototype in Piaget's developmental theory, holds up its own empirical mirror of the Rousseau-Piaget tradition. Classic developmental psychology offers as a description of "natural development," something that is a cultural historical result of Western imagination of childhood. There is of course no compulsory reason to deduce desirable pedagogy or development from this, certainly not if we cannot expect traditional imagination to fit with the modern reality of childhood.

The conclusion is as painful as it is enlightening: our children will be and will remain necessarily and unavoidably the product of our imagination. No scientific feats will be able to change this. I call this painful because it removes the last remains of optimistic progressive thinking of positivism. I call it enlightening because it places the responsibility where it belongs: with us adults. And there is also some good news: scientific research can provide a wonderful stimulus in finding possible ways for development and upbringing and can also be a fantastic help in critical evaluation of what we do in view of the chosen aims. We will, to be brief, have to accept Herbart's scheme: the normative, ethical considerations will have to provide the aims; the empirical sciences will show us the way, the means and the obstacles.

This is how we came to the end of the century of the child, how we arrived beyond that century, and how we discovered a new millennium of imaging childhood stretching before us.

The History of Childhood

Chapter 2
The Child in the Middle Ages
and the Renaissance

Barbara A. Hanawalt

Medieval and renaissance historians have been part of the twentieth-century fashion for studying childhood, as Zuckerman points out in his conclusion to this volume. The first impulse to study children came from psychoanalysis and the general vogue of psychoanalytical history just after the mid-century. Interest in Freud and the appearance of Erik Erikson's *Young Man Luther* (1962) inspired new historical biographies that included childhood influences on great men's lives. Piaget also had a strong influence on historians, leading one historian, Charles Radding (1985), to describe the Middle Ages as growing through Piaget's developmental stages. Philippe Ariès's *Centuries of Childhood* (1960, 1962) and the development of social and cultural history in the 1970s moved the study of childhood away from the more introspective, individual approach toward a discussion of general child-rearing practices, including those of previously neglected historical subjects such as women, peasants, and workers. Koops's opening chapter to this volume characterizes Ariès's two main hypotheses as "discontinuity" and "change." Medieval and renaissance historians have for the most part argued for continuity. While not disagreeing that the "image" of childhood and the sentiment toward childhood qua childhood has changed over the centuries, the historians surveyed in this essay have been eager to refute Ariès's statement that the Middle Ages did not recognize a life stage of childhood.

The statement that has spurred medieval and renaissance historians to enter into intensive research on childhood was Ariès's argument that people in the Middle Ages and Renaissance did not recognize a particular life stage of childhood nor distinguish the teenage years from those of adults.

In medieval society the idea of childhood did not exist; this is not to suggest that children were neglected, forsaken, or despised. The idea of childhood is not to be confused with affection for children: it corresponds to an awareness of the particular nature of childhood, that particular nature which distinguishes the child from the adult, even the young adult. In medieval society this awareness was lacking. That is why, as soon as a child could live without the constant solicitude of his mother, his nanny or his cradle-rocker, he belonged to adult society. (Ariès 1962, 128)

On first encounter, medieval and renaissance scholars found Ariès's startling conclusions problematic because of his careless use of historical evidence. He drew primarily from sixteenth- and seventeenth-century writers such as Molière and Montaigne, reading their portrayals of childhood back into earlier periods (1962, 36). The medieval and renaissance evidence he did use was limited and did not accord with their knowledge of the same sources. Historians who work with the limited sources of earlier periods of history tend to be very careful about interpretations of sources, and Ariès's cavalier use of them led to the initial criticism.

Ariès's dismissal of a medieval concept of childhood ultimately led to a much more comprehensive consideration of the question. It inspired scholars to reexamine the sources they already knew, such as art, sermon literature and other church writings, poetry, ages-of-man literature, and advice books. It also pushed historians of the period to look for other sources on children and the parent-child relationship that they had not previously used, such as saints' miracles, coroners' inquests into accidental deaths, private letters and papers, and other social history sources. The research of the last forty years has provided a rich account of childrearing practices in the medieval and renaissance period, the sentimental attachment of parents to their children, the culturally defined period of adolescence and how it changed over the 1,500 years the first section of Ariès's book covered, and the ideas of childhood that people held in the Middle Ages and the Renaissance.

In this chapter I examine some of the empirical research that has been done on the history of childhood and speculate on why this material has not entered into the mainstream of either the historical study of childhood or related fields such as psychology, sociology, and education. The works I discuss indicate where Ariès misinterpreted medieval evidence and show the new types of evidence that historians have used to elucidate the history of childhood.

Early Proponents of Ariès's Views

Ariès's convenient dismissal of an idea of childhood during the Middle Ages and Renaissance served as a basis for historians of the early modern and modern history of the family to dismiss discussion of the earlier period. Ariès's thesis could be used to confirm their view that the medieval period was the "bad old days," as Edward Shorter (1975) put it, and that children suddenly became more important only in the early modern period. Lawrence Stone (1977) accepted these conclusions in his book on the family in 1500. What is immediately apparent about this first phase of historical interpretation of childhood is its inherent Whiggism; the experience of children in history was getting better and better from the dark times of the Middle Ages to our present glorification of childhood. In relying on Ariès's evidence for the Middle Ages, these historians subtly changed his more value-free assessment of changing ideas of childhood to one that made the modern idea the enlightened one.

Lloyd de Mause, taking a psychoanalytic approach to the history of childhood, is the most vehement Whig interpreter. In his introductory essay to *The History of Childhood* (1974a), he characterized the ancient world as "infanticidal," the period of the fourth to the thirteenth century as one given to "abandonment," and the era from the fourteenth to the seventeenth century as "ambivalent." Following the glorious progress of his chronological chart, the latter stages depict parenting as "intrusive" in the eighteenth century, "socializing" in the nineteenth, and "helping" in the twentieth (51–53).

In addition to the obviously Whiggish nature of these interpretations of childhood in history, medieval and renaissance historians have taken exception to the ways Shorter, Stone, and de Mause used their evidence. Variations of Ariès's flawed historical approach are even more apparent in the Whig historians of the family. Like Ariès, they sought to portray the indifference of people in the Middle Ages to the loss of children with quotes from Montaigne and Molière. None read medieval texts, and de Mause simply trusted to his own intuitions that the foundling hospitals of the seventeenth through the nineteenth century were typical of the Middle Ages (1974a, 29). Like Ariès, de Mause used artistic evidence on a completely random basis, depending on how particular representations of children fit with the thesis he was proving. The Whig historians of childhood spent little time on issues of social class and the effects it may have had on child rearing; they took evidence almost exclusively from elite sources including literature, letters, diaries, and fine art. In the most flagrant case, Hunt (1972) generalized about childhood from a medical account of the rearing of the heir apparent to the French throne—hardly a typical childhood. In common with Ariès, the Whig historians did not make gender differences in rearing of girls and boys part of their picture. Nor did they attend to national or local variations, though in this regard medieval and renaissance historians are only beginning to have sufficient information (Schultz 1995; Finucane 1997).

One of the most perceptive critics of Ariès and the Whig history of childhood has been Linda Pollock (1983, 1989). She pointed out that the extended-family model, which Ariès used to explain the integration of children into the adult world, simply did not describe the typical European family structure. She also observed that, because Ariès emphasized education, he did not investigate the period before the age of seven as a life stage or the training of those not entering educational systems (1983, 54–55). In general, she argued that historians who maintain the historical change hypothesis have not really investigated the conception that medieval people had of children and therefore do not know whether it was different from the modern concept. Her own works have drawn on letters and diaries that point to more continuity than change in the treatment of children by parents in early modern and modern England.

Despite its cavalier treatment of sources, the Whig hypothesis of historical change stimulated questions about childhood in the medieval and renaissance periods that engendered a number of studies of childhood, including my own. The questions these studies raised centered on whether people in the Middle Ages and the Renaissance had a concept and practice of treating children as children, whether people in these periods distinguished between childhood and adolescence, whether high child mortality meant that child deaths were emotionally neutral events for their parents, whether medieval and renaissance society had a culture of nurturing the young, and whether earlier positive sentiments toward children were the same as those of the twentieth century.

Did Medieval and Renaissance Society Recognize a Period of Childhood and Adolescence?

The area in which medieval and renaissance historians have done most of their research on childhood has been in proving that Ariès was wrong in concluding that people of those times did not recognize the life stages of childhood and adolescence. Ariès argued that medieval illustrations of children pictured them as little adults. He also held that the very language of the period did not use the term "adolescent" as we do, and that words such as "boy," "girl," and "child" were used in reference to persons of any age. His argument was that because people of the Middle Ages and Renaissance used the terms in such an all-inclusive way, they did not have a concept of childhood or adolescence. Ariès contended that by the age of seven children entered directly into the "great community of men." In short, the modern period invented the definitions of childhood and adolescence (1962, 18–32, 411).

Historians studying this period of childhood have argued against his thesis. They find that the two life stages of childhood and adolescence appear in learned medical and scientific texts, in literary works, and in the folk terminology of the period (Burrow 1988). European society had formal and informal mechanisms for marking the entry and exit of individuals as they passed through successive life stages. By the late Middle Ages Europe was preoccupied with rearing and educating children and youth for successful passage into the adult world. Advice manuals proliferated (Riddy 1996). City laws expanded to include young people (Hanawalt 1993, 89–107; Nicholas 1983, 110–13). Court records show youth appealing for clemency on the basis of their tender years. In England a youth who wanted to gain the hearing of an official couched his or her request in such terms as "I was but a child then" or "I was a youth and new to the city" or "being of tender years," so as to evoke a sentimental picture of helplessness in adult listeners (Hanawalt 1993, 6). In artistic works, children became a favorite topic and were represented with toys and dress appropriate to their age.

Among the historians who have contributed most to the study of visual and textual representations of medieval children are Pierre Riché and Danièle Alexandre-Bidon (1994). Their work shows that medieval writers were well aware of the life stage of childhood. Both literary and educational texts commented favorably on the games children played, on their obvious interest in their own bodies, and on their early attempts to walk and talk. Riché and Alexandre-Bidon also present visual imagery to confirm the textual evidence: pictures of children nursing, playing games, interacting with adults, and being disciplined. Unlike Koops, they did not look only at depictions of the Christ child or individual youths, but instead looked at children in miniatures, particularly in the margins. They also advanced artifactual evidence drawn from archaeology—dolls, toys, bowls and feeding tubes, cradles, and other objects—to confirm the pictorial representations. Children were swaddled or naked in their early years. They wore long, loose gowns as they grew older. And they wore the costumes of adults only when they entered into their teenage years.

Ariès did not peruse the large number of illustrations Riché and Alexandre-Bidon used, but he modified his views later when he saw more pictorial evidence (Alexandre-Bidon 1997). He continued to claim that portraits of children appeared only in the sixteenth century, but that argument is also difficult to sustain, since portraits of adults, even of kings and queens, were themselves a late medieval development. Even the Italian Renaissance portraits of the fifteenth century were something of an innovation. Was it simply a change in general taste rather than a change in attitudes toward children that dictated the new subject for art?

In an earlier work Alexandre-Bidon and Monique Closson (1985) did extensive research into archival texts as well as published ones that mention childhood. These texts discussed all aspects of childhood from conception of the child to death. They touched on children's health and feeding, clothing, games, and participation in family life (Alexandre-Bidon and Lett 1997). They indicated that a period of protected childhood prevailed until the age of seven (at least for boys, about whom the texts offered more information). At this age boys began to receive some training, either in school or with their fathers. They began adult work or more serious apprenticeship at twelve or older.

Alexandre-Bidon and Closson used many medieval literary sources and some manuals on childrearing. Mary Martin McLaughlin (1974) relied on learned writing on childrearing. The material in these treatises, such as the encyclopedia of the Englishman Bartholomew Anglicus, *De proprietatibus rerum*, can be interpreted in a variety of ways. De Mause used Bartholomew's views on swaddling to underscore the cruelty of the medieval practice. He emphasized that the medieval learned tradition assumed that children were born defective and insisted that they have their limbs straightened by bindings that inevitably left them passive and dirty. McLaughlin, as well as Alexandre-Bidon and Closson, read Bartholomew as a writer who showed great compassion toward and understanding of small children. In their view, Bartholomew advised swaddling to keep the child in a womblike environment and protect it from cold and falls. As in all historical studies, the writer is not simply a fact-gatherer but also an interpreter.

The French response to Ariès has been a particularly rich one. The foremost French historian of medieval childhood, Pierre Riché, has taking the lead in pointing out the problems in Ariès's views on medieval childhood. Robert Fossier (1997) has edited a collection of essays on the history of childhood that has an introduction by Riché and Alexandre-Bidon conveniently summarizing the current state of the debate in France and the new materials available for study.

Among the new materials that historians have explored in an effort to understand medieval and renaissance childhood are the lives of saints. Saints may seem an unusual group of children to study. Their childhoods were not necessarily representative of ordinary experience, and their relationships with their mothers and fathers were not the most usual. Nonetheless, authors of the hagiographies called on the everyday experiences of more conventional children to flesh out the childhood years of these miracle workers. Weinstein and Bell (1982) have shown that saints did not assume the status of adults at the age of eight; even they had relatively normal childhoods. They might have ceased to play childish games when they were young, but only because they became "sad and wise," not because they were gainfully employed or exploited for their labor.

Perhaps more interesting than saints' lives for the glimpses of medieval children they afford are the miracles the saints were said to have performed. The ones I have used, the miracles of Henry VI, are full of asides such as "The boy, given his liberty, was playing about somewhere, as boys will, while his grandfather was all intent upon his work," or "The boy climbed up a tree about ten o'clock in the morning, bent on some childish prank—perhaps birds'-nesting," or, "The girl, careless and mischievous as children will be" (Hanawalt 1998, 163). The majority of the miracles concern curing children or raising them from the dead. The accounts offer full descriptions of children's activities and how they were miraculously saved.

I must not pass over without mention of an important miracle which, I am told, took place through the merits of the renowned King Henry some time ago in Wiston, a Susssex town. For though I have known some of the dead coming back to life, in spite of all reluctance of nature, at the Saints' intercession, I can scarce restrain my pen: the greater the wonder which the mind feels, the richer is the matter for discourse, although in my case the emotion of my full heart is far greater than my capacity for writing the record. A girl of three years old was sitting under a large stack of firewood, in the company of other children of that age who were playing by themselves, when by a sudden and calamitous accident a huge trunk fell from the stack and threw her on her back in the mud, pinning her down so heavily as to deprive her instantly of the breath of life. It was not possible that the breath should remain in her when her whole frame was so shattered; for the trunk was of such a size that it could scarcely be moved by two grown men. You may be assured that the horror of the sight soon scattered the company of the child's friends, who forthwith ran to and fro in all directions, shewing that something untoward had occurred by their screams or their flight, not by words. Perhaps it was this warning which made the child's father come up to see what had happened: and he, looking from some distance off, could see that it was his little Beatrice who lay stretched out there. Not a little alarmed, he hastened forward and, on drawing near and finding her already carried off by so cruel a death, found his face grow pale, and his heart wrung with an agony of grief: yet lifting the log with some difficulty, he raised her in his hands. Then the fountains of his eyes were loosed, and calling his wife, he put the poor corpse in her arms. She took her unhappy burden and laid it on her bosom; and so, almost fainting in her grief, and giving expression to it with heavy groans and loud wailing, made for the church that stood hard by.

The mother called on King Henry and vowed a pilgrimage to his tomb, and the breath came back to the child. "She spoke to her mother, albeit with difficult utterance, complaining of the pain she felt." Suckled with her mother's milk, she was made whole again (Know and Leslie 1923).

As the example shows, the miracle stories are full of detail. They tell of the activities of the young victims and of the adults and children who were around. They reveal the first finder of the child and the one who prayed to the saint. They speak of the grief of the parents, and they even inform us that a female child of three was still nursing at her mother's breast. In a new study of the miraculous cures of saints, Didier Lett (1997) analyzes miracle stories of the twelfth and thirteenth centuries. He notes that the miracles are more likely to give the ages of children than are other sources and that they tend to be precise (a tendency which, in itself, speaks to the special horror of losing a child). He finds that in 60 percent of the miracles the saints cured children or raised them from the dead after a domestic accident or illness. Another study of European miracle stories of the later Middle Ages by Ronald Finucane shows that 74 percent of the miracles involved sickness and 26 percent involved accidents (Finucane 1997, 8, 100).

Lett's careful analysis of the language the stories use to describe children destroys Ariès's argument that the medieval imprecision in language for the different stages of childhood meant that these stages were not recognized (Ariès 1962, 128). Lett, however, found that miracle stories written in both Latin and French used precise terms for age, although the Latin sources tended to be much more exacting. Latin sources used *infans* only for boys from 0 to 2 years old while French texts used *enfant* to refer to boys from 0 to 12 years old. By 13 to 16 *enfant* was less popular than *vallet*. The Latin accounts used *puer* for boys of all ages but reserved *adolescens* and *juvenis* for those 13–16. With girls the Latin accounts used *infans* only from birth to age 2, while the French versions used *enfans* for 0–7 years. *Puella* was the most popular Latin term for girls, and its application ran from newborns to 16-year-olds. In French, however, *pucelete* and *pucelle* were reserved almost exclusively for girls 1–7 years old. *Virgo* in the Latin sources was used almost exclusively for girls 8–16 years old. The redactors of miracle stories, therefore, had distinct words for the different ages of the children, indicating an awareness that the words described different developmental stages (Lett 1997, 362–63).

Along with this verbal differentiation came different expectations for the stages of childhood. One of the most dramatic conclusions of Lett's research was that the type of miracle changed substantially with the age of the child. From birth to 2 years old, over 40 percent of the miracles involved resurrection. From 3 to 7 years, the proportion involving resurrection dropped to about 25 percent. Between 8 and 12 years the proportion fell to about 17 percent, and by 13 to 16 to just 2 percent, or similar to the adult rate. Lett attributes the greater number of resurrections among newborns and babies to the belief that these children lived in a state of *demi-monde*. On the one hand, the newborn had to undergo an exorcism along with baptism to rid it of the devil; on the other hand, the innocent infant was between the mortal state and that of angels. Both the fragility and the innocence of a newborn made it a particularly fit subject for miracles.

The place of the miracle was also instructive. Children from birth to 2 years experienced the miracles in their home, whereas from 3 to 7 and 8 to 12 fewer than 40 percent experienced the miracles in their home and by 13 to16 years only 20 percent. Lett argued that the figures represent the greater vulnerability of infants and the immediacy of intercession by the saint when the parents called upon him or her for divine aid (1979, 57–90).

Finucane investigated the pattern of childhood accidents preserved in miracle stories. Children from birth to 2 had 70 percent of their accidents at home. The percentage drops quickly as the children reach ages of 3 and 4 and are only at about 10 percent from 5 to 9 (Finucane 1997, 147). Finucane explained the place of accident as indicative of childrearing practices and the development of motor skills among the growing children. By the age of 2 to 4 children were more mobile and more likely to wander outside the house.

The patterns of spiritual curing and resurrection closely followed those I found in the coroners' inquests into the accidental deaths of children. Indeed, the very form of the miracle story and that of the inquest are similar.

Saturday before the Feast of St. Margaret [20 July 1322] information was given to the aforesaid Coroner and Sheriffs that a certain Robert, son of John de St. Botulph, a boy seven years old, lay dead of a death other than his rightful death in a certain shop which the said Robert held of Richard de Wirhale in the parish of St. Michael de Paternostercherch in the Ward of Vintry. Thereupon the said Coroner and Sheriffs proceeded thither and having summoned good men of the Ward and of the three nearest Wards, viz.: Douegate, Queenhithe, and

Cordewanerstrete, they diligently inquired how it happened. The jurors say that when on Sunday next before the Feast of St. Dunstan [19 May] the said John (Robert?), Richard, son of John de Cheshunt, and two other boys, names unknown, were playing upon certain pieces of timber in the lane called "Kyroundeland" in the Ward of Vintry, a certain piece fell on the said John (Robert?) and broke his right leg. In the course of time Johanna, his mother, arrived, and rolled the timber off him, and carried him to the shop aforesaid where he lingered until the Friday before the Feast of St. Margaret when he died at the hour of Prime of a broken leg and of no other felony, nor do they suspect anyone of the death but only the accident and the fracture. (Sharpe 1913, 63–64)

Much of the same material that appears in saints' miracles is included, such as the activity of the child, the place where the accident occurred, and the first finder of the child. What is missing is the happy ending in which the child is restored to life.

As in the miracle stories, ages are given almost routinely for children up to the age of twelve, and the ages tend to be exact rather than rounded off. Thus six months or one year two months is not unusual. Twelve was the age at which children were legally responsible for their criminal acts, but the coroner was not called on to give the ages of children below twelve nor of those who died in accidents. As in the miracle stories, the children's ages were part of the special quality surrounding childhood. Ages of adolescents and adults became part of the inquest records only after 1350, and they were more likely to be rounded, such as "forty and more."

The places of accidents and the ages at which they occurred are similar to those Finucane outlined. Among the 58 children under age one who appeared in the coroners' inquests, home was the most common place of death; 33 percent died in fires in their cradles. Only 14 percent of the one-year-olds and 1 percent of the two-year-olds died in this manner. Unattended babies who were not in their cradles also died in their homes, and 21 percent of their deaths occurred in fires. These fires were frequently described as being caused by chickens. Chickens pecked about the open hearth for food. Sometimes they picked up a burning straw or twig and dropped it into the cradle. Sometimes their feathers caught fire and they flailed around, setting the cradle or house afire. As in the miracle stories, parents were usually the first to find the child. The most common period for child deaths was May through August (47 percent of these were babies), when the parents were in the fields planting and harvesting. Babies were swaddled and left in cradles. This was a perfectly safe precaution except for the possibility of fire or animal bites (Hanawalt 1976, 1986, 175–77).

The place of accident and the activities of children again parallel Lett's and Finucane's data (Lett 1997, 91–106; Finucane 1977, 147). While babies under age 1 had 80 percent of their accidents in their homes and 20 percent just outside their homes, the place of accidents gradually changed with age. From 1 to 3 years old only 53 percent of the children had fatal accidents at home. By then they were beginning to wander about; 14 percent had their accidents near their homes, and 31 percent were in more public areas such as the property of neighbors, village greens, and bodies of water (Hanawalt 1986, 272). The accidents, like the miracles, show that young children were highly mobile and that they were mostly playing around their house or outside, either alone or with other children.

Lett did not address the type of children's activities, but Finucane did analyze the activities of children who had fatal accidents in the miracle stories. These stories parallel the coroners' inquests in showing that children were playing with balls, or trying to get a feather or flower out of a body of water, or climbing on logs or tables when they had their accident (115–21). From ages 1 to 6, 60 percent of children's fatal accidents recorded in the coroners' inquests involved play; from age 7 to 12 the percentage dropped to 24. In teenage years play still represented a portion of the accidents (3 percent), but the play was at adult games such as target practice, wrestling, football, or knife throwing. Besides these play-related accidents, teenagers began to have an increasing number of work-related accidents (Hanawalt 1986, 271–73). In both the coroners' inquests and miracle tales, play predominated well beyond Ariès's eight-year limit. But as children grew older a new element entered—playing at and imitating the work of adults.

It is particularly interesting that by the age of two or three children's identity with their parents' work began to emerge in the pattern of their activities at the time of accidental deaths. Little girls were already becoming involved in accidents that paralleled their mother's routine, working with pots, gathering food, and drawing water, even though these accidents only involved playing at such tasks, as in the case of the two-year-old girl who tried to stir a pot of hot water but tipped it over on herself. Little boys were more actively involved in play outdoors and observation of men working. One three-year-old boy was following his father to the mill and drowned; another was watching his father cut wood when the ax blade came off the handle and struck him. The division of labor by sex began very early in children's life and was part of their early identification with the roles of their parents (Hanawalt 1986, 157–58).

By four and five, work became a part of the coroners' inquests.

Youngsters of that age were often assigned to babysit and go for water. For instance, a one-year-old boy was left in the care of his five-year-old brother, but the older boy was "a poor custodian," the inquest recorded, and the cradle caught fire. Other children took bowls to fill with water and slipped into ditches or wells and drowned. Even if children of four and older were simply sitting and observing their parents work, they were beginning to be socialized into the tasks they would eventually perform, such as cooking, brewing, milking, splitting logs, and digging (Hanawalt, 186, 158–59).

During the years from six through twelve, children began to have real chores around the house and beyond it. They aided their parents in work and supplemented the income of the household through fishing and gathering food (6 percent of their fatal accidents involved such activities). From five to twelve, fishing was a common pastime for boys. Herding was a traditional occupation for boys between ages of seven and twelve and accounted for 7 percent of their fatal accidents. Boys also took horses to be watered, and their daring with these animals accounted for 8 percent of their fatal accidents. But these boys were not doing men's tasks. Their work was chores and not field work. Only 2 percent of their accidents were in fields or pursuing a craft (Hanawalt 1986, 158–59). In the miracle stories as in the coroners' inquests, children under twelve had accidents while doing errands, tending animals, and the like (Finucane 1997, 115).

Girls from six to twelve also began to contribute to the household economy. They gathered fruits, herbs, nuts, and shellfish, and these activities led to 5 percent of their fatal accidents. Drawing water accounted for 32 percent of their fatal accidents, and cooking and laundering accounted for 14 percent. Girls were prone to accidents while fetching water for a couple of reasons. Wells were built without superstructures, so it was easy to slip on the wet clay surrounding them. And the girls themselves were often not physically able to lift a vessel full of water. Thus the jurors concluded in the case of one ten-year-old girl that the full water bowl was simply too heavy for her to lift and she fell in the pit (Hanawalt 1986, 157–59).

Contrary to Ariès's claim that teenagers behaved like adults in the Middle Ages, their accident pattern shows similarities to those of both children and adults. Adolescents still lived and worked around the house. Male adolescents spent time fishing and gathering rather than following the pattern of their fathers in working primarily in the fields or at a craft. Like younger children, and unlike adults, they still had more accidents in the home than in a workplace. When they did move into adult areas of work, they did so gradually, only taking up plowing and heavy fieldwork in their late teens. Even the games of teenagers were ball games and target practice, not archery contests and wrestling (Hanawalt 1986, 159–61). Urban records, particularly those dealing with apprentice contracts, provide even more convincing evidence for an adolescent life-stage. Apprenticeship in London began at about age 14 in the fourteenth century and increased to 18 in the fifteenth century. Parents putting their children into apprenticeships and masters receiving them made a contract that bound the youth to rules of behavior proscribing "adolescent" misbehavior. They were not to wear fancy dress, participate in gaming and theater, or waste their master's money (Hanawalt 1993, chapters 7–8).

The abundant evidence of manuals devoted to children and stages of life, art and archaeology, miracle stories, and coroners' inquests indicates that medieval and renaissance Europe recognized a distinct period of childhood and had exact words that applied to different stages of childhood. Thus while children were still in swaddling clothes and under two years old they were called by particular names and accorded particular treatment. From two to four or five, they were assumed to spend their time playing. At six or more likely at seven to twelve, they had chores to do to help their mother or father, but they were still not entering into the "great world of men" to labor. Children simply lacked the motor skills and judgment to plow or pursue a craft. They could herd, weed, carry water, and tend other children, but they could not pursue heavier work. Adults recognized the physical and psychological limitations of children and adolescents and were not willing to risk their crafts, capital, and crops in their hands. They also valued their children and adolescents too much to risk losing them in tasks that were beyond their skills. The miracle stories indicate the emotional commitment of parents and communities to children's survival by calling on saints to restore these precious souls to life.

Infant Mortality, Social Class, and Gender Differences

Although quantitative evidence from the Middle Ages and the Renaissance is sparse, it is quite clear that infant mortality ran from 30 to 50 percent. In an environment in which harmful bacteria were prevalent and medical knowledge slight, children were prone to diseases that caused extreme dehydration through diarrhea (Carmichael 1986). Finucane (1997, 163–64) found that curing children of illnesses was far more common in southern European miracle tales than in those of northern Europe. He speculated that the greater density of urban population and the presence of such diseases as malaria probably contributed to the greater morbidity among southern children. Child survival was closely related to conditions of feeding or nursing. Children who were nursed had a greater chance of survival simply because breast-feeding was more sanitary than the alternatives—feeding tubes and pre-chewed pap. Since male babies were usually nursed longer than female ones, the chances of male survival were greater.

Social class, economic prosperity, and sex made a considerable difference in the survival of children. In rural Pistoia, before the Black Death, peasants living on the hillside terrain were kept poor by the avarice of landlords who charged too much rent and did not encourage capital investment in either land or technology. The gouging landlords so depressed the standards of living of these people that married couples failed to replace themselves. Wives may have dropped below the weight necessary for fertility, or they miscarried, or their children were too weak to survive. Peasants on better land, however, had substantially larger families (Herlihy 1965). In rural Tuscany in 1427 after the Black Death, the size of the household was relatively large, with a mean of 4.4 to 7.5 persons. In urban environments Florence had a mean household size of 4.18 in 1380 and Verona 3.68 in 1425 and 5.89 in 1502 (Herlihy and Klapisch-Zuber 1985, 69, 91). In all age groups in Tuscany, the children of the rich were more likely to survive than those of the poor (Herlihy and Klapisch-Zuber 1985, 244–46).

But survival depended not only on the wealth of parents but also on the sex of the child. The Florentine materials show a bulge in reporting of children two and three years old to the tax collector and a smaller number of newborns and one-year-olds. In all age categories, the number of girls registered was smaller than the number of boys. The male/female ratio for children under one year old was 129/100, at 1 year it was 119/100, at 2 years 116/100, at 3 years 120/100, and at 4 years 118/100. Christiane Klapisch-Zuber, who compiled and analyzed these figures, suggested that there were more two-year-olds than newborns registered because parents of children under one year old were so hesitant about their survival that they did not always mention them, even though they would get a tax reduction for a larger number of children (Klapisch-Zuber 1985, 98–99). As for the preponderance of male to female children, several explanations are possible. More female children than male were abandoned and put into Florentine hospices. Treatment within the hospices was also differentiated: male babies were more likely to be nursed in the hospitals, female babies were more likely to be placed outside the hospital with wetnurses in the country (Trexler 1973a, b).

This differential treatment of males and females was true of the wealthy Florentines as well as of the desperate ones who abandoned their children. Klapisch-Zuber used the private record books, the *ricordanze*, to show the great pains that fathers took in selecting an appropriate wetnurse for their sons. They preferred to have their sons in their homes, but if the child was put in the country the father kept watch over the condition of the wetnurse. Not so with their female children. While 23 percent of the male children had nurses in their household, only 12 percent of the females did; 55 percent of the male children and 68 percent of the female children had nurses in the countryside (Klapisch-Zuber 1985, 132–64).

The picture in England is similar in that the conception and survival of children depended on the wealth of their parents. In Halesowen in the pre-plague period land was so scarce that sons inheriting small holdings or cottages were unable to increase either their income or their holdings. Consequently, they had small families, while wealthier peasants with more land had larger families (Razi 1980, 85–88). In post-plague England, although land was readily available, infant mortality kept household size low until the end of the fifteenth and the beginning of the sixteenth century.

Child abandonment, however, is not apparent in England. Unlike Florence, London and other English cities did not have foundling hospitals. Outright infanticide was rare. In rural jail delivery rolls and coroners' inquests, I have found only three indictments for infanticide among approximately 5,000 cases of homicide. In London, I have found only one suspected infanticide in the coroners' inquests (Hanawalt 1993, 44–45). Since a mother was not guilty of homicide in killing her infant until the mid-sixteenth century, jurors may have been unclear whether an indictment was appropriate. No woman was convicted of infanticide in the medieval records I surveyed. But the pattern of infant and early childhood accidents does not indicate a pattern of concealed infanticide. Slightly more male than female children died in the first few years of life. This is a pattern consistent with modern accidental death patterns and indicates a greater adventurousness on the part of male children (Hanawalt 1986, 102).

If infanticide was not a criminal offense, evidence of it nonetheless might have appeared in church court records, since the church required a penance for infanticide and was particularly concerned about overlaying. But again the evidence is slight. Although few ecclesiastical court records are preserved for London, a series from the late fifteenth and early sixteenth centuries reveals fewer than one allegation of infanticide a year, none of which ended in conviction (Hanawalt

1986, 44). Other studies of church courts in England have shown that infanticide was rarely reported (Helmholz 1969).

One London source with which I have worked suggests a pattern of selective care that is similar to that found among the elite of Florence and in the miracle stories. London had a law that provided for the protection of the property and persons of the citizens' orphans. These were usually children who had lost their father but still had a mother alive. The children, male and female, and their mother came into court with an account of the property willed to the children. At the time that they entered wardship, 780 (45 percent) of the orphans were female and 951 (55 percent) were male. The disparity in the number of males and females varied over the fourteenth and fifteenth centuries, reaching its high point in the plague of 1349 and dropping to a bare 2 percent difference in the second half of the fifteenth century. As in Florence, the pattern was probably not willful infanticide so much as a difference in the nursing and nurturing of male and female children (Hanawalt 1993, 58). Curiously, in the miracle tales 69 percent of the children cured were boys and 31 percent girls in Lett's study (1997, 165) and 65 percent were male and 35 percent female in Finucane's (1997, 141). Furthermore, the girls tended to have been sick for a longer period of time than the boys (Hanawalt 1998, 163). While Finucane does not give figures, he does note that parents were more likely to have contacted a doctor for boys than for girls in the miracle cures (Finucane 1997, 95–99).

Infanticide and abandonment are notoriously difficult to document, particularly for the Middle Ages and the Renaissance. While records of the hospices of Florence paint a grim picture of death (Trexler 1973a, b), the very establishment of a haven for abandoned children indicates a moral commitment to save the foundlings. Because the evidence of infanticide is weak, historians have read their own optimistic or pessimistic views onto the past. On the pessimistic side is de Mause's dramatic but unfounded statement that "the latrines of Europe were screaming with the cries of murdered infants" and that there was a "widespread infanticide component . . . present in the medieval personality" (de Mause 1974b). Other than in urban areas, monasteries, and castles, archaeological evidence for latrines is minimal, so this pessimistic reading of medieval personality traits is factually wrong even on the "toilet seat" (his term) level.

In contrast, John Boswell provides the most remarkably optimistic view. "Most abandoned children were rescued and brought up either as adopted members of another household or as laborers of some sort. Whether they were exposed anonymously . . . sold, donated, substituted, or 'fostered,' abandoned infants probably died at a rate only slightly higher than the normal infant mortality rate at the time." Boswell argues that the value of human labor was such that these abandoned children were saved by the "kindness of strangers." He sees parents making hard decisions, such as selling children, because they saw this terrible expedient as the best hope for the child's survival (Boswell 1988, 428–34).

Whether one takes the optimistic or the pessimistic view of child death by disease, abandonment, or infanticide, I would ask a learned audience not to jump to conclusions about an "infanticidal medieval personality." The lack of evidence for widespread infanticide does not permit the conclusion that it was widespread nonetheless. With child deaths at 30 to 50 percent and with the fertility of the poorest very low, infanticide might not have been necessary. In a largely rural economy, which Europe had throughout the period under discussion, all labor was essential; wealthier households often did take into their care the superfluous or orphaned village children. The Florentine evidence may not be the best available for an understanding of Europe as a whole. Even in the urban environments of Florence, Ghent, and London, stringent laws guarded children of citizens and their properties. We do not have enough evidence to argue for a conclusion that all children were valued and society attempted to save them or, on the contrary, to assume a murderous propensity on the part of medieval society toward children. One can only suggest that legitimate children and male children of prosperous parents had a better chance of survival than poor children, bastards, and girls in general. It is best to move on to arenas that can enhance our knowledge of the culture surrounding childrearing and the value that medieval people put on children.

Emotional Response to the Death of Children

Did medieval and renaissance parents mourn the loss of their children? Did they have a sentimental attitude toward children as children? Again, I am reluctant to see modern studies read back into the medieval and renaissance period. Nancy Scheper-Hughes has argued that mothers shield themselves from maternal bonding in northeast Brazil because they lose so many children and the social norms permit selective neglect (Scheper-Hughes 1985). She is not talking about a rural society but about a densely populated urban slum. The medieval and renaissance sources make clear the depth of emotion over the loss of children for both mothers and fathers. Elite fathers' reactions to the death of their children are recorded, sometimes even in their own handwriting. The reactions of mothers are amply apparent in miracle stories. On the question of a sentimental attitude toward children, a variety of sources point to medieval feeling for the special quality of that life stage.

Medieval miracle stories afford some of the best evidence of the emotional attachment parents of all social classes had to their children and of their outpouring of grief for the loss of these children. Lett's analysis of miracle stories shows that the relationship of parents to sick and dead children was very close. Before the age of eight, the presence of parents in the course of the miraculous event is marked. The mother was more likely than the father to be the first finder of the infant and to initiate the intercession of the saint. But after age eight, the father was more likely to take this role (Lett 1997, 165–78). Finucane found that the mother was the person who called for saintly intercession in both accidents and illnesses of children (1997, 162). In the coroners' inquests as well, the mother was usually the first finder of young children, but the father was the first finder of a greater proportion of the boys because they were following him around or working with him (Hanawalt 1998, 164–67). None of the records give a prominent role to extended family (uncles, aunts, grandparents) or even siblings. Neighbors were more important than kin. Extended family, even in southern Europe, where that household structure was more common, apparently did not play a major role in rearing children.

The miracle tales permitted the outpouring of misery on the part of parents, particularly mothers, at the loss of their child in a way that an official record such as the coroners' inquests did not. The stories spoke of tears, cries, anxiety, tearing of hair, falling down with grief. Of course, they also spoke of joy when the child was restored to health or life (Lett 1997, 200–203).

Margaret King (1994) has traced the tragedy of the death of an eight-year-old son of Marcello, a soldier from a leading Venetian family. The death dominated the father's life until his own early death. He collected a book of paeans to the boy from leading humanists. He sought the consolation of talking to other fathers who had lost sons. He could not reconcile himself to the death and could not accept comforting words about the loss.

From the fourteenth through the sixteenth century Italians expressed an increasing interest in and tenderness toward children and childhood (Ross 1974). One sees it in the art of the renaissance painters and in the *ricordanze,* and especially in Leon Battista Alberti's treatise, *I libri della famiglia* (Alberti 1969). Louis Haas (1998) has documented the sentimental attitudes of renaissance Florentine fathers toward their children and their recognition of the special needs children had as they passed through different life stages.

While there was considerable sentiment about children and the loss of them on the part of medieval parents, both in particular instances and in their admiration for childhood innocence, one still detects differences in the conception of childhood as a life stage in the Middle Ages and the twentieth century. Medieval and renaissance parents, artists, and writers expressed a sentimental attitude toward childhood and recognized it as a distinct phase of life separate from adolescence and adulthood. Boys and girls needed protection in their young years and regulation in their teenage years. Medieval parents and their surrogates were realistic about training youth to provide for themselves in a harsh world. They did not have false expectations about the amount of work a child could do, but they did train their children to work, to take responsibility for themselves, and, when they reached sufficient years, to give obedience to their superiors. In a hierarchical society, learning to live and work within the hierarchy was important for male and female children, nobles' and peasants' children. Medieval parents were aware that sentimentality about childhood would not extend into adulthood. Self-sufficiency was ultimately most important for their youngsters' success, but training for this preferred state required parental oversight and discipline. Corporal punishment was thought to be essential to train children, and fostering and apprenticeship were considered ideal ways to train noble children and artificers (not peasants) to make their way in the world.

To give some perspective on the treatment of youth, it is useful to cite one of the most popular parables of the Middle Ages, that of the divided horse blanket. The father instructs his son to take the horse blanket out to his grandfather, who is sleeping in the stable on a cold night. The son returns with half a horse blanket, and the father inquires why he has done that. The boy replies that he is saving it for his father when he is old.

Conclusions

One can conclude from this brief and far from complete survey of the study of medieval and renaissance childhood that historians have been actively engaged in research on the subject. They have found sources that Ariès did not consider, and they have gone much further with studies he barely began. Some firm conclusions can be reached. In medieval and renaissance art, artifact, and dress, the period of childhood was distinguishable from the stages of adolescence and adulthood. In the very language by which they referred to children, people made distinctions between those under seven or eight and those over that age. Children were not put into the harsh world of men to work when they reached eight. They might enter service if they were poor, but the expectation was that they would do chores commensurate with their strength, motor skills, and judgment. The investment in such a young servant was in future skilled work that the child would be able to do in the household. High infant mortality seems to have induced in medieval and renaissance parents more of a sense of sorrow than of callousness over the loss of life. Even the medieval lullabies speak of the tenuousness of the child's existence (Hanawalt 1986, 179).

While not arguing that the medieval and renaissance experiences of childhood were exactly those of the twentieth century in Europe or America or even those of the twentieth-century child in Calcutta, historians of childhood in these periods are adamant that Montaigne and other early modern authors do not represent "artifacts" of medieval belief and custom regarding childhood. Scholars of the Middle Ages have drawn data and arguments, not from seventeenth-century intellectuals but from medieval records, miracle tales, art, and learned writing. Yet medieval and renaissance historians face the frustration of having their studies ignored by the rest of the scholarly community. The tenacity of Ariès's picture of medieval childhood and adolescence, and of medieval attitudes toward childhood, as it appears in modern textbooks of psychology and social work as well as daily parlance, deserves some consideration.

Part of the reason for the robustness of the negative view of medieval childhood comes from our folk culture, which calls everything undesirable "medieval" whether or not the practices had anything to do with the Middle Ages. An educated woman once asked me how I could work on childhood in the Middle Ages when there was no period of childhood then, because "children were put into factories immediately." She had conflated the nineteenth century, when there was child labor in the factories, with the Middle Ages, when there were no factories at all. It seems to comfort people to embrace a Whig interpretation of history. Such an interpretation implies that there is progress in human development and that we have evolved beyond what we consider "medieval" or what my students call on their exams "mid-evil." The authors who adopted Ariès's model found a ready audience of believers among the reading public as well as educated academics.

Much of the same thinking prevails in textbooks of psychology and social work. Once the subject of children in the Middle Ages and the Renaissance has been written off, it is possible to move on to our more modern, enlightened period. Either using Ariès or quoting the same sources he used to establish medieval practice and medieval concepts of childhood, we can dismiss the Middle Ages. One author wrote: "During their early years children were little noticed by society. As late as the sixteenth century the French essayist Montaigne casually remarked of his own baby, 'I don't count the little one' " (Greenleaf 1976, 32). The persistent use of Enlightenment thinkers to establish medieval practices makes writers such as Locke and Rousseau look as if they were offering a new view of childhood that did not exist in the Middle Ages. Textbook writers simply have not bothered to read the more accurate accounts in modern historiography. As Pollock (1983) pointed out, the writers of learned treatises of the Enlightenment and Romantic era give a very different picture of their times than do the letters and diaries of the same period written by more ordinary people. Intellectuals are not our best guide to everyday practice, then or now.

But for those who would be more reflective about changing attitudes toward childhood and changing definitions of it, I would ask why it is necessary to posit hypotheses of discontinuity or change? Why is it essential for reflective arguments on modern concepts of childhood to cling to Ariès's or the Whig historians' distorted picture of medieval childhood? If medieval and renaissance historians have demonstrated that all levels of society—intellectuals (mostly clergymen), nobles, urban dwellers, and peasants—had a well-articulated concept of childhood and adolescence, then the relevant question is not whether they had an idea of childhood, but what it was. Historians of earlier periods have pointed to understandings of physical and emotional development that are commensurate with our modern understanding of the development of motor skills and judgment. We cannot ignore, nor did the medieval parents and theorists ignore, the basic biology of the child, which has not changed over the few centuries we are discussing. To be sure, the cultural attitudes toward children and images of them change over time, but basic to any concept of childhood and childrearing are children themselves.

What medieval and renaissance scholars have shown is that parents and communities valued, protected, and taught their children, although gender and social class distinctions influenced what was taught and how much effort went into protecting. Training, apart from the formal education that was the real focus of Ariès's work, varied depending on what the child's position in life would be in adulthood. That this social world and culture of childrearing was different from that of the twentieth century should be no surprise to historians, sociologists, or psychologists. Does a modern scholar of child development or of the modern idea of childhood need Ariès at all? Is it not possible to see a continuity of parental and societal formulations of an idea of child-hood that derives from both human biology and a shared cultural heritage from the Middle Ages and even earlier, and at the same time to demonstrate that concepts of childhood are structured to prepare children for the social reality of their own particular historical time period?

Chapter 3
Early Modern Childhood in the Dutch Context

ELS KLOEK

"Kinderen hinderen." That is to say, children are hindrances. Young people nowadays don't know them any more, but only a few decades ago almost all Dutchmen could tell you that these were the words of our seventeenth-century politician and poet Jacob Cats (vadertje Cats). So in the seventeenth century Dutchmen still thought of their children as hindering creatures. Still? Or should we say "already"?

On the other hand, old stories may be quoted stressing the preciousness of children. For instance, the poet Daniel Heinsius, in his collection of stories of exemplary women (1606), told the classical story of Cornelia, the mother of the Gracchi, who refused to buy jewelry, pointing to her children and saying, "my children are my jewels." Or in Dutch, "mijn kinderen zijn mijn schatten" (Moerman 1974). This story of the good mother, who loves her children more than luxury, is known in different versions.

These two expressions about the child (and its parents), both cited from seventeenth-century Dutch literature, have been known to us for centuries. But only in the second half of the twentieth century, after Ariès's interpretation of the history of childhood opened the debate on family history, did these historical utterances of feelings toward children force us to ask the same questions again and again: What do such expressions tell us about attitudes toward children in the past? Do they imply love or indifference? When was the concept of childhood "invented" anyway?

The central question of this volume is whether we have come to an end of the century of the child. As an early modern historian asked to write about the Dutch child of the seventeenth century, I think it beyond the scope of my discipline to attempt to answer this question, for the answer as to whether Ellen Key was right in proclaiming "the century of the child" is not to be found in the seventeenth century. But in one important and obvious way, Key's prediction, or even wishful thinking, turned out to be right. It was only in the twentieth century that historians became aware that topics like family life, childhood, and motherhood should be studied alongside the traditional topics of kings, queens, and battles. Although there had already been a modest rise in the historiography on family, children, and women at the beginning of the century (for the history of the Dutch child, see Knuttel-Fabius 1906; Pomes 1908; De Vletter 1915; van den Eerenbeemt 1935), the real boom started only in the second half of the twentieth century.

Philippe Ariès opened the discussion in 1960 with his pioneering study *L'enfant et la vie familiale sous l'ancien régime*. So, seeing the twentieth century not so much as "the century of the child" but as "the century of family history," I will deal with the question how historical knowledge about the Dutch attitude toward children in early modern times may contribute to the international family history debate. First, I will discuss the way Ariès used Dutch materials—that is to say, genre painting—in his theoretical model and the way other historians followed his example by using these "indirect" sources in the historiography of Dutch family life. Second, I will summarize some historical data on Dutch society in early modern times, in order to sketch the historical context in which a possible "Dutch case" of family history should be seen. Finally, I will focus on some examples of Dutch advice literature of the sixteenth and seventeenth centuries, treating them as "direct" sources to inform us at least about pedagogical thinking itself.

Historiography

Ariès

According to Ariès, medieval society knew neither our idea of childhood nor any other awareness of a distinct child nature. The attitude of parents toward their children was one of indifference. But between the thirteenth and the seventeenth centuries a new sensibility toward children came into existence. Ariès draws this conclusion by looking at different sources: paintings, manuals, and didactic sources. The emergence of paintings showing children as individuals and the institutionalization of schools and their discipline stand at the core of Ariès's argument. They are for him the first signs of the setting apart of children, a process he characterizes as a typical "modern" phenomenon.

In the fifteenth and sixteenth centuries, Ariès argues, a lay iconography eventually detached itself from the medieval religious iconography of childhood. Themes like the ages of life, the seasons, the senses, and the elements became favorite subjects of painting as well. The child became one of the characters in these anecdotical paintings. On its pictorial side, Ariès formulates his theory as follows:

These subject paintings were not as a general rule devoted to the exclusive portrayal of childhood, but in a great many cases there were children among the characters depicted, both principal and secondary. And this suggests the following ideas: first, children mingled with adults in everyday life, and any gathering for the purpose of work, relaxation or sport brought together both children and adults; secondly, painters were particularly fond of depicting childhood for its graceful or picturesque qualities. (1962, 37–38)

Of these two ideas, the first, according to Ariès, is "out of date" because nowadays we tend to separate the world of children from the world of adults. It is the second that foreshadows the modern idea of childhood.

For Ariès, the most important change in the pictorial representation of the child is to be found in the seventeenth century. It was then that artists began to paint individual child portraits (42), and then too that the older genre of the family portrait began to plan itself around the child (45), as in the work of Rubens, Frans Hals, and van Dyck (42, 45). Most of the Dutch paintings discussed by Ariès are mentioned in the chapter on games and pastimes. They show adults and children playing the same games, having the same feasts, having fun, and staying up very late together (79–81). Paintings produced in the Low Countries also show special children's celebrations, like May festivals and Saint Maarten. In both cases, whether with adults or set apart by themselves, children of different ages behaved as one age group: the youth. According to Ariès, this new attitude is even more clearly to be seen in a Dutch painting by Vinckelbaons (Ariès means Vinckboons) of a hurdy-gurdy man, where a man has a little child on his arm in order to let the child see as much of the performance as possible (80).

In the last part of his book, Ariès deals with the "image of the family." As early as the second half of the sixteenth century, Dutch painters composed family portraits more dynamically; they changed the family portrait into the genre piece. These genre paintings, according to Ariès, were inspired by something totally new: the sense of family. They are about the child and its expression of a happiness that makes the rest of the family happy too. Dutch painters such as Jan Steen depicted family feasts that differ from traditional feasts in one important aspect: they are organized by adults for their children. This new, modern attitude toward children, this "sensibilité de l'enfance," caused another new attitude: the "sensibilité de la famille" (353–62). The point Ariès wants to make is that modern family life was the result of new attitudes toward children, and not the other way around. Modern family life did not cause modern "child centeredness." It was the result of it.

This groundbreaking theory of Ariès about historical change in the

Western family over centuries opened a lively debate among family historians from all over the world during the 1970s and 1980s. Obviously, Ariès should be praised for that. But I am afraid that Ariès's model was not the most suitable starting point for this scholarly debate, because essentially his approach was ahistorical. He paid hardly any attention to the historical setting of his sources. He used whatever was available to him to unfold his general theory about the development of a "sense de la famille." For instance, the part of his argument related to the system of schooling contains only French and a few English sources, while the parts on painting consist mainly of Dutch and Flemish materials. Ariès does not say anything specific about the Dutch culture of the seventeenth century. To him the Dutch (and Flemish) were relevant only so far as the development of genre painting and family portraiture was concerned. And even then his argument in these interpretations of paintings is not always clear, because his examples seem to contradict each other. Sometimes he seems to be saying that these Dutch paintings show the child as part of the adult world, while at other times he stresses that these paintings show children as a group on their own.

I think it was because of the lack of historical context that Ariès's book opened the door to endless speculations about (the lack of) feelings in the past, detached from any historical setting other than that of his theoretical model of change itself. In other words, this debate among family historians focused too much on the question of the right or wrong of Ariès; thus it overlooked the larger issue of the limits and perspectives of a general history of childhood itself.

VAN DEN BERG AND HEIJBOER

Four years before Ariès published his *L'enfant et la vie familiale*, the Dutch psychiatrist J. H. van den Berg dealt with similar questions concerning the development of childhood in his theoretical work *Metabletica: Of leer der veranderingen: Beginselen van een historische psychologie* (van den Berg 1956; English edition, *The Changing Nature of Man: Introduction to a Historical Psychology* 1961). According to van den Berg, the child only *became* a child in the eighteenth century, the age of Rousseau. Van den Berg's essay is based very little on Dutch sources, although he did ask someone else to dig in the history of Dutch literature to find relevant quotations to sustain his argument. In the end, he decided not to use them, so this assistant, M. E. Heijboer-Barbas, published the materials she had found in a separate booklet entitled *Een nieuwe visie op de jeugd uit vroeger eeuwen* (*A New View of Youth in Ear-*

lier Ages 1956). It is astonishing how much her argument resembles the first element of Ariès's developmental model: in the past, children were pocket-size adults because the world of children and the world of adults were not yet separated. Children from the elite were forced to learn their classics when they were very young. Adults talked about anything and everything without taking notice of the presence of children, as if they were equals. Careers commenced in adolescence.

Now the interesting point I would like to emphasize is this: almost all the examples Heijboer mentions to support her thesis that a modern notion of childhood was absent in traditional society are derived from seventeenth- and especially eighteenth-century sources. She writes that only at the end of the eighteenth century did the Dutch start to create a certain distance between youth and adulthood, imitating foreigners like Locke and Rousseau. Even the writings of typical representatives of the Dutch Enlightenment, such as the famous author/educational reformer Betje Wolff (1738–1804) or the first Dutch writer of children's books, Hieronymus van Alphen (1746–1803), are used by Heijboer to prove the strength and persistence of this traditional conception of children as pocket-size adults. She does not refer to iconographic sources, so it is difficult to compare her analysis with Ariès's, but one thing is clear: according to Ariès, a modern notion of childhood already could be seen in seventeenth-century Dutch genre painting, while according to Heijboer this modern notion was still totally absent in late eighteenth-century Dutch literature.

How are we to reconcile the way Ariès makes use of Dutch paintings with the way Heijboer uses Dutch literature of the seventeenth and eighteenth centuries? Should Dutch culture get credit for being the first to discover childhood, or are the genre paintings it produced exceptional artifacts proving the rule that the general awareness of childhood as a life stage did not exist yet, even among the Dutch? In that case, the question remains whether iconographic sources really inform us about attitudes toward children in former times.

DURANTINI AND HAKS

Ariès's interpretation of pictorial sources caused a lively debate among scholars, but his example of using them for the purpose of writing family history had few followers. The use of paintings turned out to be more complicated than he suggested. Diane Hughes put it: "Ariès's discovery of childhood has been questioned, . . . but Ariès's confidence in the validity of iconographic evidence has not been challenged" (1988, 8). She formulates her conclusion as a serious warning:

"Stylistic habits and concerns, along with the emblematic nature and didactic purposes of so much family portraiture, should encourage us to approach with caution the family history that it seems to tell" (36).

Maybe such caution about entering the art historical field explains why the Dutch case did not get the attention among family historians that it might have received after Ariès's references to Dutch painting (Burton 1989). For if Ariès's use of pictorial sources was to be accepted, then the Dutch case should have been one of the first to be explored in a more detailed way. A few years ago, the historian van de Woude (1991) figured out that at least five million paintings were produced by Dutch painters in the seventeenth and eighteenth centuries, and a rough 10 percent of these were genre paintings. So we are talking about 500,000 genre paintings, without even counting the portraits of families and of children. And in fact family historians have repeatedly pointed out the importance of seventeenth-century Dutch painting as a mirror of friendlier attitudes in family relations (for instance, Stone 1979, 259; Arnold 1980, 65). Nonetheless, it was quite a long time before family historians paid further attention to the Dutch and their family life in early modern times.

The only monograph that deals with the question how Dutch genre paintings reflect attitudes toward children is the thesis by Mary Frances Durantini, *The Child in Seventeenth-Century Dutch Painting* (Durantini 1983; for art historical articles, see van Thiel 1987; Bedaux 1990; Franits 1990; Dekker 1996). Without explicit reference to Ariès's model, and seemingly without any awareness of it herself, Durantini attacks the model at the core of its cultural representation of children by saying that the large number of paintings of children by Dutch artists does not reveal anything about attitudes toward children as children. According to Durantini, there was in those paintings no fundamental interest in childhood, no attempt to understand the child's world, no effort to depict the complexity of children's nature itself. As she puts it, "childhood was not regarded as a fully independent stage of life. It was a preparatory stage prior to the more perfect end: adulthood" (3). Her argument in itself underlines the vagueness of criteria that have been used to measure the feelings of adults toward children in former times. For what is wrong with thus seeing childhood as a stage prior to adulthood? I would say that it is exactly this notion that makes people aware that childhood is special. But more than that, Durantini's argument actually undermines the iconographic pillar of Ariès's theory itself: as she sees it, the cultural representation of childhood does not inform us about changing attitudes toward children.

As I have said, Ariès did not pay any attention to the historical context of his Dutch sources, for he was not interested in the question of national differences in the history of childhood. Only with the work of Donald Haks, *Huwelijk en gezin in Holland* (*Marriage and Family in Holland* 1982) was the idea of Dutch family history as an exceptional case introduced in the international debate on family history. Haks asks explicitly whether a "modern" family already existed in Holland in the late seventeenth and eighteenth centuries. (He defines a "modern family" as one with little contact with relatives, a free choice of partner based on affection, and a certain degree of equality and intimacy between partners and between parents and children.) To answer his question, he explores judicial case records and prescriptive literature. He does not refer to the paintings of the seventeenth century. He focuses on specific aspects of family history, such as relations with neighbors and with wider family connections, premarital sexuality, choice of marriage partner, relations within the household, and possibilities of divorce.

Unfortunately for us, he does not take the raising of children as one of his topics. Indeed, Holland was a very modern region of Europe in those times, as regards its economic and social structure and its degree of urbanization. So there is no need for amazement at Haks's conclusion: the modern family prevailed among broad segments of the population in Holland. His main findings are that Dutch moralists pleaded for partner choice based on affection and hence that Dutch youth had more freedom of choice than anywhere else to find their future mate. The explanation he advances for such modernity lies in the fact that Dutch society underwent its process of "specialization" rather early: already in the sixteenth century most Dutch households had reached a high level of specialization in earning their living. Self-sufficient households had already become an exception. This situation implied that young people could leave the household of their parents quite easily, starting a household on their own without the help of their family.

SCHAMA

Since Haks's work was only published in Dutch, Simon Schama's anthropological account, *The Embarrassment of Riches* (1987), had a much greater impact on the international study of family history. (For a recently published English monograph on Dutch childrearing practices in the seventeenth and eighteenth centuries, see Roberts 1998.). Schama's work is a monograph on the mentality of the Dutch in their Golden Age. It is based on both literary sources and iconographic evidence such as genre painting and prints. According to Schama, the main problem for the Dutch in the Golden Age was how to be rich and moral at the same time. With respect to raising children, this problem manifested itself in the polarity between liberty and obedience. That tension explains why the Dutch of the seventeenth century were fixated on their children to a degree and in a manner arrestingly unlike men and women of other European cultures. Leaning heavily on the work of Haks, Schama says that the Dutch of the seventeenth century were the first to approach children in a modern, love-oriented way. The home was for them an important element of their culture. It was a place where these Calvinists could worship God on their own and, at the same time, keep themselves morally safe from the evils of the harsh world outside. According to Schama, Dutch families were much more reluctant than those of other contemporary cultures to relinquish their hold on the young. The Dutch home was supposed to be an ideal school for the world.

But Schama does not see this fixation of the Dutch on their children as a "benign liberation" from medieval hardships (486). When we see children running riot in a genre painting, he says, we have more than mere snapshots from a Dutch family album. We glimpse "scenes from the interior of the Dutch mental world," a world obsessed by the process of growing up and trying to reach (political) adulthood. In his eyes, the dominance of children in Dutch genre painting is a metaphor for the Republic itself. Schama formulates it as follows: "To be Dutch at all, at least in the seventeenth century, was to be imprisoned in a state of becoming: a sort of perpetual political adolescence" (495). Only the Dutch of the eighteenth century were to be released from this preoccupation, thanks to the precocious decadence of their Republic.

So Schama understands the extraordinary abundance of child-picturing in the Dutch Golden Age mainly in a metaphorical way. By doing so, he refrains from taking a position in the general family history debate, stressing only the shortcoming of the developmental model family historians have been using since Ariès. He interprets the iconographic and literary sources on Dutch child raising against the historical background to which they belong. I would criticize him only because he did not approach his sources with an open mind. He knew what he would find in advance, no matter what subject he studied. While Ariès used Dutch genre painting to support his theory about a growing child-centeredness in early modern family life in general, Schama only needed those paintings to support the prevalence of moral tensions and uncertanties within the young Dutch Republic. But Schama's usage also makes clear the elasticity of iconographic material, especially when it is used to prove a theory of historical change.

"Typically Dutch"?

What do we know about "the Dutch case" in the history of childhood? Is there a Dutch case, and, if so, what is so special about it? To answer these questions, some historical facts should be considered.

DUTCH SOCIETY IN EARLY MODERN TIMES

In the sixteenth century, the Low Countries already formed a peculiar region in Europe. In the first place, they composed the most highly urbanized region in Europe (Israel 1995, 113). In 1525, 44 percent of Holland's population was living in cities; by 1675 this figure had risen to 61 percent. This extraordinary degree of urbanization was not confined to Holland. For the whole Republic, including the rural parts of the eastern provinces, the proportions were still 32 percent urban in 1525 and 45 percent urban in 1675 (van der Woude and de Vries 1995, 84–85). By comparison, in seventeenth-century England only 20 percent of the population lived in cities (Laurence 1994, 133). A second peculiarity of the early modern Low Countries, and especially of the northern part, was the dispersion of cities. There was no single metropolis toward which its urbanization tended. On the contrary, the Low Countries experienced a proliferation of middle-sized towns, so even rural people lived very close to "the city." In other words, the whole Dutch population was familiar with city life by 1600. This both reflected and reinforced the wide distribution of wealth and commerce throughout the region.

A third peculiarity of Dutch society in early modern times was the size of households. They were remarkably small. According to van der Woude, the average size of households in Holland—servants included—was 5.9 persons in the sixteenth century. It had dropped to 5.3 in 1630 and to 4.3 in the first half of the eighteenth century, the rural areas included (van der Woude 1972a, 1: 149). Cities in the sixteenth century had an even smaller household size. In Leiden, for example, the average household in 1581 had no more than 3.8 persons (Daelemans 1975). In the seventeenth and eighteenth centuries 49 percent of the Dutch population lived in a household that consisted of one to four people, while in England 31 percent did so. The differences are most marked between the groups of households of eight or more persons. In Holland only 10 percent of the people lived in such large households; in England more than 25 percent did (van der Woude 1972b, 309–10).

The small size of the household implies other peculiarities of Dutch family life in the seventeenth century. First, it meant that a great many people in early modern Holland were living on their own. No fewer than 19 percent of the households consisted of one person. This is a high figure, which can be explained only partially by the postponement of marriage until the age of twenty-five to twenty-seven (van der Woude 1972b, 311). Second, only 17.5 percent of the households had servants living in. This relatively low figure can be explained by the fact that the Dutch did not have the custom, common in other European countries, of exchange between households of growing children who had to learn a trade. Even when the children of the Dutch were sent away to acquire artisanal skills, they usually returned home every night (312–14).

Beyond these demographic peculiarities of early modern Dutch society, its political and religious situation should also be mentioned. In 1566 the Low Countries became involved in a religious war with Catholic Spain. After 1585 the northern parts alone continued this struggle, proclaiming themselves a republic. (Most European nations recognized the proclaimed independence within a few years. For Spanish recognition, the Dutch had to wait eighty years: peace was signed in 1648.) The political structure that arose out of this situation was a loosely organized federation of autonomous cities, "buurtschappen," and provinces. This decentralized structure lasted for over 200 years, as a "counter-model to absolutism" (Davids and Lucassen 1995, 8).

The revolt against Spain did not result in the establishment of a Calvinist state church. To be sure, the Dutch Republic was a Protestant nation and the Reformed Church received a privileged status. Nonetheless, a sharp division of state and church was introduced. The only prescription was that public offices were confined to people of the Reformed Church. And even then, many statesmen of the seventeenth century were very moderate Protestants who disliked dogmatic Calvinists. Other famous Dutchmen of that period, including writers, poets, and painters, were Catholics or Mennonites. So the new Republic should not be seen as a Calvinist society. Freedom of religious choice was maintained, and Catholics and other dissenting groups were tolerated, though officially they were not allowed to have religious services in public.

The war against Spain lasted until 1648, but it was during the years of that conflict that the young Republic gained its importance, its colonies, and its riches. So the seventeenth century is considered the Golden Age of the Netherlands. It was a time of political and commercial prosperity, and literacy, literature, and painting prospered as well. This prosperity began to reach its end in the last quarter of the seventeenth century. In the eighteenth century, the Dutch became very

aware of this decline. They wondered why the nation fell from dominance, and they criticized their own loss of virtue and courage. Dutch
culture became a culture of self-pity and nostalgia, proud of its ancestors but not of itself.

SPOILING CHILDREN: AN OLD REPUTATION OF THE DUTCH

The Dutch way of raising children seemed to be peculiar as well. In
the seventeenth century, foreigners were already recording their as-
tonishment at the laxity of Dutch parents. A Frenchman wrote that
the Dutch knew only one rule, "celle d'un laisser-faire presque illim-
ité" ("that of almost unlimited laissez-faire"; Murris 1925, 110). In 1735,
another French witness described the Dutch as being fond of their
children, not because they thought it in the interest of the children,
but only because they were weak themselves. To his amazement, they
preferred to close their eyes to the faults of their children, and they refused to use corporal punishment. Yet another Frenchman noted that
Dutch children were adored and spoiled and that they lived under
conditions of almost total liberty (Murris 1925, 111). The same criticisms were also made by Germans and Englishmen, and they continued in the eighteenth century. The German traveler Benthem (1687)
wrote that the love of Dutch parents for their children was like blind
love (*Affenliebe*) because they did not dare to whip them. When the
Dutch were faulted for not punishing their children, they would reply: does anybody spoil his own face, or cut off his own nose? (Bientjes
1967; van Strien 1989, 158; see also Schama 1987, 486; Rang 1990,
91). In the eighteenth century (1769 and 1777) some foreign travelers
began to praise this liberal childraising. The French doctor Daignan
observed, "on donne (aux enfants) de bons maitres, sans les presser
d'apprendre. Ils apprennent cependant aussi bien que d'autres; ils
sont absolument libres de suivre leur goût" ("one provides a good
teacher for the children, without urging them to learn. Still, they learn
as well as other children; they are absolutely free in following their
own taste"; Murris 1925, 111).

Besides this spoiling of children, foreigners remarked on something
else: since the sixteenth century, most Dutch children—girls as well as
boys—had been going to school. According to Guicciardini, this was
just "normal practice." Of course these accounts written by travelers
from abroad may not be trusted at face value, for travel journals should
not be understood as spontaneously written documents. Travelers knew
exactly what to observe, and obviously the permissive manners of the
Dutch was one of the topics to be noted when one visited the Netherlands. This does not imply that these descriptions are useless. They prove

the early existence of an international stereotype of Dutch child raising, at the very least.

Dutch Advice Literature

And the Dutch themselves in the seventeenth century, how did they
think about child raising? Of course, we cannot ask them personally or
observe their childrearing practices, but we might find some clues to
their attitudes as educators in sources that deal with the subject explicitly: moral treatises, medical manuals, letters and diaries, observations
by contemporaries, and so on. It is impossible to review all these sources
in detail, so I will restrict this overview to a selection of moral and
medical advice literature. (For information on Dutch childrearing practices as they can be gleaned from diaries and family archives of the seventeenth and eighteenth centuries, see Dekker 1995, and Roberts 1998.)
Manuals on raising children presuppose the notion of childhood, that is
certain. But the question is whether this notion of childhood showed any
change over time. To focus this question, I will concentrate on a few issues: discipline, coddling and the necessity of corporal punishment, paternal love, and the role of fathers and mothers.

ERASMUS AND THE SCHOOLMASTERS

The first advice on education to mention here was written by
Desiderius Erasmus (1467–1536). He published his *Declamatio de pueris
statim ac liberaliter instituendis* in 1529 and *De civilitate morum puellum* in
1530. Erasmus stresses the importance of getting an early start on the
education of children (see also Riemens, Reurslag, and Yzer 1930).
Why should we leave little children to their mothers and nurses, who
do nothing but coddle and spoil them? It is better to teach them to
read and write as soon as possible, for children have excellent memories when they are young. Some people—especially women—think it
is unhealthy for children to be forced to study, but Erasmus insists that
this danger is exaggerated. As long as teachers do not behave like
bogeymen but teach children as if their lessons are games, there will
be nothing to worry about. Erasmus sharply warns against corporal
punishment. The Bible does say: "spare the rod and spoil the child"
(Proverbs 13: 24). But we should interpret these old Jewish words
more mildly: "onze roede zij een welgezinde aansporing, somtijds ook
een berisping, maar gekruid met vriendelijkheid, niet met hatelijkheid"
("Our rod should be like a friendly incitement, sometimes a repri-
mand too, but flavored with kindness, not with hatred"; Riemens,

Reurslag, and Yzer 1930, 61). The most important tools of the educator are shame and praise.

Of course, we should not treat Erasmus's advice as typically Dutch. He formulated his ideas in the international context of humanism, so the "internationality" of his ideas is beyond dispute. Still, it is noteworthy how strongly later Dutch moralists, ranging from libertines like Dirck Coornhert to Calvinists like Cats, were influenced by the work of Erasmus. Even the thinking of Dutch puritans fitted in this Erasmian tradition, though obviously more indirectly (Groenendijk 1984).

In the years between 1590 and 1630, at least five textbooks by schoolmasters were published. Remarkably, all five of them dealt with the problematic relationship between schoolmaster and parents, especially mothers. Parents are too indulgent and they forbid the teacher to use corporal punishment to discipline the schoolchildren, with the frustrating result that all that is "implanted" at school in the morning is wiped out at home in the afternoon (Rang 1990, 90). As the Calvinist schoolmaster Valcooch complains in 1591: "D'ouderen gevense hedendaechs al haar willekens, men straft haar niet, men spaert haer billekens" ("Parents nowadays always give in, they do not punish, they spare their buttocks"). Still, he too advocates treating schoolchildren gently, pleading only "sachte hantplaxkens en proper grauwen" ("gentle tiny ferules and accurate growling"; Kruithof 1990, 30). This caution regarding corporal punishment is not restricted to Protestants. Catholics also advise against the use of violence, because otherwise children will become obstinate (Polman 1965; Garrer 1889).

JACOB CATS

In his famous and very popular treatise *Houwelyck* (*Marriage*) (1712 [1625]), the poet Jacob Cats wrote thousands and thousands of verses on married life. His work became known as the "huwelijksbijbel," the "marriage-bible," for an enormous number of Dutch families possessed a copy of Cats's *Houwelyck* as if it were as important as the Bible itself. Implicitly as well as explicitly, Cats deals with the ins and outs of family life. This means he especially deals in great detail with love, fidelity, and sexuality. Obviously, in the eyes of Cats harmony between the sexes deserved the highest priority. The chapters of *Houwelyck* are arranged around the successive stages of a woman's life. One part deals with motherhood, and in this part he dedicates some pages to the question of how to raise children (395–98). A mother has to look after her children until they are seven years old. She should be a serious educator, preparing her young as a farmer tills his land, so the father may then seed successfully in this healthy soil. She should teach her children to be good Christians, to obey their parents, to speak the truth, and to follow her virtuous example. She should teach them moral lessons they can understand: "prijst veel de ware deugt, en spreeckt'er dikmael van, / en let op yder kint, hoe veel het dragen kan" ("praise true virtue a lot, and talk about it many times, / and take notice of every child, how much it can bear," 396). Parents should teach children a trade or craft that suits them personally, so they will be able to earn a living when they grow up. They should not be forced to learn a trade they dislike; it will not work out well. According to Cats, the best means to teach children is through play: "het is een soete vont, en weerdig om te prijsen, / de jeught door enckel spel te onderwijsen" ("it is a sweet device, worthy of praise, / to teach the youth only by play"). For instance, the best way to teach children a foreign language is by having a governor speak this foreign language with the children while they play.

Like Erasmus, Cats warns against corporal punishment: "Het kint dat harde tugt en droeve slagen vreest / krijgt dofheyt aan het breyn, en domheyt in den geest" ("the child that fears severe discipline and sad drubbing / gets dullness in its brains and dumbness in its mind"). It is better to evoke children's ambitions. Nonetheless, parents should not be afraid to punish, for "wie streelt, en flickefloyt, of boven reden mint, / en krijgt maer enckel leet, oock van een aerdig kint" ("who fondles, and coaxes, or loves beyond reason, / will only receive sorrow, even from a nice child," 397). But punishing parents should never be dominated by anger: "want daer een korsel hooft is besig met de tugt, / Daer wort een heylig werk geoeffent sonder vrugt. . . . Waer toe in dit geval soo byster ongebonden? / Een die sijn kinders straft, kastijt sijn eygen sonden" ("where a crabby head is at work on discipline, / there a holy job is done fruitlessly . . . . For what reason in this case be so exceedingly unbound? / One who punishes his children, chastises his own sins.") Cats thinks it is of no use to punish children when they are small. They will not understand. The right time to begin such discipline is when children start playing with dolls. From that time on, their upbringing becomes a serious matter. Be aware, Cats says, that a child is a blank slate. Try to keep it away from bad influences.

In the end, Cats offers some practical advice to the young mother. When she and her husband have visitors, she should not let the children join the company, because they do not belong to the world of adults. She should not let the children be frightened by the maid telling stories of ghosts or bogeymen, because they might retain their fears. It is better to tell a nice story. And she should not favor one child above the other. Cats also offers a piece of advice for the young father.

He should not teach his children to fear the devil, but to fear God (398). In other words, Cats thinks children sensitive to positive influences. He never mentions the necessity of breaking the will of the young. He explicitly urges that discipline and gentle tactfulness go hand in hand.

DUTCH PURITANS

A more pious tradition of educational thinking is also to be found in seventeenth-century Holland. I am referring to the prescriptive literature produced by the Nadere Reformatie, a seventeenth-century pietistic movement among the Dutch Reformed that criticized the Reformed way of living, while taking the Dutch climate of freedom and tolerance for granted. Like the English Puritans, representatives of the Nadere Reformatie tried to make religion a matter of the heart and to bear witness to this by leading a pious lifestyle. The home and the ideal of a "godly household" were immensely important to these reformers. Families had to be transformed into "little churches." Since these pietists believed that most evil had its roots in the family, it was there that they proposed that reformation should begin. An early manual produced by the pietists was *De geestelijke queeckerije* (*The Spiritual Nursery*) by Joannes de Swaef (1740 [1621]). In his introduction, de Swaef emphasizes original sin. Babies at the breast sometimes already look pale because of their anger, proving the necessity for parents to break their depraved will as early as possible. Still, it is astonishing to note how much de Swaef's advice is like that of Erasmus. Children should be treated as equals, and parents should choose a trade for their children that suits them best. Moreover, to raise them as good Christians, parents should start as early as possible, knowing "datse kinderen sijnde ook als kinderen dencken" "that children, being children, also think in a childish way"). Corporal punishment is only a last resort; it is much more effective to make children behave by appealing to their pride (Kruithof 1990, 42). In 1679, Jacobus Koelman published another pietistic manual, *De pligten der ouders* (*The Obligations of Parents*). The title itself is interesting: for the first time, parental responsibilities are stressed without mention of their traditional counterpart, the duties of the children. In 281 items, Koelman urges parents to start the religious education of their children as soon as possible, to teach them to be obedient, to talk with them about God, to break their will, to train them in an attitude of self-denial, to be modest in corporal punishment, and to deal with them "naer proportie" (proportionally), all in order to reach salvation. Koelman also modernizes the old theme of dealing with children according to their character. Since some children need only one word while others have to be beaten before they obey, parents always have to decide whether to use love or rigor to convince the child (Kruithof 1990, 47).

Late Seventeenth-Century Advice

At the end of the seventeenth century, two other interesting texts were published. The first was a medical manual, Stephanus Blankaart's *Verhandelinge van de opvoedinge en ziekten der kinderen* (*Treatise on the Upbringing and Illnesses of Children*) (1684). This treatise turns out to be a medical manual almost *tout court*. Only one short chapter contains advice on rearing. It is the same Erasmian story. Children should not be nagged, because they will become aggressive. They should not be scared by stories about monsters and ghosts, because they will stay frightened forever. The middle of the road is again the best way to go. One should not be too severe or thrifty, because children will get jealous, steal, or become lonely. One should not give the young too much or be indulgent, for they will end up in the pub. One should not break their will by hitting them, only by gentle warning ("soete vermaninge"). But Blankaart does advance two new arguments in this advice book. First, he says that adults should not talk about things between man and wife in the presence of their children. In the next century this advice will be repeated again and again, becoming one of the most important elements of good childrearing. Second, Blankaart puts forth a new way of understanding original sin. "De ouders selfs moeten de kinderen niet te hard vallen, in dit of dat, gelyk ik weet, dat veele de gewoonte hebben; want de kinderen is het quaad van jongs aan genoegsaam ingeboren, so dat men het daar niet hoeft in te dragen" ("parents themselves should not get angry with their children about this or that, as I know a lot of them are used to do; for evil is in children from the moment they are born, and we do not need to introduce it into their lives ourselves," 30–31). This is the first time that original sin was used not as a reason to be severe but in defense of gentleness in raising children.

The second work was the anonymously authored *Algemeene opvoedinge der hedendaagse kinderen of mal moertje mal kindje* (*General Education of Nowadays Children, or Silly Mother Silly Child*) (1690). From the title one might expect another manual, but it is nothing of the sort. It is, instead, a long lamentation on the decline of good manners among the Dutch. A great number of very good families are being ruined by the misbehavior of their youth, the author complains. And his explanation is simple. In all social classes, but especially in the middle and lower middle class, girls as well as boys in the four successive stages of growing up are spoiled by their mothers. This spoiling begins as soon as they are born, but the author is especially worried about the behavior of children in their third and fourth stage of development (*wasch-dom*). Girls get pregnant. Boys become idlers. In the sixteenth century, a golden age when trade flourished ("dat het te dier tyden een Goude eeuw, en een florizante tyd was dat als toe de coopmanschap te recht floreerde," 83), people knew how to raise their children, and the "overmatige burgerlijke wijse van leven" ("excessive middle class way of living") we see nowadays did not exist yet (86). In the late seventeenth century, decline has set in because of the mother's love of ostentation and money. This repetitious complaint explains the subtitle of the book, "Mal moertje mal kindje" ("silly mother, silly child"). The father should be involved in raising his children to a much greater degree than he is, so the children may feel his authority and his discipline (100).

CONTINUITY AND CHANGE IN DUTCH ADVICE

A great deal of continuity is to be found in Dutch advice literature in the sixteenth, seventeenth, and eighteenth centuries, despite the fact that some of it is especially concerned with sin and hell while some is more concerned with a more general goal of Christian life. All of it agrees on the principle that young children have to be formed to become good Christians. Discipline is always invoked as an important element in rearing children, and coddling is disapproved; but corporal punishment is also discouraged by most advisers or recommended only on a modest scale.

On close reading, however, some shifts can be observed, especially in regard to parental love. In the beginning, parental love hardly seems to be an issue in the advice literature. It is simply taken for granted. Children, on the other hand, are charged again and again to love their parents. So in the sixteenth and seventeenth centuries love for children is a non-issue, while love for parents is an embattled one. Only in the second half of the seventeenth century do advisers begin to demand of parents that they love their children, a new accent that was to be continued in the advice literature of the eighteenth century. And this clearly has to be seen in connection with the already mentioned obsession with decline, once the "Golden Age" was over. Advisers despise parental laxity. They admonish parents to love their children, and in doing so imply that they should be severe to them as well, as the Dutch used to be in the past. It is in this context that fathers are criticized for leaving the education of their children to their wives. That is why young people in the Netherlands are spoiled. Fathers should take part in the child's education to a larger extent, helping to discipline it in an authoritative way, as only men can do.

Obviously, the question whether these manuals and advice books reflect the daily reality of Dutch family life in the early modern era remains. We simply do not know. But one thing is clear: they inform us of mainstream pedagogical thinking a lot more directly than painting and prints ever will.

Conclusion

There is an old Dutch expression: "in het jaar der kinderen," in the year of the children. It is a way of referring to a time that will never come, an impossible prophecy. Ellen Key's proclamation of the "century of the child" reminds me of this old expression, though I am sure Key herself did not doubt her prophecy! Declaring the century just begun "the century of the child," as Key did in 1900, she declared her optimism. She expected tremendous results from the natural raising of children. They would grow up to be good, well-educated, self-confident adults. They would make the world better, that was certain. And look at us: talking about "child centeredness" or the lack of it, we only declare our deeply felt concerns. It seems as if parents nowadays have nothing but worries. Does the child get enough love and attention? Will it learn useful things to survive in this harsh world? Will it be intimidated by other kids or sexually abused by the teacher or babysitter? In short, we are no longer certain that the adult world is able to offer a pleasant life and a good future to our youth.

A historian should never try to predict the future. So I will not answer the question whether we are at the end of the century of the child. But I can be affirmative in one way. Yes, I think we should end the century of the child, that is, the century of this family history. For I think the central question of the debate—were children in the past seen as children or as pocket-size adults?—does not do justice to the people of the past. Ariès set the tone of this debate. His interpretation of history was meant as an argument against the child-centeredness and crumbling parental authority of modern life. That is why he stressed the harshness of family life in former times, when parents treated their children as little adults. But instead of being used as a plea for rehabilitation of the old-fashioned ways of raising children, his family history has been embraced by those who condemn the harshness of these old-fashioned attitudes toward children and urge the necessity of even more autonomy, rights, and love for children. So reformers have used these stories about the harshness of raising children in the past to underline the necessity for change. People from the past were condemned as adults without love for or interest in their children, or they were defended as people who, on the contrary, did love their children, despite the harshness of the circumstances of their day.

We should be aware that generalizations like these cannot be falsified and therefore tend to an anachronistic and ahistorical approach. Family historians who try to imagine the past in such a broad way, while using the debates of their own time as a starting point, are very likely to write a "Whig interpretation of history," as the contradictory interpretations of the history of Dutch childhood cited at the beginning of this chapter illustrate. Of course, speculations may be useful in stimulating debate, but I think the time has come to put an end to them now. Questions to the past can be too large to yield answers, like the questions Ariès introduced with his daring history of childhood. Family historians should leave growing pains behind and develop a more specific sort of historical knowledge. They should look for empirical facts, do justice to historical contexts, and formulate refined theories that can be tested by looking at those historical facts. As a historical discipline, family history should grow up.

Chapter 4
Patterns of Childrearing in America

KARIN CALVERT

Members of any society carry within themselves working definitions of childhood, its nature, limitations, and duration. In fact numerous, even contradictory conceptions of the nature of childhood may exist simultaneously in a society, a family, even an individual. Adults may not explicitly articulate such paradigms or even consciously conceive of them as an issue, but they act on their assumptions in all their dealings with, fears for, and expectations of their children. The process of education in the broader meaning of the term is one in which children who have reached the age of reason learn to adapt themselves to accepted personas, to be feminine or masculine, obedient or mischievous, humble or arrogant, innocent or worldly, as their society or their parents expect of them. The degree to which any particular child meets such expectations and his or her ease in doing so depends on a wide range of factors including the compatibility between the child's personality and the roles assigned by social convention, the level of commitment of the parent to those conventions, and the consistency and clarity of the expectations.[1]

Infants and toddlers, however, lack the necessary comprehension and skills to conform to social expectations in even a rudimentary fashion. Children do not always look or act in accord with prevailing social constructs. Where little children are unable to conform, caregivers rely on exterior means, including material objects, to maintain the accepted images and ensure the desired behavior of their children. In fact, only a small part of children's physical environment deals primarily with their physical needs. A great deal, including much of children's furniture, is used to direct, contain, and control a child's behavior. Similarly, toys underscore or encourage specific class or gender roles. Artifacts are also used to maintain a perception of the child compatible with common cultural assumptions regarding the nature of childhood. Clothing, for example, often conveys social signals regarding a child's gender and age, and may either link children to the adult world or set them apart from it in accord with cultural assumptions. Conventions of dress may go further, suggesting qualities not yet apparent in young children. For example, precisely because of the androgynous appearance of babies, parents in a culture that puts great significance on gender may use gender-coded clothing to distinguish sons from daughters. Deciphering the rationale behind such conventions can tell us a great deal about cultural expectations of children and their place in society.

The commonly accepted artifacts of childhood present in America in the first century after European colonization gradually disappeared from common use, to be replaced with new forms, which in turn gave way to entirely new constellations of furniture forms, clothing styles, and playthings less than a century later. Such wholesale changes in the accouterments of childhood suggest equally significant changes in methods of childrearing, assumptions about the nature of children, and perceptions of childhood itself. Dates are little more than rough indicators of such broad and fundamental changes in childrearing practices, because the rate of change varied for city and countryside, religious affiliations and ethnic communities, and socioeconomic levels. A nearly constant influx of immigrants kept alive traditional practices that had all but disappeared from most American homes and simultaneously introduced innovations as yet unknown here. The result was that at any given moment in American history a number of childrearing systems were in operation.

General trends nonetheless are evident, and it is those trends that I wish to consider here. Setting chronological parameters on deep social change must be an approximation at best. The dates used here for each era in American childrearing represent only the point at which a significant portion of middle-class families had adopted new methods of childrearing.

The Colonial Child: 1620–1770

Adults in colonial America viewed infants as rather inadequate creatures, extremely vulnerable to accident and disease, irrational and animalistic in their behavior, and a drain on the family's resources and energy. To the seventeenth-century mind, human beings were literally made, not born. The newborn infant appeared as unpromising material, a shapeless "lump of flesh, " "a round ball" that had to be molded into human form by the midwife (Buchan 1809, 44).[2] Adults believed that such unpromising material would not develop on its own but had to be humanized through direct adult intervention.[3]

That intervention began moments after birth when the midwife placed the newborn on her lap and began molding and smoothing the head and pulling the arms and legs to their full extension, rubbing and shaping them so that the child would grow straight and tall. She then preserved her handiwork by swaddling the infant in bands of linen wrapped tightly around the legs and torso. Another band held the child's arms straight against the body. Yet another piece of cloth, the stay band, she secured at the forehead and shoulders with additional strips of cloth. The end result was an immobile little mummified package, about the size and shape of a loaf of bread, which could be placed in a cradle or basket or even hung from a peg on the wall. Swaddling protected the child and freed the mother to attend to the endless responsibilities essential for the family's comfort and survival. A swaddled baby could not kick off the covers on a cold winter night or roll off its resting place, and it could be left safely in the often perfunctory care of a servant or older sibling. There was no risk to the weak little neck or back, since, no matter how the child was carried, it would remain fully supported within its rigid wrappings. Support came from the costume, not the attendant.

Beyond the perceived physical benefits from swaddling, adults believed that, without swaddling bands to keep the legs extended and the back straight, the naturally curving infant body would never grow into an upright human being. Parents feared that, without the direct intervention swaddling represented, children would never learn to stand erect but would, as the physician François Mauriceau warned in 1675, "crawl on all fours like little animals for the rest of their lives" (Mauriceau 1675, 130). In his *History of the World*, Sir Walter Raleigh (1694, Book 1, 31) compared each age of man with one of the planets. Mercury symbolized the second age of schooling and soldiering and Venus the third age of love and courtship. Infancy, the first age, which he considered categorically different from the rest, he compared to the moon, since the moon was a celestial body but not truly a planet, just as an infant was not truly a human being. It could become one, but, in a world of miracles, witchcraft, changelings, and spontaneous generation, there was no assurance that an infant would develop into an upright, rational adult without aggressive parental intervention.

The swaddled infant slept in a cradle, a term that referred to any bed prepared for a babe, whether it was a wicker basket, old box, chest, or specially constructed bed on rockers. What really mattered was that any separate bed was believed better for the infant than being put to sleep with its mother, nurse, or some other older person. Adults, exhausted by hard physical work and commonly dulled with alcohol, could all too easily roll on an infant in the night and smother it. Since "laying over" was a highly feared form of infant mortality, the child who slept alone slept most safely. A "purposely made" cradle was a portable piece of furniture of wicker or board construction affixed to wooden rockers and often hooded at one end. It could be placed close to the fire or within the curtains of the parent's bed for additional warmth. Babies were laced into their cradles with tapes laced "from hole to hole in the Cradle which they tie very hard; for should they not do so, they believe their Child would not stay in the Cradle . . . whereby the inlaid Child is packed up like a pack of Wares" (Wurtz 1656, reprinted in Ruhrah 1925, 202–12). In this manner the cradle also became a means of ensuring that children would grow straight and stand erect.

Babies outgrew both swaddling clothes and cradles by the end of their first year. Long petticoats helped to keep infants warm and effectively foiled any attempt the baby made to crawl. Parents and physicians alike viewed crawling on all fours, not as a natural stage of human development, but as a bad habit that, if not thwarted, would remain the baby's primary form of locomotion for the rest of its life. As late as 1839, when babyish behavior had gained considerable acceptance, the American childrearing authority William Alcott noted that many American mothers still prohibited their little children from crawling (Alcott 1839, 232).

As the common form of locomotion for most animals, crawling raised too many fears and negative associations. It distinctly emphasized the difference between children and adults and seemed to be development in decidedly the wrong direction. Parents wanted their children to become more like them, not less.

Most of the handful of traditional furniture forms designed expressly for children encouraged early standing or walking and prevented crawling. Parents pushed children to stand at as early an age as possible, partly to strengthen their leg muscles to ensure early walking and partly from the common belief that it was unlucky for a child to learn to speak before it had begun to walk. At about the same time that mothers freed their children from swaddling bands, they began to make use of standing stools. The standing stool looked like a normal wooden stool, with somewhat shorter legs and a round hole in the top into which the child was placed. The device supported babies just finding their feet but did not allow them the opportunity to sit down. Most such devices were homemade, the simplest being a hollowed out tree trunk: "the inside and upper edge are smoothed, and a child just able to stand is put into it, while the mother is at work by its side, or going after the business of the house" (Loudon 1839, 351). Standing stools of whatever configuration kept infants off the cold and dirty floors and strengthened the leg muscles. Colonial society had no faith that children would naturally take to walking when they were ready, but instead firmly believed that children needed to be forced upright. Dr. William Cadogan urged that "a child, therefore, should be pushed forwards, and taught to walk as soon as possible. An healthy child a year old will be able to walk alone" (Cadogan 1769, in Buchan 1809, 123).

To get the child walking was the first major goal of parenting in the colonial era, and swaddling bands and standing stools were tools in that endeavor. The walking child reassured parents that their infant would make the necessary transition to complete humanness and marked the true beginning of life as a human being. "This we may call the era of their deliverance; for this great difficulty surmounted they generally do well, by getting out of the nurse's hands to shift for themselves" (Cadogan 1769, in Buchan 1809, 123). To ensure and hasten walking, parents relied on a variety of additional devices. The simplest were leading strings, ribbons or cord fastened to the shoulders of young children's clothing or passed under their arms. An adult holding the strings could guide the child's steps and guard against both falls and any inclination the baby might have to drop down to the floor and crawl.

Another device to encourage early walking was the walking stool or go-cart, which was essentially a standing stool with wheels attached. Even those who worried about babies being left to stand too long on unsteady legs in standing stools approved of go-carts, since "in those stools the children can hold out longer, because they can stir and move in them" (Wurtz 1656, 220). Unlike standing stools, go-carts did not protect little ones from accidents. Children in walking stools, if unattended, could and did walk into open fires or down stairwells. The urgency parents felt regarding the necessity of getting children up and walking, however, tended to override any misgivings regarding safety.

Once walking on their own, children essentially entered the adult world and no more special equipment was considered necessary. Colonial parents expected their young ambulatory children to accommodate themselves as best they could to the world around them. Children slept wherever there was space—with parents, siblings, servants, or guests, in full-sized beds or on pallets on the floor in often crowded rooms. They ate sitting on an adult's lap or standing by the table in order to reach their plates. They played with balls, whistles, cards, and whirligigs, which were made as much for adult amusement as for children, or went without toys if their religious sect disapproved of play in general.

Colonial society viewed early childhood as a vulnerable, frustrating period of human inadequacy, best gotten through as quickly as possible. Infancy represented such a precarious existence that parents regarded it essentially as a state of illness. Babies needed to be protected assiduously and pushed beyond infancy as quickly as possible. Growing up meant growing strong and gaining sufficient autonomy to be able to take care of oneself. Conscientious parents wanted to see their children out of the dangers and miseries of infancy and safely on their way to secure positions in the world. Furniture that would hasten the process—equipment that got infants up and walking as quickly as possible—had great appeal. Autonomy and self-sufficiency were considered better for both the children themselves and their overworked parents.

The independence parents desired for children, however, was a physical one. Parents wanted their children independent of external restraints and controls, but able to internalize the rules of conduct, obedience, and deference and act appropriately. Ambulatory children remained dependent on and obedient to their parents for many years, but they were increasingly responsible for the own actions and no longer dependent on external control or close supervision to conform to familial and social rules.

The Republican Child: 1770–1830

Beginning about 1770, Americans began to take more interest in their families. Increasingly, marriages were based on affection rather than economics, and parents took delight in the peculiarly childish natures of their children. Middle-class mothers wrote letters to absent fathers detailing the baby talk and antics of their infants, and both parents more often enjoyed playing with their little ones. While colonial portraits of children depicted them standing or sitting with adult solemnity, in portraits after 1750 they were more often shown playing on the floor with a toy or dancing about in childish glee.

A growing interest in the natural sciences and in direct observation of the world led eighteenth-century scientists to hypothesize that each species developed through a series of predictable and immutable stages and that from such natural law not even man was exempt. It followed that infants would learn to sit up, stand, and even walk without parental intervention, because it was their nature to do so. A new generation of childrearing experts argued that children needed more freedom and less restriction or coercion. They wrote that children would grow straight and tall if left unbound, would learn to walk in their own good time, and would remain altogether healthier if not protected so assiduously from the cold and damp (Locke 1693; Rousseau 1762; Buchan 1809; Cadogan 1769).

Philosophers and scientists of the period turned from a static conception of the world to a dynamic one, in which all things, whether individual organisms, animal species, or even human cultures, were understood as progressing through observable stages, each with its own needs and characteristics. Leading proponents of a dynamic progression of stages in natural history included Carl von Linnaeus, F. W. J. Schelling, and Johann von Goethe. Within this trend, the two men most influential in altering American childrearing patterns were John Locke, who stressed the malleable nature of the young, and Jean-Jacques Rousseau, whose fictional Emile offered the first popularly recognized alternative to the adult model of appearances and behavior. Both men viewed children not as incomplete adults but as immature human beings with both limitations and abilities appropriate to their stage of development. They believed that play was not frivolous and should not be forbidden. Rather, they encouraged children's inclinations to play as a natural part of the learning process. American middle-class parents gradually abandoned much of the tight bandaging that had shackled earlier generations of infants. Babies and young infants wore light muslin frocks that permitted them freer use of limbs and lungs. Educational toys and children's books gained acceptance as suitable possessions for children.

The perception of childhood had changed from one of a period of vulnerability and deficiency, through which fearful parents pushed their children as quickly as possible, to one of a vital preparatory stage, in which children needed only freedom and gentle guidance to develop their own natural talents and inherent moral nature. Children needed time to develop at their own pace, and an extended childhood provided that time. There was no need to rush children into adult behavior; indeed, it was counterproductive to do so.

During the second half of the eighteenth century, middle-class parents stopped swaddling their babies and abandoned standing and walking stools. Dr. William Buchan, a respected authority in America, declared that "dwarfishness, deformity, diseases, or death" often resulted from swaddling a child like "an Egyptian mummy." Instead, he advocated dressing babies and toddlers in light cotton frocks both summer and winter to give them freedom of movement and harden them against the elements (Buchan 1809, 48). What comfort babies gained in freedom from restrictive clothing, they lost in exposure to the cold. Buchan echoed John Locke in warning that "children be not too warmly clad or cover'd, winter or summer," citing the observation that "the face when we are born is no less tender than any other part of the body. 'Tis use alone hardens it, and makes it able to endure cold" (Locke 1693, 10). Another physician took this line of thought even further by arguing that infants were not more delicate than adults but actually hardier. A baby actually required less clothing and fewer covers at night, "because it is naturally warmer and would bear the cold of a winter's night much better than any adult person whatever" (Cadogan 1769, 111). Not surprisingly, many American parents adopted the firm belief that cold baths protected and invigorated small bodies. With the enthusiasm for fresh air and cool sleeping quarters, traditional enclosed cradles gave way to new forms whose slatted or spindled sides permitted a free flow of air around the baby. Swaddling was no longer needed to keep an infant from kicking off the covers, since exposure to the air was thought to be beneficial.

Whether a cradle had closed or pierced sides, it almost invariably had rockers. Traditionally, rocking was thought to imitate the gentle motion of the womb. Seventeenth- and eighteenth-century physicians assumed that the fetus hung suspended from the umbilical cord within the womb. As the mother moved, her baby swayed gently back and forth. Babies therefore enjoyed being rocked in a cradle because it reminded them of in utero sensations. Unfortunately, there were many tales of harried attendants who, "in the excess of folly and brutality," rocked the cradle so violently that the baby became insensible from the prolonged vertigo and sensory bombardment. Such hard rocking, as it was called, could quiet a fussy infant for several hours (Buchan 1809, 71). The cradle that had been championed as a safe haven from the dangers of infant overlayment came to be perceived as too easily a tool of infant abuse. Gradually the cradle fell from favor, to be replaced by the cot or crib, a stationary infant bed that could not be rocked.

By the beginning of the nineteenth century, most middle-class American homes had grown larger and contained more rooms. More rooms meant more specialization of function for each room. With separate, permanent sleeping chambers, there was less need for a portable cradle to be moved about as wanted. Gradually the cradle with open sides and without rockers took up permanent residence in a back chamber designated the nursery. The redesigned furniture, termed a cot in England and a crib in America, offered a baby a safe, if chilly bed. For older children, however, parents still believed it better to room them with adults whenever possible, rather than with siblings of similar age, since the more time children spent with reasonable adults, the more likely they were to develop rational minds. The wealthy Virginia planter Robert Carter, for example, assigned his son to sleep in a room with the children's tutor, and his young nephew shared a room with Carter's secretary. Likewise, George Washington's grandson shared a room at Mount Vernon with Washington's secretary.[4]

Although many similar changes in the philosophy and manner of childrearing were occurring in England and parts of Europe, youth took on special meaning in America in the last quarter of the eighteenth century. Americans of the Revolutionary era and the new Republic had become accustomed to a new political rhetoric in which America was the child colony or the young nation, as opposed to the decadent and feeble European mother country. The advantage lay with youth, innocence, and vigor. As childhood became more a period of preparation for life and less one of vulnerability, the healthy, natural state of freedom before the constraints of civilization, parents took greater delight in their children's childishness. Gradually the years of childhood increased. Childhood was no longer viewed as an age when the child was unproductive and at risk, but as an important stage in human development. A longer and less encumbered childhood would better prepare the future citizens of the new country.

Victorian Childhood: 1830–1900

The new recognition of the special nature of children that emerged in the last decades of the eighteenth century found wider acceptance during the nineteenth century. The special needs and general welfare of children became a major concern of a newly emerging professional middle class (Wiebe 1967, 111–32). A growing number of professionals in the fields of law, medicine, education, and social welfare slowly came to regard minors as individuals entitled to certain basic rights under the law and not merely as possessions of their parents. This radically altered viewpoint made possible a growing number of state and local child-protection laws, child-labor laws, special institutions for the orphaned and delinquent, and the formation of Societies for the Prevention of Cruelty to Children. In the field of education, universal and compulsory schooling became the goal, if not always the reality. The average number of years of schooling and the length of the school year both expanded significantly over the course of the century as prominent educators stressed the importance of both kindergartens and high schools. At the same time pediatrics became a recognized medical specialty. Interest in the needs of children spread beyond professional circles to include much of the middle-class public. Indications of concern for and fascination with children included the expanding genres of childrearing manuals and children's literature, the creation of child-centered holidays, and the profusion of toys and other artifacts marketed expressly for children.

Many influential American theologians of the nineteenth century no longer regarded children as tainted by original sin, but saw them as essentially pure and innocent gifts of God.[5] The perceived innocence of children made them distinctly different and separate from adults, who had been corrupted by the world. Middle-class parents, influenced by the pervasive sentimentalized image of the child as cherub, felt pressured to raise children who lived up to that ideal. Any failure on the part of the child was automatically the fault of the parents. Such socially imposed apprehensions about childrearing were compounded by popular misunderstandings concerning the nature of heredity. Nineteenth-century scientists believed that dishonesty, insanity, alcoholism, and talents were all equally inheritable; similarly, the physical and mental condition of the parents at the time of conception, a mother's emotional state during pregnancy, and even a father's youthful excesses before marriage could all affect the offspring. The popular writer and phrenologist Orson Fowler warned, "Willing or unwilling, you are *compelled* to predetermine [your children's] future virtues or vices, talents or foolishnesses, happiness or misery. Ignorant or informed, you cannot escape the momentous responsibility" (Fowler 1870, 817). Wise parents protected the inherent angel and suppressed the inherited devil in their children.

Nineteenth-century American society was one of self-restraint and control, where appearances counted greatly and ceremony was valued above spontaneity. "We are constantly required to sacrifice comfort to conventionality," an authority on etiquette reminded readers, "and the discipline is good for us" (Harcourt 1907, 83). Parents were responsible for teaching their children both the specific rules and the self-discipline necessary to function satisfactorily in polite society, certainly no easy task. Such authorities as Catherine Beecher advised mothers that teaching morals and manners (the two were definitely linked in Victorian minds) could neither start too early nor be pursued too diligently. "There is no more important duty devolving upon a mother," Beecher warned, "than the cultivation of habits of modesty and propriety in young children. All indecorous words or deportment should be carefully restrained and delicacy and reserve studiously cherished" (Beecher 1848, 33). Civilization depended on standards maintained by everyone, and even "babies must be taught to be decent members of society" (Panton 1893, 231). For children too young to have developed a reliable degree of self-discipline, the nineteenth-century mother required external forms of control to ensure that her offspring functioned within the accepted bounds of decorum.

One of the most important training grounds for both manners and morals was the Victorian family's dining table, where little children were most visible to family and guests. While many English and European upper- and middle-class children commonly took their meals apart from adults, the majority of American children joined their elders for all but the most formal social occasions (Wells 1890, 423). Family meals, the authors of childrearing manuals believed, were excellent opportunities for teaching children etiquette and self-restraint. Successful internalization of the rules of civilized behavior mattered because the physical well-being and future character of the child were at stake, as was the family's claim to gentility and refinement. "Good conduct at meals," declared one expert in "nursery discipline" early in the century,

is with children, a fair criterion of manners and meals may be made use of, as favorable opportunities for inculcating propriety of behavior. Children should be taught to sit down, and to rise from the table, at the same time; to wait, whilst others are served, without betraying eagerness, or impatience; to avoid noise and conversation, and if they are no longer confined to the nursery, to be able to see delicacies without expecting or asking to partake of them. (Hoare 1826, 83)

Most authorities and parents firmly believed that a child's diet should be simple and wholesome, free of all delicacies and rich foods. Bread and milk, plain vegetables, unsweetened puddings, and cereals were regarded as the most healthful food for children, while rich or spicy food would stimulate them, making them restless or sick or prematurely awakening their sexuality. Children had to learn to sit quietly at the table, eating their milk porridge, while their elders indulged in meats, rich sauces, and sweet desserts, a hard lesson perhaps, but one that many parents considered essential to the health of the child.

High chairs of any form were rare in America before 1830. Most children too young for a proper chair sat on an obliging lap or were raised up with books or pillows. The high chairs that did exist were simply that, a high chair that brought the child up to a comfortable dining height. By 1850 high chairs had become common in American homes, but these were high chairs with a difference. For the child too young to master sufficient self-discipline, the Victorian high chair came complete with its own attached tray, which not only held the child securely in place but also separated the young person from direct contact with the dining table. The separation of the toddler from the main dining table suppressed or at least contained any display of bad manners. Babies could not grab food or objects or smear sticky fingers on white tablecloths. The new tray provided access only to those items someone else saw fit to place on the tray's surface. As the *Furniture Gazette* of 1870 advertised, a high chair with a tray promised "well regulated demeanor" at the table.

Since nineteenth-century infants were no longer forced on their feet by their first birthday, the go-cart and standing stool lost their usefulness and disappeared from middle-class homes. The nineteenth-century home, however, filled as it was with furniture, decorative objects, bric-a-brac, and curiosities, was not a safe environment for unsupervised infants. Babies who grabbed at the ubiquitous fabric draped over every table in the house risked toppling statuettes, vases, and kerosene lamps down on their heads. Although parents no longer tried to rush their children into walking, they were still reluctant to regard crawling as a natural part of human development. Nowhere in the paintings, photographs, prints, or childrearing manuals of the day were children depicted as creeping, for this form of locomotion was still too animalistic for a society that prized self-control and genteel deportment.

In the Victorian home, the baby swing or the many variations on the baby jumper replaced the go-cart as the object of choice for exercising a baby. Advertisements for swings appeared regularly in catalogues and ladies' magazines, and childrearing manuals extolled their usefulness. The common swing was a simple wooden chair without legs that was suspended from a doorway by four ropes. A jumper essentially was a swing attached to a spring to give it bounce. The nineteenth-century mother feared as much for the immediate safety of her toddler as that of her baby. A swing was a satisfactory solution, for it offered children amusement while protecting them from mishap by tethering them to one spot. The swing, like the go-cart before it, was a simple device, easily made at home or cheaply purchased. While the go-cart had forced the baby to stand on its own two feet (however unsteady they might be) and had offered a sense of independence at the risk of possible injury, the swing was designed with the physical limitations of nonambulatory children in mind. It offered support, security, and amusement. Parents and manufacturers were quick to realize that any device that could restrain a crawling baby could limit the movements of a toddler just as well. Advertisements for swings stressed that their products could easily hold children as old as six, providing them with exercise and amusement while protecting delicate household furnishings (*Sears, Roebuck Co. Catalogue* 1897, 142). For children of the nineteenth century, the price of safety was frequently a loss of independence.

If the swing and high chair held babies secure during the day, the

crib safely contained them at night. After the Civil War, the crib replaced the cradle so completely that the 1890 volume of the *Upholsterer*,
under the unequivocal heading "The Cradle Is No More," asserted
that "a cradle is a thing unknown nowadays. Go to the furniture store
and ask for cradles, and they will show you cribs, perambulators, ham-
mocks and bassinettes" (*Upholsterer* 1890). Cribs were housed in the
nursery, a bedroom/playroom for all the young children of the family,
usually located as far from rooms of adult activity as possible. The controlled atmosphere of the nursery was meant to protect children's innocent natures and physical well-being, and it provided an area in
which they learned the discipline of regular habits. "It is in the nursery, in a great measure," advised an eminent Philadelphia physician,
"that the habit of early or late rising is generated—this is a matter of
much importance, and the greatest regularity should be observed"
(Dewees 1832, 11). Orson Fowler was in full agreement forty years
later: "Periodicity should be faithfully observed in everything. They
should be bathed quickly at one specified hour, . . . put to sleep at
regular intervals, and nursed by the clock" (Fowler 1870, 847). Catherine Beecher, like most nineteenth-century authorities, favored confining children while still awake to their cribs for scheduled periods, as
this would "induce regularity in other habits, which saves trouble. In
doing this, a child may cry at first, a great deal, but for a healthy child,
this use of the lungs does no harm, and tends rather to strengthen,
than injure them" (1848, 219). She then went on to assure the young
mother that the child would soon become accustomed to lie or sit in its
crib much of the time, freeing the mother for other activities. Training
a child to the clock was a very useful discipline in an industrialized society that required punctuality and respect for schedules to function
effectively.

The crib was admirably constructed to contain the child who might
object to confinement. The tall legs and high sides made escape difficult and dangerous, especially when compared to the old-fashioned
and discarded trundle beds that rested only inches off the floor. Cribs
measuring three feet wide by five feet long were not only large enough
to give a baby room to exercise but also ample enough to comfortably
sleep a four-year-old. Like the swing and jumper, the crib could confine
the toddler as well as the infant until the intricacies of self-discipline
were mastered.

Eighteenth-century physicians had encouraged putting young children to bed with older siblings or "some handy reasonable servant"
(Cadogan 1769, 219). Nineteenth-century childrearing authorities,
however, increasingly agreed that children should be separated from

others while they slept. "When practicable," advised one physician in 1832, "children should sleep in separate beds; and these should be large for it is injurious to have them cramped together when they sleep, as well as indelicate to crowd opposite sexes together" (Dewees 1832, 110). Near the end of the century, a popular childrearing manual asked, "Should a child sleep in the same bed with its mother or nurse?" and answered "under no circumstances if this can be avoided. Nor should older children sleep together" (Holt 1894, 110) Descriptions of how to arrange the furniture in a nursery were predicated on the assumption that each young child would sleep in a separate crib (Dewing 1882, 164).

Ideally, once children grew too old for the nursery they moved into rooms of their own. This seems to have been a particularly American custom; most European cultures continued to room young children together. "At a suitable age, a child may be removed from the nursery to a separate sleeping chamber," wrote William Alcott in 1839. "Here, if circumstances permit, it should sleep by itself" (1839, 272). "Where your dwelling will admit it," Walter Houghton agreed nearly fifty years later, "give each child a room to himself or herself" (1883, 51). Experts and parents believed that children given their own rooms would study better without interruptions, take greater pride in their room and keep it clean and neat since it was really their own, and appreciate a private place to entertain friends or pursue hobbies. American parents wanted to encourage in their children a sense of independence and individualism, and they believed that spatial separation fostered both traits. As Orson Fowler explained, "sleeping by themselves is also a first-rate plan, both for health, and to prevent their imbibing anything wrong from other children" (1853, 62–63). Victorian parents believed that children sleeping with others were vulnerable to both the transmission of disease and sexual awareness.

If social perceptions of children were predicated on a belief in their perfectly innocent and pure natures, then anything that compromised that innocence destroyed the child, for the loss of innocence was nothing less than the loss of childhood as Victorians defined it, and therefore the loss of a state of grace that enveloped and protected the child. Parents were obsessive in their zeal to safeguard their children. Permitting children to sit with their legs crossed, ride on hobbyhorses (especially for girls), or bounce on a paternal knee all could lead to "degrading sexuality" (Walker 1839, 74–75). Cautious parents saw to it that their children avoided rich and spicy foods, red meats, overly warm beds or sleeping rooms, inadvertent genital stimulation from clothing, toys, or games, and intimate contact with servants or worldly wise children. Such homely items as the crib, high chair, unsweetened bread pudding, and footed pajamas were all weapons against contamination from both the outside world and the child's own internal weaknesses.

Nineteenth-century Americans were preoccupied with the concept of loss. The sentimental cult of mourning, tragic love stories, and fears of the gradual decline of the human species were common fare. Childhood fit well into this romantic pattern; it was something bright and fleeting, to be cherished while it lasted. Maturity, in the new schema, was a corrupting process from which no one emerged unscathed. Perceiving childhood as a time free of guilt, regret, or care, parents tried to build a separate and safe world for their children. The separate nursery was a safe haven, and the newly available high chairs, swings, and cribs confined the innocent to protect them from corruption. Freedom had become dangerous and safety lay in isolation. The inevitable age when children outgrew childhood was perceived as a loss, a kind of expulsion from the Garden of Eden, to be avoided as long as possible.

The Modern Child: 1900 to the Present

During the last decades of the nineteenth century, an alternative perception of the nature of children emerged. Some scholars, writers, childrearing authorities, and parents began to doubt the absolute innocence of all children. Mischief, according to this view, was natural, normal, and healthy, especially in the development of young boys. Mark Twain, for example, expressed the new sentiment when he described Tom Sawyer and Huckleberry Finn as basically good and likable boys even though they were almost always in trouble. Sigmund Freud later codified the new perception in his descriptions of infants as born with desires, instincts, and selfish impulses. Growing up was a process of experimentation in order to discover the individual's strengths and talents. Since no child was perfect, parents did not have to guard their children quite so assiduously, and any display of disobedience, stubbornness, or selfishness could be treated as natural and correctable, even harmless, rather than as the first sign of worldly corruption. As parents came to accept that every act of disobedience did not represent a fall from grace, infant naughtiness could actually seem comical and endearing. The cherub of the nineteenth century had become, by the turn of the century, "King Baby," "the little emperor," or "the little tyrant," whose demands could sometimes be indulged without fear of permanently damaging the child's character. Twentieth-century parents wanted their children to be more independent and self-assertive, and they sought environments that would stimulate and channel youthful energy.[6]

Parents who accepted the newer perception of childhood believed that it was no longer necessary to protect their little ones quite so diligently from contact with the world around them. In fact, they believed that the intellectual stimulation derived from exploration and experimentation would help children adapt and mature. Parents could give children freedom to benefit even from their own mistakes. Changing parental perspectives led once again to changes in many of the popular artifacts of childhood. The playpen replaced the baby swing, providing a secure, contained environment, but one that allowed little ones to sit, stand, crawl, or lie down as they wished. Articles in women's magazines encouraged mothers for the first time to make their homes safe for their babies, so that toddlers could be given free run of the house without fear of injury. Americans of the early twentieth century came to see their children as mischievous, curious, adventurous, and impulsive beings who needed a stimulating environment that integrated them into the life of the family while offering safety and protection.

Parents were encouraged to fill their children's lives with stimulating environments. Separate playrooms became increasingly popular, furnished with child-sized tables and chairs, blackboards, bookcases, and toys. Since the 1770s, parents had provided children with educational toys to encourage their development. The Victorian nursery contained moral or educational board games and miniature versions of adult artifacts, such as carpentry sets to develop manual skills in little boys and diminutive tea sets to foster domestic instincts in little girls. The purpose of such toys was to prepare children for the roles they would one day assume as adults. The popularity of educational toys continued and expanded in the twentieth century, but what was really new was the acceptance and encouragement of a fantasy world for children. Colonial and Victorian parents shunned make-believe as the propagation of falsehood. At best, make-believe confused children; at worst, it was lying. Only with the gradual acceptance of the mischievous child in the twentieth century did middle-class parents accept fantasy as a harmless pleasure for children. To the traditional stories of children facing moral dilemmas now were added the stories of *Peter Pan*, *Alice in Wonderland*, *Winnie the Pooh*, *The Wizard of Oz*, and the tales of Beatrix Potter. Soft, cuddly Brownies, Kewpies, and Golliwogs and anthropomorphic rabbits, mice, and, of course, bears filled the playroom. These were the first stuffed toys, and the tactile pleasure the toys offered their little owners brought a sense of comfort and security and the companionship of a little friend. Children live in a world where everyone is bigger, stronger, and smarter than they. They therefore can find relief and delight in the company of someone smaller and weaker than themselves whom they can dominate or protect. Raggedy Ann and Winnie the Pooh were important to a child's immediate sense of well-being. Soft toys have remained popular throughout the twentieth century and beyond and have become such a commonplace of childhood that we tend to forget how very modern the concept actually is.[7]

By the 1920s, the Victorian nursery had ceased to exist in most middle-class homes. Smaller families made the single large children's room obsolete. Instead, parents frequently placed the infant directly into the room he or she would inhabit throughout childhood, which they decorated to reflect the child's age and gender. The new model was a room and furnishings that could be altered to "grow with the child." Women's magazines and books on interior decorating showed mothers how to match the room to their child. A baby boy, for instance, could be given a room decorated with ducks and boats and furnished with a brightly colored toy chest. A few years later the ducks could be removed, the boats retained, and the toy chest turned into a footlocker with a fresh coat of dark paint. By the middle of the twentieth century this elaborate, artificial code of colors and images developed to designate age and gender had become commonly recognized and accepted. Rare was the modern American mother who would put her baby son to sleep in a room decorated in shades of pink or the adolescent who would accept balloons, lambs or clowns as a decorative motif. The search for individualism was conducted within an elaborate and rigid set of rules.

Separate children's rooms remained important, but by the last half of the twentieth century few parents believed that it was possible to isolate their children from the realities of the world in order that they might remain carefree and innocent as long as possible. Rather like their colonial counterparts, late twentieth-century parents saw their children surrounded by dangers from which there is no safe haven. The modern home became permeable to knowledge via newspapers, radio, television, and the Internet to a degree unprecedented in our history and, in a society of latchkey children, illicit drugs, and the horrors of child molestation, innocence had become vulnerability. The protected child was once again the child who has been prepared to cope successfully when faced with the adult world. What Victorian parents sought to preserve as innocence in their children, modern parents feared as ignorance that put a child at risk.

The development of playrooms, playgrounds, and an image of children as playful and mischievous was accompanied by the development of separate costumes designed specifically for play. In the first decades of the century, parents dressed their toddlers in rompers that were loose, bifurcated one-piece garments that left their knees bare and permitted crawling and climbing with ease. By the 1920s little girls wore very short dresses with matching short bloomers underneath, which gave them as much freedom of movement as the shorts and knickerbockers of little boys' play clothes. In the last decades of the century, play clothes became the common costume of children for all activities. At the same time, uniforms became much more common, for both school and the increasingly adult-directed sports activities of children.

One of the most striking issues regarding children's artifacts in the twentieth century was shifting rules regarding gender distinctions in clothing. Perhaps the most significant was the adoption by girls of clothing previously reserved for boys and men. Traditionally, little boys had worn anything their sisters wore. In the 1920s, baby boys still wore dresses, through they ceased to do so during the Great Depression. But the attire of older boys and men had been theirs exclusively. By the 1930s, a few girls had adopted shorts and pants for play. Through the second half of the century, girls went on to appropriate every item in the male wardrobe. At first manufacturers met the new demand by producing traditionally male items of clothing restyled slightly to distinguish them from actual boys' wear, such as pants with side zippers or shirts that buttoned right over left. By the end of the century, boys' and girls' wardrobes looked very similar, and male prerogative in the manner of dress had virtually ceased to exist. This, of course, was occurring at the same time that women and girls were stretching out into previously male-dominated areas of sports, education, and employment.

At the same time, paradoxically, gender distinctions in infants' clothing became more defined and restrictive than ever. For the first time, parents wanted clothing that unambiguously announced the sex of even the youngest baby. By the 1950s infants' clothing was clearly coded, with transportation and sports motifs decorating boys' clothes and butterflies and flowers for girls. Details that announced the young wearer to be female included gathered sleeves, ruffles, lace, jewelry, and anything worn to hold the hair in place, including barrettes, ribbons, or elastic bands. The most ubiquitous distinction of all was a system of color-coding that assigned pink to girls and blue to boys. Traditionally baby clothes had been white and suitable for either a male or a female infant. In the second half of the twentieth century, blankets, clothing, greeting cards, toys, indeed virtually anything associated with babies came in pink or blue. The reason for this sudden need for gender labeling is unclear. Perhaps, in an ever more fluid world, parents felt a need to try to establish a strong gender identification immediately. As the traditional roles of men and women blurred, parents seemed to need to establish more firmly than ever a core gender identification in their children. Studies have shown that Americans tend to treat male and female infants differently, holding and cuddling girls more and playing more vigorously with baby boys. Gender-coded clothing intended that everyone who came into contact with the infant could recognize the sex of the child and adjust interaction with the baby accordingly.

Babies in modern America were dressed according to rigid sexual stereotypes, while older girls, given free rein to borrow where they would, appropriated all the elements of dress previously reserved for men. Boys, however, were given no such latitude. While traditionally little boys dressed like their sisters, now they were forbidden to cross the gender line. They could no longer wear skirts or colors now designated as feminine or any of the other particulars of the female dress code. The rules were very precise and involved numerous details, from which way a shirt buttons to the shape of a cuff. There was an equal aversion on the part of many to boys playing with traditionally feminine toys. Gender in modern America is still an uneven playing field. Americans perceive girls borrowing from boys as an acceptable move up, while the idea of boys borrowing from girls is most decidedly an unacceptable, even dangerous or unnatural move down. Distinctions were maintained not by putting things above the reach of girls but by declaring some things below the reach of boys.

Conclusion

The actual consequence on any child of any system of childrearing is complex and predicated on a number of factors, including the compatibility of the child's and parent's personalities and the affinity of their personalities with the accepted theories of childrearing. Some children thrive when challenged; others falter. Some blossom under close attention; others are stifled by it. No single system serves all children well.

The twentieth century seems in retrospect a jumbled mixture of sensible reform and inexplicable obsessions. It is common in any age to compare the present to the past, and for most modern Americans "the past," "tradition," or "the good old days" referred to America of the Victorian era. Children then were kept childish for a long time, their innocence predicated on isolation from and ignorance of the adult world. In comparison, we fear that modern children grow up too fast, are exposed to the adult world too soon, and lose their innocence too quickly. Yet viewed from a broader perspective, children of every era except the Victorian have mixed in adult society from an early age. Perhaps the Victorian image of childhood will prove to be an anomaly, a somewhat claustrophobic idyll in the more common pattern of integrating children into family and community life. Modern childrearing practices were less of a break with or degeneration from tradition than a comparison with the practices of the Victorian era alone would suggest. The modern child's world includes not only parents but also other caregivers, teachers, coaches, and a mind-numbing range of media models. Children are once again being raised by and in a community of adults, for good or ill

Chapter 5
The Birth of the Virtual Child
A Victorian Progeny

JOHN R. GILLIS

> *Needing the idea of the child so badly, we find ourselves sacrificing the bodies of children for it.*
> —*James Kincaid,* Child-Loving *(1992)*

The Victorians taught us not only what to think *about* the child but also how to think *with* the child. They created the concept of "the child" and then used it to symbolize the meaning of life itself. People have always cared and thought about particular children, and not just their own, but it was the Victorians who constructed what James Kincaid has called that "wonderfully hollow category, able to be filled up with anyone's overflowing emotions, not least overflowing passion" (1992, 12). And we have become even more dependent on the child as a master symbol and image, so dependent that we are nearly incapable of seeing how central it is to our sense of ourselves and the world we inhabit.

The Victorians were also the first to make the child a presence in the absence of real children. They supplied Western culture with a plethora of beloved child figures—innocent, pure, timeless—but also gave us a gallery of eroticized, seductive, even savage children (Kincaid 1992). These split images have outlived not only their progenitors but also the media that first gave them life. Figures born of books and theater multiply in contemporary film and on television, taking on ever more fantastic forms over time. Victorian imaginings first colonized every segment of Western society and were then exported to the rest of the world. Now, at the beginning of the twenty-first century, the West finds itself haunted by images of children that were its own creation (Stephens 1995). Terrifying tales of street children, which were first produced in London's East End and New York's Lower East Side, are beamed back by satellite from the slums of Brazil and the Philippines to their now gentrified places of origins.

In a global economy, commodified as well as politicized images of the child circulate with ever greater velocity, contributing to one of the great paradoxes of our times, namely, that Western society has become an extraordinarily child-centered culture, even in the absence of children. Never have children been so valued, yet rarely have so many adults lived apart from children. The childless couple is no longer a rarity, and, given the longevity revolution, parents spend a smaller fraction of their lives actually living with their children. Rates of biological reproduction have been falling since the Victorian era, but what I want to call the rate of cultural reproduction has moved in exactly the opposite direction. Never have the symbols and images of the child been so pervasive. Our politics, commerce, and culture all depend on them (Holland 1992). We are extremely attentive to these virtual children, even as we neglect, even abuse real children. The virtual child has become so luminous that it threatens to blind us to real children.

While fewer adults are having children, the desire for children, often amounting to desperation, has increased. This is not at all surprising, because, beginning in the Victorian era, to be "in the family way" has meant to be expecting a child. In contemporary Western culture it is birth that transforms marriage into family, while it is said of older couples that "their family has left them" (West and Petrick 1992). Childless couples feel anomalous, but to lose a child of whatever age is an event so devastating that even very strong marriages often do not survive it (May 1995; Finkbeiner 1996).

In an era when children occupy less and less real time and space, they are an ever larger presence in the land- and timescapes of our imagination. They have been the most photographed and are now the most videoed members of our species (Spence and Holland 1991). Childhood has become the most memorable age, and children are central to all our major commemorative rituals. Childhood has become modern society's central myth of origins, our explanation of who we are and what we will become, and in the process children have assumed an iconic status, demonized as well as idolized. As Marina Warner observes, "children have never been so visible as points of identification, as warrants of virtue, as markers of humanity." They have become our image of origins, but, as Warner notes, "origins are compounded of good and evil together, battling." As the screen on which adults project their greatest hopes and deepest fears, children are imagined either as little angels or as little monsters, but rarely as just children (Warner 1995, 57, 60).

It was during the Victorian era that "from being the smallest and least considered of human beings, the child had become endowed with qualities that made it Godlike, fit to be worshipped and the embodiment of hope" (Cunningham 1995, 78). But it was also then that the child came to stand for what we find most disturbing—a symbol of forbidden sexuality, primitivism, even savagery (Kincaid 1992; Cunningham 1991). This split image of children, reflecting the ambivalence adults have felt toward them since the mid-nineteenth century, takes many forms but remains a central feature of modern culture.

Nations and families are no longer so materially dependent on their biological offspring as they once were, but are much more dependent on them in other ways. Long before and after they have ceased to live *with* children physically, adults live *by* them culturally and psychologically. Never before in history has the symbolic connection been so intense or extended. It now begins before birth and endures beyond death, for, in the contemporary Western imagination, the fetus has become the "unborn child" while the dead or lost child haunts us in ways that no other missing person is capable of doing (Gillis 1996; Beck and Beck-Gernsheim 1995).

Cultural History of the Child

This chapter is concerned with the way we imagine children to be, not the way they actually are. I am therefore more concerned with the culture of adults than with the culture of children, though in the conclusion I have some things to say about the latter subject. Philippe Ariès (1962) first explored the cultural context of childhood forty years ago. Unfortunately, *Centuries of Childhood* has found few successors. It appeared at a moment when interest was shifting from culture to behavior and the social sciences were coming to hold sway on both sides of the Atlantic. The social scientific approach to the history of childhood has shaped not just the content but the organization of the field. The history of childhood has become yet another specialization. Each age now has its own historiographical niche, and experts on the various segments of the life course find no compelling reasons to cross boundaries. Childhood, adulthood, and old age have all taken on the qualities of bounded objects, obscuring the relationships among them and ignoring the larger frame within which all their histories might be profitably understood. Ariès was right to see the culture of the family and understandings of children, death, and dying as interrelated subjects, all affected by the onset of modernity. Only by returning to this broad perspective can we begin to understand the meaning of childhood in modern culture.

Putting this historiographical Humpty Dumpty back together again will not be easy, but an excellent start has been made by Thomas Cole in his *The Journey of Life* (1992), a history of old age that deconstructs that reified category, showing how definitions of aging have been shaped by large scale cultural transformations, particularly shifts in religious belief and practice. Starting from a more psychological perspective, Carolyn Steedman (1995) accomplishes a similar reintegration of the subject by demonstrating that the idea of the child is closely identified with adult selfhood, which itself was the product of a new subjectivity peculiar to the late nineteenth century. From that point onward every adult would be required to construct a childhood appropriate to his or her sense of personal identity. Steedman's relational perspective thereby reconnects segments of the life course previously studied in isolation, showing how ideas of adulthood and childhood are inseparable, both invented rather than discovered phenomena, twinned offspring of a profound shift in the understanding of the self associated with the onset of modernity.

The Birth of the Virtual Child

How, then, do we account for the birth of the virtual child? The first step is to be very specific with respect to its lineage, in this case in the Anglo-American context. Similar developments may well be found in other northwestern European societies. Indeed, the Netherlands has a strong claim to have been the first in many respects, though the value placed on the child in its Golden Age in the seventeenth century was not to have the influence later Anglo-American developments had (Kloek this volume; Schama 1987). Ariès argued that the idea of the child was already present among the elites of early modern Europe; Lawrence Stone finds similar premonitions, while Barry Levy argues that the Quakers were the progenitors of modern notions of family and childhood (Stone 1977; Levy 1988). Many new notions of childhood can also be seen in the romantic movement of the late eighteenth and early nineteenth centuries. However, whatever the legitimate claims of these precursors, it was not really until the nineteenth century, and first among the Anglo-American middle strata, that these notions became hegemonic, embedded in an emerging class and gender system that would naturalize and universalize them, ultimately institutionalizing them in law and social practice.

This moment coincided with the industrial revolution, when the household first lost its economic functions, requiring the reconstruction of family on an entirely new basis, based no longer on material relations among its members but on entirely new cultural foundations.

The key to understanding the role of the Anglo-American Protestant middle classes in the invention of the virtual child lies in an understanding of how they coped with this change culturally as well as materially. And here their religious culture provides what I believe is the key to understanding this process.

A significant portion of the Protestant middle classes had already been intensely preoccupied throughout the late eighteenth and early nineteenth centuries with their personal relationship to God. Known loosely as Evangelicals, this group's obsession with sin and agonizing introspective quest for signs of divine will set them apart not only from Catholics but also from other more conventional Protestants, who still relied on traditional religious rites and good works for reassurance of salvation. The turning point came in the mid-nineteenth century, when many Evangelicals lost faith in their belief system and turned away from institutional religion. This crisis of faith produced among them a desperate and enormously creative search for new secular sources of grace, a quest that turned away from introspective soul searching to find signs of salvation in the most unexpected places—in nature, in encounters with "noble savages," but most of all in childhood.

Among the post-Evangelical middle classes, a strong sense of sin remained. The Fall remained for them a central myth, but a myth told in personal rather than supernatural terms. Introspection was transformed into retrospection. The Garden ceased to be a place and became a stage of life. Paradise lost became childhood lost when the quest for grace turned inward and retrospective, bypassing institutional religion and finding expression in the newly sanctified realm of the family, the middle classes' ultimate refuge of innocence and purity. "God has given us each our own Paradise, our own old childhood, over which old glories linger—to which our hearts cling, as all we have ever known of Heaven upon earth," proclaimed James Anthony Froude in 1849 (Gillis 1996, 5).

The sacred was displaced from the realm of the supernatural to the family, with the result that children along with women became objects of sentimentalization bordering on worship. This contributed immensely to the care and protection of children, but at the cost of cloistering them from the world. Thus emerged the seminal contradiction of our times: our simultaneous worship of children and our inability to recognize them as real human beings with the faults and virtues associated with the species.

The Preindustrial Household

This development can best be traced through the iconography of children. To be sure, Christian culture had accumulated a treasure trove of child images, stories, and myths, the most important of which centered on the Christ child himself, beginning in the fourteenth century (Boas 1966). But it was precisely the superabundance of heavenly children that accounts for the striking lack of images of down-to-earth children in ordinary households prior to the nineteenth century. Until that time, families showed little interest in images of their own children. To be sure, there existed a long tradition of family portraiture among the old elites. The Evangelical middle classes could certainly have afforded to patronize artists, but they were iconoclastic when it came to representations of their own family members (Gillis 1996). Until the Victorian era they felt no need to turn their children into symbols. Absent too were the child-centered rites, such as birthdays, which we have come to regard as essential to a good family life. Christmas was still a communal occasion in which children played only a small part (Nissenbaum 1996).

With the notable exception of the seventeenth-century Dutch, childhood occupied a very small place in the preindustrial European and North American imagination. Birth was a moment to be forgotten, not remembered (Kildegaard 1985). Indeed, people seem to have had great difficulty imagining very young children at all. The notion of the "unborn child" was absent; and even when a child was born it did not get what we would regard as the full cultural treatment. Naming was often delayed until after the survival of the infant was certain, and it was Christian baptism, not the physical birth itself, that marked the formal entry of the child into the world. Furthermore, baptism was not the family celebration we understand it to be now. The church rite did not require the presence of the birth parents, and it was rare for kin to assemble on such occasions. Baptism was very much a communal rite, meant to establish a broader set of social connections, for it marked the beginning of a life that was likely to be spent in several different households, a pattern dictated by the high mortality rates and scarce resources characteristic of the preindustrial era (Gillis 1996).

Subsequent stages of childhood were also given scant symbolic treatment. According to the Christian understanding of the journey of life, the believer drew closer to God toward the end of life. Old age was therefore the appropriate time to number one's days and to celebrate advanced years that were supposed by believers to be a sign of divine grace. Many children grew up without ever knowing their ages, for infancy and early childhood were largely undifferentiated by either age or sex and the idea of babyhood had yet to be invented. Medieval and early modern texts had marked the boundaries of various age groups, but this did not have a direct impact on behavior. Childhood was a generalized condition, determined more by relationships of authority and dependency than by numerical age itself. Although a high premium was placed on precocity, one could remain in the status of child for a much longer time than modern notions of aging would ever allow. The numerical boundaries of childhood were, like so many other measures of age in the premodern period, quite imprecise and wildly variable by class, region, and gender. It was not so much how old you were but who you were that determined your place in the generational hierarchy. Early childhood often ended for boys with the ritual act of breeching, but for girls it shaded into girlhood with few visible markers. Until school and work became age-graded in the second half of the nineteenth century there was no compelling reason to remember one's age, much less celebrate it.

When adults looked back over their lives, it was not the earliest but the later years that they recounted. It was death, not birth, that gave the premodern Christian life its meaning (Porter and Porter 1988). This was the moment when fallen humanity was reckoned to be closest to God. The dying person provided a window on immortality, and therefore the deathbed was an object of fascination up through the mid-nineteenth century (Cole 1992). By contrast, the childbed was regarded with dread, even horror, until the Victorian era. Childbirth was exclusively women's business, something that men were thankful to be relieved of and careful to distance themselves from (Gillis 1996).

The pain mothers endured was commonly perceived as the curse of Eve, and birth itself as a reenactment of the Fall, requiring that both mother and child be cleansed of its polluting effects. The rite of "churching," meant to purify new mothers, remained in high demand throughout the early modern period (Gillis 1996). The newborn was also regarded as a sinful polluting presence until the protective act of baptism had taken place. Even then, however, the little "stranger," as babies were often called, would be scrutinized for signs of original sin and disciplined in ways that we would find unsuited to small children.

Protestants placed less faith in ritual than did Catholics, and the Evangelical middle classes of the late eighteenth and early nineteenth centuries were the most antiritualistic and iconoclastic of all. But their rejection of the traditional rites of churching and baptism only increased the anxiety that characterized Evangelical childrearing practices. As Philip Greven has shown, Evangelical Protestants were the most obsessed with issues of childish disobedience, and the most prone to resort to harsh discipline to "bend the twig" in the proper direction (Greven 1977, 1991).

This is not to say that the treatment of children was ever as harsh as some historians of early modern childhood would have us believe, but neither was it careless or indulgent. Assumed to be neither particularly innocent nor particularly devilish, youngsters were not confused with either angels or demons (Walzer 1974). As long as devils and angels were thought to be real, and Christianity continued to provide all the compelling images and dramatic stories of good and evil that ordinary people needed to make sense of their own lives, children carried little of the symbolic load they do today.

Life in a preindustrial household was noticeably lacking in the melodramatic qualities we associate with modern families. The household itself was a functional unit, and its members related to one another on an institutional rather than a sentimental basis. Household formation did not depend on natural reproduction alone, but instead incorporated unrelated persons, as would any other social institution. None of its members were irreplaceable. The death of a child produced grief, but the household was compelled to find a substitute and carry on. Furthermore, in a world where fatherhood was quite separable from biological paternity and motherhood did not mean the same as biological maternity, parental identities depended on a relationship not with particular children but with children in general (Gillis 1996).

Effects of the Industrial Revolution

The effects of the industrial revolution of the mid-nineteenth century differed by class and region, but perhaps the most affected was the middle class household, whose functions and composition were profoundly altered when production was removed to the factory and the office. While middle class households continued to contain unrelated persons as domestic servants well into the twentieth century, a clear distinction was now made between them and the biologically constituted nuclear family. For the first time, fatherhood became exclusively associated with biological paternity and motherhood with biological maternity. The way was now cleared for a corresponding redefinition of childhood as an irreplaceable relationship between a specific parent and a specific child, drawing for the first time a sharp line between so-called "natural" offspring and adopted or fostered children.

Removal of production from the household transformed the meaning of fatherhood, limiting it to the breadwinner role, but it likewise changed motherhood, transforming it into an all-consuming identity, something transcending the act of mothering. Mothers became the symbolic centers of middle-class families at the moment when fathers were recast as strangers to the domestic realm. The mother's real and symbolic involvement with the individual child was simultaneously transformed, intensified in a manner that ultimately contributed to the reduction of the number of births (Gillis 1992). Simultaneously, the definition of family narrowed to the nuclear unit, defined by the presence of children born to it (Griswold 1993; Gillis 1996).

It was at this same moment that the cultural understanding of the child underwent a revolution that was to have an immense impact on the ideas and practices of modern family life. As a result of the crisis of faith, among the middle classes birth ceased to be a reenactment of the Fall and became a sacred moment, a kind of secular sacrament. The birthing room was no longer the exclusive domain of women; it was made accessible to fathers, with middle-class men becoming the first fathers to attend the birth of their children. These men found birth as personally redemptive as their wives found it personally sanctifying (Gillis 1996). Although working-class women continued to use the rite of churching, the middle classes, who now regarded birth itself as purifying, abandoned it entirely.

Birth and death had changed places, and it was newborns who were now the window on eternity. Infants were, wrote Wordsworth, "fresh from the hand of God, living blessings which have drifted down to us from the imperial palace of the love of God" (Cunningham 1995, 74). Birth became a purifying moment, requiring no further rites of sanctification. Infant baptism lost its traditional meaning and became the modern christening ceremony, a largely social occasion celebrating birth itself. Naming no longer waited on the survival of the infant, and the child's birthday became a family occasion for the first time (Gillis 1996). The child was now a luminous presence, itself a symbol of innocence and purity, a source of sacredness the Christian churches were quick to recognize as a source of institutional revitalization. In the second half of the nineteenth century religious ceremonies became increasingly family- and child-centered, a recognition of the shifting locus of the sacred (Joselit 1994).

Infancy had ceased to be an undifferentiated condition. By 1900 the "baby" had made its appearance in the medical literature and in popular consciousness (Wright 1987). The child was now born with age and sex already assigned. It took some time before the gendering of infants was fully accepted at all class levels, but boys' and girls' dress became sharply differentiated, obviating the need for ceremonies like breeching, which had previously endowed the young with the marks of gender as well as age.

Having become the sign of family, its sacred center, the child was now the focus of a whole host of newly invented middle-class rituals that came to constitute and maintain the meaning and sense of family from the mid-nineteenth century onward. The child's meal times, bed times, birthdays, and graduations marked the passage of what came to be called "family time," not only defining the increasingly tightly calibrated stages of childhood development but also determining the parents' sense of their own journey of life. The comings and goings of children, which in the preindustrial household had little cultural meaning in and of themselves, now became the definitive moments in the adult life course.

But the unprecedented symbolic centering of the meaning of family and adult identities on children involved a contradiction that had not been present in the preindustrial household. The old household had been impervious to the passage of time, for it replaced the children who died or grew up and left with unrelated persons. Now that the central function of the nuclear family was the reproduction and development of children, growing up inevitably produced a sense of loss, not just for the child in question but for the parents, whose adult identity was thrown into confusion or even doubt. As the number of children per family fell and life expectancy increased, the empty nest became an ever more important cause of stress, even depression, especially among women, who sometimes felt their lives to be over once the children had left home.

Childhood as a "Substitute Religion"

By the end of the nineteenth century, childhood had become what Hugh Cunningham has called a "substitute religion," but one recognizably Judeo-Christian in its elements. Childhood stood for the Garden of Eden, no longer a place but a stage in the journey of life that led inevitably to the fallen state of adulthood, especially for men (Cunningham 1991). It is little wonder that childhood had by this time become an object of intense nostalgia, attracting to itself all those longings that had previously attached themselves to the Garden itself (Degler 1980; Pollock 1983; Kincaid 1992). Childhood had come to symbolize not only uncorrupted nature but also the nobility associated with simpler times and peoples. This displacement coincided with the New Imperialism, which terminated the myth of the noble savage. Once the entire globe had been explored and all hope of finding an actual earthly paradise was exhausted, the child became the final repository of the visions of unbounded happiness that had been sought by Europeans for centuries (Cunningham 1991).

By 1900 childhood had displaced old age as the most memorable part of the lifetime. Autobiographical writings dwelt increasingly on early childhood experiences, while a whole new set of commemorative practices developed to allow adults access not only to their own childhood memories but, perhaps more important, to children, who were increasingly seen as mnemonic resources, the repository of the earliest memories of mankind itself. With late nineteenth-century evolutionary theory came the notion that each individual recapitulated the history of the human species. Thus the child was the closest thing to early man, the repository of unspoiled qualities, but also a potential source of primitive instincts, even savagery (Cunningham 1991).

Such ideas found expression in science and in the emerging family cultures of the period. The middle-class festive calendar came to revolve increasingly around children, times of renewal when adults (especially men) grown weary of the urban industrial world could return to simpler, purer things (Robson 2001). The newly invented, secularized family Christmas was thought of in precisely those terms, as a moment when adults could reconnect not only with children but also with their own childhoods. The Englishman Clement Miles remarked,

At no time in the world's history has so much been made of children as today, and because Christmas is their feast its lustre continues unabated in an age when dogmatic Christianity has largely lost its hold . . . . Christmas is the feast of beginnings, of instinctive, happy childhood. (Miles 1912; Gillis 1996, 102-3)

It was no longer the end but the beginning that now gave life its meaning. The precious glimpse of immortality previously associated with the deathbed was relocated to the cradle, but not before going through a phase when stories of dying children and photographs of dead children were much in demand. As the death of a child was already seen as the ultimate personal and familial loss, Victorians learned to prize the image of the dead child, commonly portrayed at rest from the struggles with the childhood diseases that still plagued even affluent families (Douglas 1977). Dead children were the favorite subjects of Victorian postmortem photographers; their graves were visited and their presence kept alive through spiritualist mediums who played such an essential part in middle-class culture at the time (Burns 1990; Zelizer 1985; Martin-Fugier 1990; Kildegaard 1985). The early twentieth-century hospitalization of birth brought a pause in the practice of postmortem photography, but in the last twenty years it has returned as part of new mourning rites that allow parents to cope with their loss. Bereaved parents often initially reject the photos offered to them, but then, realizing that the absence of some tangible evidence of the child's existence leads to even greater anguish (anguish akin to that when loved ones are missing or the bodies of the dead are unrecoverable), they ask for them, using them to develop a mental picture of the child they never knew (Ruby 1995; Lundin and Akesson 1996).

We remain fascinated with baby pictures, the closest thing Western culture had for a long time to an image of humanity untainted by the passage of time until ultrasound technology made the fetal image possible. As Susan Sontag (1972) has suggested, the photograph is our means of glimpsing eternity, holding time at bay. In this age of the "hurried child," when children are not allowed to linger even in their infancy, it is hard to hold on to old images of childhood. In this context, a sonogram of the "unborn child" has become for many the ultimate symbol of immortality. Existing outside real time and space, exempt from the imperfections of life itself, the image of the fetus provides all those qualities Western culture has projected onto childhood since the mid-nineteenth century. In effect, the fetus has become the newest little angel, making abortion seem for some the work of the devil (Rothman 1989; Stolberg 1998; Lundin and Akesson 1996).

Obstacles to Family Formation

Parenthood has lost none of its symbolic appeal at the beginning of the twenty-first century, even though fewer people are having children. There is no recognized role for maiden aunts and lifelong bachelors in our time, and even happily married couples often feel incomplete until they have a child. The desire of gay and lesbian couples for children is further evidence of just how powerful this particular cultural construction of family life has become.

The reasons for having children are always complex, and parents are not always conscious of their own motives, but in this low-fertility culture children are central to the construction of adult identity. As British survey researchers were already finding in 1945, "first children are mostly born for the sake of the parents; second children often for the sake of the first—to keep them company" (Mass-Observation 1945, 72–73). Until quite recently, having children was more important to the construction of female than male identity, but with the emergence of the "new fatherhood" this seems to be changing (Busfield and Paddon 1977). It is also worth noting the phenomenon of the "new grandparenthood," which is suggestive of how older adults have also become more rather than less dependent on children for their identities (Furstenberg and Cherlin 1986). The fact that for most of the time grandparenting is a virtual rather than a real activity does not make it any less appealing.

Over the past twenty years or so the obstacles to family formation have multiplied. The age of marriage rises; childbearing is postponed;

and the number of childless couples increases. There are fewer children, but contemporary society has become increasingly obsessed not just with lost children whose images appear in posters and on milk cartons but also, if the recent spate of books on the disappearance of childhood is any indication, with losing childhood altogether (Postman 1992; Sommerville 1982; Winn 1984; Kotlowitz 1991). As Paula Fass has noted, "That dream of personal resurrection—to live once more through our children—has made them dearer to us, while their loss has become all the more unbearable, to outlive them, a modern curse" (Fass 1997, 255).

Conclusion

And so at the start of the twenty-first century the pace of iconization, ritualization, and mythologization of childhood quickens. New child-centered holidays, resorts, and products proliferate, yet they seem not to be able to satisfy our insatiable need to pay homage to the idea of childhood (Cross 1997). But, as Peter Stearns points out in Chapter 6, we have become less trustful of children and subject them to ever greater control. The contemporary child, long since isolated from nature and no longer allowed access to the street, inhabits a series of worlds—daycare center, kindergarten, playground, summer camp—purpose-built to satisfy adult hopes and allay adult fears, but not always serving the best interests of children (Nahban and Trimble 1994).

As adult relations with children become increasingly mediated by images, rituals, and products, the social as well as the material costs mount. For children, the price is the loss of autonomy. I am not confident in judging whether children behave worse or better now, but it is clear that children today lead increasingly scripted lives. And when they do not conform to adult idealizations they are perceived as fallen angels or, worse, little monsters. Contemporary culture's ambivalence expresses itself in wildly opposite reactions to children—on the one hand excessive indulgence, and on the other chronic indifference and episodic abusiveness. As John Demos has argued, in a situation where adult identities are so dependent on idealized notions of parent/child relations, childish misbehavior becomes especially threatening, producing anger and violence directed toward otherwise beloved children (Demos 1986; Beck and Beck-Gernsheim 1995).

Our attempt to live by the icon of the child makes it all the more difficult to live with real children. We have to become aware of the way our cultural constructions, once reified, blind rather than enlighten us to the true nature of our relations with children. We need to invent new images and find different stories to tell ourselves, but, most important, we need to attend to the conditions that make adulthood it-self so problematic and produce the longings that are projected onto children. We might start by heeding Marina Warner's caution that "with-out paying attention to adults and their circumstances, children can-not begin to meet the hopes and expectations of our torn dreams about what a child and childhood should be" (Warner 1995, 62). Pay-ing more heed to adult needs would in the long run be of great bene-fit not only to them but also to children.

Chapter 6
Historical Perspectives on Twentieth-Century American Childhood

PETER STEARNS

Given the number of factors that shape childhood, it is not surprising that key twentieth-century developments took a variety of directions (Elder, Modell, and Parke 1993). Prior adult roles were rethought, amid growing criticism of past repression, and some previous latitudes were also reined in, particularly for boys (Rotundo 1993; Hawes and Hiner 1982). At the same time, novel developments were complicated by the persistence of earlier patterns. Long-standing American emphasis on children's independence and voice, amid unusual labor needs and frontier alternatives, continued to affect the experience of childhood, though in new ways. No simple model of liberation or regulation works well; there was no coherent package.

Nevertheless, a new tension in the experience of children did emerge from the early part of the century onward. Adult constraints on children became more detailed and demanding even as children's outlets through consumerism expanded.

The New Dualism

This central tension informed basic childhood experiences, socialization results, and adult-child contacts. Its distinctive interplay between constraint and release differed from the most widely articulated nineteenth-century patterns and constituted the most important new twentieth-century framework.

On the one hand, earlier assumptions of children's strength, accompanied by considerable freedom from adult supervision, yielded to new anxieties and new efforts at parental and adult control (including, of course, the expanding role of schools). Childhood became associated with a host of potential problems as novel forms of expert advice blended with changes in the actual structure of childhood. On the other hand, opportunities for escape from worried guidance, particularly through new consumer outlets available for children and new forms of peer culture, increased greatly. Childhood became divided between stricture and latitude, preparing an interaction that would be carried to adulthood. Subsidiary innovations in childhood, such as changes in familial work responsibilities, flowed from efforts to accommodate this tension.

This framework was different from that of the nineteenth century, although nineteenth-century idealizations persisted and caused confusion. (The idealizations were those discussed by John Gillis in Chapter 5, but their durability was far more qualified than his essay suggests.) To take an obvious instance, Victorian middle-class insistence on morally uplifting reading and entertainments for innocent children (though admittedly incompletely carried through in practice), now yielded to a more uninhibited media culture, catering to interests in violence and incipient sexuality. Of course moralizing materials remained available, and even more obviously fears about corrupting children, inspired in part by Victorian continuities, responded to the change. The fact was, however, that change predominated. Most of the leisure fare offered to children escaped parental control.

Or, to take a more subtle instance, though parents continued to echo nineteenth-century praise for children (while bemoaning, as Victorian observers did, actual problems with the current younger generation), the place of children in family life slipped. Rising divorce rates, the ultimate decisions of mothers to enter the workforce (Chafe 1991), and, after the 1950s at least, actual polling data all reflected growing adult interest in other goals, which meant that the undeniable commitment to a semi-Victorian rhetoric embraced an important values dilemma.

A New Context

Several factors shifted the framework in which adult-child interactions occurred. The three major birth rate periods in the twentieth century set up distinctive issues. During the initial decades of the century, and particularly the 1920s and 1930s, the intensification of earlier reductions in rates led to many families with only one or two children, which increased parent-child contact, and reduced available sibling relationships. The result enhanced parental anxiety about their own adequacy and increased the demands individual children placed on parents, developments that reflected adult concern for children but also created a potential source of dissatisfaction. The baby boom period, largely a product of positive decisions for a more child-centered family environment, led to crowding of families and growing competition for adult attention, particularly because the spacing between children was characteristically close—another basis for new adult concerns and childhood tensions. Finally, the subsequent decline in birth rates was marked by a measurable reduction in the valuation of children, at least compared to other indices of family success; both genders began to cut back their claimed appreciation of children as against the importance of the marital tie. The fact that Americans did not move as readily as Europeans to alternative systems of child care, partly because of greater hostility to the state and partly because of attachment to traditional maternal imagery, complicated parents' lives while adding a sometimes hectic element to the experience of children themselves. Older rhetoric persisted, but key facts pointed in a new direction—including, by the 1970s, the expansion of communities for mature adults in which children were prohibited altogether save as occasional visitors (Van Horn 1988; Easterlin 1980; Elder, Modell, and Parke 1993; Veroff 1986).

A second element in the context for twentieth-century childhood, like birth rate trends novel but not brand new, involved schooling. The identification of childhood with schooling had clearly begun in the nineteenth century, but its complete articulation awaited the early part of the twentieth. The full impact of schooling on childhood in the United States is a contemporary phenomenon. It was only after 1900, for example, that southern states moved toward formal school requirements. It was only in the 1920s that school attendance began to be vigorously and systematically enforced on the urban lower classes. It was only at this point that child labor, before adolescence, began virtually to disappear, save in highly selected settings. Newspaper delivery, for example, was shifted from lower-class urban youth, who might depend on it for part of their family livelihood, to middle-class boys recruited on the assumption that work would be good character training. In ways only tentatively sketched in the nineteenth century, the twentieth century saw the full linkage between childhood and schooling and, at the same time, a more rigorous definition of what schooling entailed.

The shift to a fuller commitment to schooling often also involved a move away from rote memorization, relied on for its disciplinary qualities, to a somewhat more demanding effort to train children in some analytical skills. This shift, along with an increase in the length of the school year and other innovations such as homework and the systematic use of grading and report cards, introduced widely in the 1920s, affected a number of social classes, not just the rural and poor. For several decades, many observers expressed great concern about the deleterious effects of modern schooling on children, arguing that the burdens were too great, the deprivation of freedom too extensive, the physical consequences too confining. A significant battle, for example, developed over the idea of homework after 1910, as older conceptions of a free, innocent childhood only gradually gave way to complete acceptance of childhood as a period of major learning responsibilities. More recently, widespread interest in Attention Deficit Disorder (a disease entity formalized in the 1970s, though identified under different headings from 1900 on) reflected the tremendous impact of contemporary schooling as an adult-imposed determinant in children's lives (Schlossman and Gill 1996; Kohn 1989). Changes in schooling also introduced more competition among children, complicating student bonds common in the nineteenth century.

The ubiquity, intensity, and academic demands of schooling constituted important new components in American childhood and adult-child relationships. There were connections with the past, beyond the obvious middle-class rhetorical esteem for education itself. American schools in the twentieth century were asked to take over key moralization efforts, as confidence in parental fitness waned. Athletic programs proliferated (continuing a trend launched in the later nineteenth century), and while several factors were involved, a desire to discipline and build character through sports played a key role. Americans also showed unusual willingness to see schools drive home standards of morality and hygiene. With the collapse of Prohibition, for example, lessons against drinking became common, just as, later in the twentieth century, schools would teach against smoking and drugs. Education about sexuality became another hesitant staple, though experiments in the 1920s to broaden sexual horizons, against real or imagined Victorian repression, quickly moved to more inhibitive fare. This aspect of schooling, unusually extensive in the United States, involved important Victorian-style commitments to moralization of children, but, equally significant, a sense that major innovations were required in the methods of delivery.

Children as Problems

A key ingredient of shifts in both parent-young child contact and schooling involved a new assessment of children themselves and an openness to a novel problem-seeking brand of expertise. Even as rhetorical valuation of children soared, at the end of the nineteenth century, detailed discussions implicitly identified a growing range of disturbing issues. A new spate of childrearing manuals reflected the need to explore a new paradigm. New levels of adult anxiety took many forms. Careful emotional control was one. Beginning in the 1920s, childrearing manuals began to warn parents against provoking guilt in their offspring, lest this undermine their confidence. Jealousy among siblings provided an even more intense target. Parents were responsible for controlling this newly identified rivalry, lest children seriously injure each other and a damaging emotion be allowed to fester in ways that could poison adulthood. Here, indeed, was the general theme: children harbored a variety of counterproductive emotions that they could not properly manage on their own. Studies showed, for example, that many children suffered from unaccountable fears, which meant that parents must carefully avoid fear-provoking situations and must develop strategies, including bribes, to help children afflicted with fears of strangers, animals, or other potential threats. Merely telling children to be brave, in the Victorian mode, would not suffice and might indeed make matters worse. Assisting in emotional management was vital, furthermore, not only for childhood itself, but to provide the basis for emotionally healthy adulthood. Finally, the management process must begin when children were quite young. Strategies to defuse intense jealousy, for example, might target two-year-olds. By the 1930s parents were citing issues of this sort as leading concerns (Stearns 1994; Zelizer 1986).

Health and hygiene formed another set of issues. Children must be taught regular habits in these areas, even though it went against their inclinations. A vast amount of time must be devoted to internalizing cleanliness and control of odor. By the 1920s, school programs, promoted by soap companies, were prodding teachers to inspect children's washing habits, as a means of extending middle-class intensity into working-class life. Questionnaires and lessons drove home the need to bathe at least twice a week. Regular toothbrushing was another new target. As the pediatrics specialty gained ground, taking children for regular medical checkups became part of standard routine, extending from the middle class; here was another occasion to review the habits for which parents were responsible.

Children's bodies and emotions, then, were seen as immensely vulnerable, requiring both protection and discipline by parents, schools, and other organizations. Despite some ongoing use of nineteenth-century rhetoric about children's competence unless corrupted by adults, of the sort Karin Calvert discusses in Chapter 4, the fact was that a sense of the need to supervise and worry increased. Except for a religious minority, no return to ideas of original sin was involved, but childhood became problematic in new ways (including, of course, the new category of school competence). Special counseling might be invoked when appropriate habits could not be formed. A torrent of child-rearing advice began to emerge in the 1920s, including the creation of the new *Parents' Magazine*, signaling a need to drive home a new set of messages. As with school programs, manuals and magazines turned away from the generalized morality typical of the nineteenth-century genre. Far more specific problems, and in a far wider range, now commanded attention. Manuals not only proliferated but also expanded in size because of the multitude of potential concerns. Overall, the basic approach to children as suggested in mainstream prescriptive literature shifted. Dominant nineteenth-century middle-class advice had urged the fundamental strength and innocence of children, so long as misguided adult messages did not interfere. While echoes of hoped-for innocence lingered in the twentieth century, confidence declined: children were now problems, or at least by their very nature often harbored an array of problems, even in the best environments. They needed greater supervision and control.

Not surprisingly, this new approach encouraged a proliferation of programs to provide adult guidance of children's activities, and these programs in turn provided the context for the redefinition and extension of moralization in the schools. In the early decades of the century, efforts to use not only schools but also settlement houses to create organized activities for immigrant children incarnated this approach most obviously. But much the same approach was applied to middle-class children as well. The scouting movement, though a substantial failure among its initial adolescent targets, caught on strongly among boys and girls of grade school age, providing a range of activities to teach skills and control the use of time. Organized lessons began to proliferate, building on the nineteenth-century precedent of music training for girls. The encouragement of hobbies gained new energy from the 1920s onward. Leisure time could be used for self-improvement, with adult guidance providing the initial impetus for children who could learn about the world by collecting stamps and coins or building radio sets from specially provided kits. Amid this barrage of guidance—headed, of course by the intensification of schooling itself—the independence of middle-class children, particularly boys, seems to have declined (Platt 1969; Cavallo 1981; D. Macleod 1983; Gelber 1991; Tyack and Hansot 1990).

Several factors promoted this new approach and the less confident beliefs about children it incorporated. New expertise was crucial. Psychological and medical research produced novel information about children. G. Stanley Hall's research, for example, first created knowledge of the intrinsic, irrational fears that beset many young children, even in benign settings. Dissemination of the germ theory prompted obvious concerns about protecting children from these unseen enemies. A host of popularizers, plus the new efforts of government agencies like the Children's Bureau (whose pamphlet *Infant Care*, frequently re-edited and expanded, became the most popular single government publication), helped spread the word. Growing professionalization of teachers, including physical education instructors, provided another prescriptive channel. Historians like Christopher Lasch (1977) have argued that the growing array of expertise—based on scientific credentials rather than the religious-moral credentials of the less detailed nineteenth-century experts—undermined parental confidence in their own impulses concerning children. Certainly the popularizers were at pains to tell parents that many commonsense beliefs, including undue reliance on children's own strengths, were misguided. Attacks on real or imagined Victorian traditions helped create a sense that new approaches were necessary. Changes in expert emphases—from behaviorism to somewhat greater permissiveness—added to the potential anxiety: it became harder to keep up with the latest wisdom but seemingly increasingly imperative to do so (Ross 1972).

Expertise, however, was supported by other changes in context, without which it could not have found an audience. The dramatic reduction in infant mortality after 1880, for example (which would drive mortality rates below 5 percent by 1920), combined with the steadily declining birth rate, increased parental attachment to individual children and made children's deaths increasingly intolerable: hence, somewhat ironically, the growing interest in precise and anxious instructions about health and hygiene. Safety concerns increased, in part because of new dangers from home appliances and automobiles (the American vehicular death rate in the 1920s was spectacularly high), but partly because of the new responsibilities associated with keeping children alive now that no death could seem inevitable. Changes in living arrangements contributed: with growing suburbanization, children had to rely more on adult transportation, which provided another basis for redefining controls (Burnham 1996).

Another set of shifts entered in for three reasons; parents, and particularly mothers, now had greater contact than before with individual children, particularly in the middle classes. Use of live-in servants declined dramatically. Grandparents began to move out of the homes of their adult children at a fairly steady rate beginning in the 1920s. Finally, smaller family size and growing school obligations reduced the amount of child care available from older siblings. Fathers may have begun to provide a bit more help with children in middle- and upper-class families, though they usually adopted a role as pals that reduced their disciplinary contributions (Marsh 1990; Griswold 1993). Overall, many parents began to find the task of dealing with young children more arduous than before, which heightened their receptivity to detailed advice and also made it easier to focus on the myriad problems of childhood. The context facilitated a belief that early childhood was an important but difficult stage, which the new expert advice then confirmed and elaborated. Shifts in context also affected children directly. Sibling rivalry increased with the falling birth rate (and then, in the baby boom, with close child spacing), simply because there were fewer intermediaries between child and parent and more dependence on adult attention and affection. Perceptions that early childhood was problematic reflected some objectively increasing difficulties (Sennett 1970; Stearns 1989).

Changes in adult policies also helped to generate new childhood experiences and problems directly. Dramatic shifts in sleeping arrangements followed from new concerns about individualism and adult leisure (Stearns 1996). Until the 1890s infants were usually lodged in cradles for sleep, near an adult, whether parent or nursemaid, who could rock the infant easily if it stirred. Adult activities in evenings focused on family tasks that were compatible with this kind of attention. In the 1890s, however, infants began to be placed in separate bedrooms and in cribs rather than the less structured cradles. Many crib designs proliferated, and by 1915 cradles had become objects for nostalgia. Cribs, in contrast, were widely approved, touted for their safety and contributions to good posture and to sleep. They had the advantage of allowing a young child to be safely placed in a separate room, freeing adults for other leisure or work activities; presumably, the child would learn more independent sleep habits in the process. After the crib years, children were increasingly housed in separate bedrooms rather than the multiple-sibling rooms common even in the upper middle class during the nineteenth century. Sleeping with other children declined, as part of the insistence on greater individuation and, probably, the growing concern about homosexuality. The result, not surprisingly, was that children's sleep deteriorated, or at least sleep problems began increasingly to be identified. Interestingly, the amounts of time recommended for children's sleep extended as well, which was consistent with growing concern about vulnerabilities. Here was a vital area for adult anxiety and expert pronouncements; the result, well-intentioned, added up to a decline in certain comforts and group ties available as part of growing up.

Finally, adults in the early twentieth century seem to have projected onto their children some new concerns affecting their own lives. In an economy increasingly focused on service sector jobs and corporate management, many adults were being instructed to curb their anger and other emotions at work: it was small wonder that these restraints were translated into growing impatience with children's anger. Growing constraints on adult jealousy, as social interactions with women increased, contributed to the otherwise oddly intense concern with regulating this aspect of children's emotion. Even guilt at rapid birth rate reduction, as parents increasingly sought consumer enjoyments, could feed into the new protective stance toward children and the desire to provide more adult supervision.

Important changes in family and adult environments thus coalesced with a novel expertise that sought to heighten parental concerns in order to sell new advice and services. The result was a less confident, more problem-focused approach to children, with expert definitions and parental responses increasingly stressing difficulties. In this context, efforts to increase adult supervision of children's activities, to make sure that the array of goals and standards were being met in areas such as emotion, sleep, safety, and health, increased. Free-floating children's groups declined in favor of organized activities, school programs, scouting, sports and hobby clubs, and music and dancing lessons. Monitoring and also formal and informal checkups on children's progress increased, facilitated by lower birth rates.

Goods and Entertainments as Outlets

Paralleling this development, however, was increasing targeting of children as consumers, which allowed children to form attachments apart from full parental or adult supervision. Consumerism also underwrote new bases for attachments in peer groups, devoted to similar consumerist or leisure activities. Here was another trend initially sponsored by adults, but in directions designed to convince children to buy (or have bought) goods and services rather than directly to monitor and train. As part of this development, the effort to provide children with more modest but also uplifting consumer fare characteristic of the nineteenth century declined in favor of pleasure, diversion, and entertainment. To put the case over-simply, nineteenth-century middle-class parents had emphasized selective standards for children, mainly associated with manners, gender, and sexual restraint, which were reinforced by moralistic reading and uplifting recreation, while at the same time allowing considerable latitude to children's separate play. Adults in the twentieth century, as the middle class expanded, multiplied the goals attached to monitoring and guiding children, while at the same time reducing moralistic controls over consumption, which increasingly provided a world of fantasy alternative to daily reality.

The new offerings were framed in a language of escape, sometimes even of defiance of adult norms. They did, obviously, provide activities different from schooling, with imagery that contrasted vividly with the imposition of manners, hygiene, and emotional norms. The freedom was partly illusory, of course. Adult provision remained essential, and media fare often served to distract children from concerns about regimentation that might otherwise have loomed larger. The child who returned from school grumpy but consoled himself with hours in front of radio or television was not necessarily a liberated child. Unquestionably, much of this new, alternative space was passive, teaching children to consume the fruits of others' imagination rather than indulge their own. But a sense of contrast informed the new developments, and parental anxieties reflected their sense that this adult-created world was not exactly aligned with the framework they wished to urge on their offspring.

The increased linkage between consumerism and childhood showed in many ways. The provision of allowances, designed to reward children and train them in the use of money, formed a crucial basis for separate consumer activities—a development from the 1890s onward. Purchases of consumer gifts for children proliferated. Again by the 1890s, Christmas became a time for lavish purchases rather than exchange of simpler items. Reading matter cheap enough for children to buy was another crucial development, running from cheap boys' novels, racy and violent, in the late nineteenth century, to the comic books from the 1920s onward. Radio fare became an even more important venue, allowing extensive advertisement direct to children, for their own purchases but even more as the basis for pressing parents to buy (Nissenbaum 1996; Stearns 1998).

Parents participated actively as well. Goals of emotional training depended increasingly on consumer props from the 1920s onward. Advice materials urged parents to use purchased items to help distract children from fear—put a desired object near the frightening item to lure children in. Separate goods for each child played a vital role in reducing jealousy; an intriguing, increasingly common practice saw adults bringing presents for a sibling on the occasion of the other child's birthday, to distract. Infancy was now surrounded by soft dolls and other items, part of the movement toward reliance on cribs. This occasioned worried debate in the early years of the twentieth century, as children were seen as becoming too dependent on things, but the debate was soon resolved in favor of goods: an article in 1914 approvingly noted that "children's affections have come to center around the toys with which they have lived and played" (Hill and Brown 1914).

Habituated to varied goods in infancy, children readily moved to greater attachments to purchases, acquisition, and consumer-spectatorship as they matured. Growing dependence on commercial media formed a vital part of this pattern, as radio and movies designed explicitly for children evolved into ubiquitous, escapist children's programming on television, noteworthy particularly for its routine violence. Schools joined in as well. Providing new sources of adult discipline over children, schools also encouraged consumer displays as part of peer culture. They provided an array of leisure activities as part of their full-service approach to childhood. Even textbooks, lavishly illustrated to please the eye, tried to combine learning and fun, contrasting revealingly with the sparer products common in other industrial countries. Using children as a market—the pattern opening up by 1900—not only accelerated its pace but also increasingly induced children themselves to define much of their lives in terms of acquisition and spectatorship.

The Central Tension and Its Results

Childhood thus changed in two somewhat contradictory directions, with more detailed standards and parental controls vying with consumer diversions. At times, the two trends could conjoin, and this was where some of the most striking specific changes in childhood occurred. Both impulses, though for different reasons, could push for new forms of indulgence. Parents who worried about vulnerable children could warily ally with sales pitches designed to make children's lives easier. This alliance may account for some otherwise odd exceptions to the regime of careful discipline. American parents and experts alike, for example, were notoriously lax in regulating children's eating habits, save in urging more food, and American children grew fatter as a result, particularly after the 1950s. Here was a clear contrast to European standards, which did not regard ubiquitous snacking as a logical prerogative of childhood. Relaxation of posture standards, after a flowering of programs through the 1940s targeting schoolchildren, flowed from a desire not to add further burdens to childhood plus a recognition that new leisure patterns required a more relaxed body style.

Somewhat similarly, in merging anxiety and indulgence, efforts to regulate children at home often emerged as loosely guided consumerism. Beginning in the 1920s discussions of play turned increasingly to the idea of having playrooms (later, recreation rooms) in the home, so that parents could supervise the toys and entertainments involved. But the result actually cleared the way for further purchases and increased interaction with media and goods. The same applied to the intense preoccupation of suburban parents with the training of children in leisure skills: both monitoring and consumerism were served (Jacobson 1997; Cross 1997).

Reconciliations of indulgence and constraint could involve new levels of isolation of children themselves. This was not true of sports training, where avid parents prided themselves on watching their offspring and shouting detailed instructions on performance. But providing snacks easily turned into letting children regulate more of their own eating habits, while playrooms frequently became spaces in which children could be alone, with parental supervision involved in organizing the room itself but not in regular presence.

A clear decline in work expectations also resulted from the strange alliance of adult concerns and children's new leisure world. Parents worried about school demands and insisted on regulating children in other respects, but steadily reduced the amount of work in the home—chores—expected of children, partly of course because work itself in the domestic sphere declined. The 1930s depression briefly expanded obligations, but then they fell back again. Children, lured by the media and consumer playthings, eagerly joined in, becoming too busy as spectators to respond to work requests. The result was that school and lessons served as primary work training, rather than work itself. At the same time parental annoyance at noncontributing children—an annoyance all the greater in that parents connived at the indulgence—could easily increase.

Grade inflation, which began in the 1960s, reflected a similar combination. Parents sought higher grades to reduce children's tensions—by the 1970s, the reigning concept involved sustaining precarious self-esteem—while children themselves, as consumers, increasingly sought greater ease in their school experience, assuming at the least that any effort should be readily rewarded. These developments occurred, of course, in an atmosphere of growing emphasis on school results, including college placements, so the net effect did not necessarily ease pressure on children or increase parental satisfactions, but the shift in behavior and expectation remained significant.

In other areas, however, the tensions between new concerns about regulating and monitoring children and the provision of an alternative, commercialized fantasy world clearly warred. Most obviously, parents and experts concerned about molding vulnerable children agonized about their lack of control over children's consumer culture. In the early 1950s, attacks on comic books as promoters of violence and sadism helped establish a recurrent theme among those responsible for children: clear and demanding goals were being countered by media presentations and violent toys. Subsequent battles focused on television and music. The conflict was clear, but it was never, save in aberrantly strict individual households, resolved. The tensions were complex, of course. Many parents simultaneously worried about their children's sexuality and urged sexual precociousness in dress, dating, and makeup. Some were involved in marketing sexual materials to the children of others. Ambivalence, in other words, conjoined with conflict. But from the standpoint of children themselves, the result was an opportunity to create vital distance from demanding adults—the adults they encountered personally—by pursuing consumer and spectator choices explicit to the peer group, at once providing a common vocabulary with other children and delightfully provoking adult disapproval. Consumerist outlets also encouraged young children to "grow up" faster, mirroring teenage tastes and leisure styles as a means of personal and group identity.

While objections to escapist media and music produced the clearest trend clash—allowing children important wiggle room by insisting on tastes differing from those of their parents—media themselves played off parental strictures. As efforts to control children's anger and prevent informal fights among young children intensified, radio and television violence escalated. A few control taboos were honored, to be sure—homosexuality, for example—but in key areas toys and shows were clearly if indirectly based on the new or heightened targets of discipline—deliberately courting audiences by presenting alternative fantasies.

In a larger sense, the conflicting trends prepared children for the experience they would face as adults, tied to often demanding behavioral standards at work that were juxtaposed with escapist, often clearly fantastic leisure—a largely make-believe world of violence and (for adults) sexual indulgence. To this extent, the dual trends of twentieth-century childhood were functional and oddly consistent. More immediately, the conflict may have conditioned changes in adolescence, heightening the need for defiance while providing, through media signals, some of the guidelines. In the final analysis, while children's and youth culture became separated and distinct, there was no separate childhood; adults and their offspring were enmeshed in a common pattern of daily constraint and spectator release.

Diversity Issues

Interpreting twentieth-century American childhood, including some of its distinctive comparative features, involves testing the interplay of new frameworks on the experience of children themselves. Internal periodization must be played against longer-term trends.

Key divisions among children raise important issues even for the ubiquitous basic tensions, and they did not hold steady over time. Adult standards for children did, at least from the 1920s onward, reduce overt gender differentiation, as against Victorian emphasis on distinctions in principle. Childrearing manuals spent less time on gender and more on common goals such as avoidance of fear and systematic restraint of temper. Emphasis on gender-distinctive clothing persisted a bit longer, but by the 1960s this too began to merge. Partly in advance of adult role changes, partly accompanying them, blatant insistence on gendered socialization declined.

But American childhood remained a gendered experience as new, if slightly more subtle, differentiations arose. Coeducation spread at all school levels, but reading matter and actual courses in high school continued to emphasize domestic skills for girls and more work-oriented subjects for boys. Again at the high school level, activity groups largely separated boys and girls. This was prepared for in the grade schools by distinctive conversational patterns, with boys increasingly identifying each other through sports interests and knowledge, girls through fashion and more verbal friendships. Toy choices differed markedly, as did entertainment fare after the earliest years. A heightened anxiety about homosexuality for boys, which took clear shape from the early part of the century onward, also led to new forms of insistence on avoiding androgynous characteristics (D'Emilio and Freedman 1988). Even feminist efforts in the 1960s to reduce the gender gap had surprisingly little impact, as separate social patterns continued in school settings and most activities, though girls' growing sports participation breached the divide in one area. Overall, in fact, the consumerist opportunities for children often increased gendered signals, with toys and shows emphasizing violence for boys, romantic escapism for girls. Here, too, a tension emerged between admittedly hesitant changes in formal standards, in which greater gender equality was urged, and fantasy releases. Gender factors in childhood changed, but the result was an enduring tension both for children themselves and for the adults who sought to guide them.

Issues of class and race were more complex still, for this is where, after the 1950s, the most crucial divide occurred in the framework for American children's experience in the twentieth century (Bronfenbrenner 1958). For about sixty years after 1900, childhood experiences and adult approaches to children became increasingly homogeneous across class and ethnic lines. School experience was increasingly shared, despite wide differences in levels depending on areas of residence and a pronounced tendency toward test-based tracking. Schools and other agencies, including advertisements, inculcated common standards in hygiene and appearance (Vinikas 1992). Explicit "Americanization" programs pressed middle-class values vigorously, with treatment of children high on the list of goals. Shared participation in lower birth rates—the conversion of Catholic Americans to the use of artificial birth control devices by the 1930s or 1940s was a crucial development—indicated some common beliefs about children and what they deserved and facilitated common treatment as well. The new children's media were offered across class and ethnic (if not racial) lines. Wide differences depending on income and cultural background persisted. Even social workers, increasingly involved in counseling immigrant and working-class families, often showed considerable tolerance for distinctions in childrearing patterns, though they also helped bring information about middle-class values (Horn 1989). Nevertheless, considerable convergence occurred, facilitated by the massive reduction of immigration after 1922.

Developments after the 1960s opened new gaps. New and varied immigrant populations automatically increased the diversity of childhood experiences, at least for a generation. New gaps in economic experience and birth rate (including illegitimate birth rate) were at least as important. Inner-city childhood moved farther from suburban, middle-class experience, thanks to greater dependence on welfare, lower real wages, and larger families. (The basic divisions stemmed from social class but disproportionate minority involvement added a racial component.) Government protection of children declined after the "Great Society" programs of the 1960s. The percentage of children living below the poverty line grew rapidly (Kelso 1994). With growing disparities, plus more general attacks on the limited American welfare state, came increasingly implicit disdain for poor children by the middle and upper classes. Beginning with the Reagan administration in 1981, expenditure on support for poor children diminished and children became the age group most likely to live in poverty. Clearly this pattern of growing divergence looms large in any discussion of twentieth-century American childhood.

Yet even growing class/race divisions did not erase the fundamental tension of twentieth-century childhood, though they greatly affected its applicability. If only through school demands, children generally remained acquainted with some of the exigent expectations of middle-class parents. Through commercial outlets, they were even more widely acquainted with opportunities for apparent release, and consumerist enthusiasms among even disadvantaged children spread astonishingly widely.

Conclusion

Assessing the impact of gaps in the experience of childhood, in historical perspective, remains a vital task. But tracing the complex results of the tensions within the socialization process, at all or most levels above starkest poverty, requires attention as well. The interaction of more anxious monitoring and a larger fantasy world has created important choices for children themselves, with new opportunities to form groupings and individual styles based on differential responses to the available cues. The lure of escapism draws some, regardless of social class, while that of more overt conformity attracts others. Quiet battles are fought in areas such as sexual behavior, where norms are unusually nuanced and where young people themselves have altered group behaviors in the interest of new kinds of community control.

The tensions introduced into the experience of childhood obviously affect wider American patterns. Adults maintain more concern for the standards of personal discipline instilled in childhood than some observers credit; the learning experience of combining passive leisure and a surprisingly demanding set of behavioral controls bears important fruit. Further inquiry into the impact on childhood itself is clearly warranted. In a century that defined the child both as educational vessel and as market opportunity, children had to develop navigational options of genuine ingenuity.

Chapter 7
The History of Children and Youth in Japan

Hideo Kojima

The main task of this chapter is to compare theories and practices regarding Japanese children and youth in two historical periods. Taking the time span between the seventeenth and twentieth centuries (the early modern and modern periods), when, in my view, meaningful comparison in this field can be made, I will focus on the period from 1700 to 1870 to represent non-Westernized, preindustrial Japan, and the period after 1910 to represent Westernized, industrial Japan. I will take the intervening four decades between 1870 and 1910 as a transition period during which Japan transformed itself from a feudalistic, preindustrial country to a modern, industrial nation.

The objectives of this investigation are to understand childhood and youth in Japan and, more important, to understand how psychological inquiry into the child is organized in Japanese society. I will characterize the developmental study of the child as a joint endeavor by agents with different roles in the society. Lay persons, practitioners, expert advisors, and academic researchers all participate in the construction of child development theories and practices. This view is the outcome of my rethinking of psychological research on the basis of two decades of historical inquiry into child development and family life in Japan. I hope that my delineation of our discipline in its relation to other disciplines and other people in society will point a path for studying the child in the twenty-first century.

I begin with an explanation of a traditional method of counting age in Japan. For example, when people in preindustrial Japan said, "Before seven, among the gods," their age of seven was not ours. The following sections deal with folk beliefs concerning the place of human life in a cycle of the transmigration of soul and the place of childhood and youth in the total age grading systems of preindustrial and industrial Japan. Thus childhood and youth are nested in the human lifetime at the level of the social system and human life is nested within the transmigration cycle of the soul at the level of folk belief. It is my view that a deeper understanding of childhood and youth in Japanese society can be attained by taking note of their double embedding in the social system and folk beliefs.

I then turn to the construction of Japanese ideas and practices related to the child in the two historical periods. The main conceptual framework for this comparison is the distinction of four social roles related to human development. These analyses lead to why I came to rethink the place of developmental psychology in society.

How Was Age Counted?

The traditional way of counting ages in Japan was a convention on which the social perception and treatment of people and age-related rituals were based, and thus it influenced the age- and self-awareness of children and adults. Ages in Figures 1 and 2 below are shown in the older Japanese reckoning system, which had come from China. In that system, every newborn was reckoned to be one year of age; on the next New Year's Day (usually in late January or early February of the Gregorian calendar) the cohort born in the previous year became two years of age irrespective of whether they were born only a few days or nearly a year ago. In this way people belonging to a birth-year cohort all aged together. Age-related rituals, entry into and withdrawal from age-graded social groups, and the legal and customary treatment of people were mostly based on this age.

The prevalence of this convention, however, does not mean that a child's actual birthday was irrelevant. In preindustrial Japan, the first birthday of a child was celebrated by the extended family and community members. There is also evidence that in the early nineteenth century some families celebrated children's later birthdays annually and that in some districts people celebrated actual sixty-first and seventieth birthdays. The introduction of Western systems in such spheres as education, medicine, the armed forces, law, and demographics, followed by the development of the child study movement and child psychology, led to the introduction of age counting based on the child's birthday. This age was called *man nenrei* (real age), and for a time it coexisted with the old *kazoe doshi* (counted age). After World War II, counted age was gradually replaced by real age; nowadays it appears to have vanished altogether.

HUMAN LIFE AND THE HEREAFTER

Traditional folk conceptions of human life and the hereafter in preindustrial Japan were the outcomes of centuries of complex interactions among native Shinto beliefs and practices, Confucian and Buddhist innovations introduced after the mid-sixth century, and other religious beliefs and practices. Inevitably, they contained diverse and heterogeneous components and differed by region, historical epoch, and social class. Historical ethnography and folklore research, however, reveal common features of folk beliefs in eighteenth- and nineteenth-century Japan. The core components of these beliefs appear to have been maintained to the very present.

Figure 1 schematically shows the traditional folk conception of human life and the hereafter in Japan. Like people in many other cultures, the Japanese conceived of life in this world and also in the other world. The soul of the dead was believed to make a journey to the land of the dead. Because death was regarded as a state of impurity, contact with it was avoided. The Japanese held the animistic view that the soul of the newly dead might have a malevolent influence on them. People who had just lost a person of significance to them felt an ambivalent mixture of loss and fear. They believed that the soul in this transitional phase after death needed special attention so that it could migrate to the stability of the next stage and thus do no harm to people.

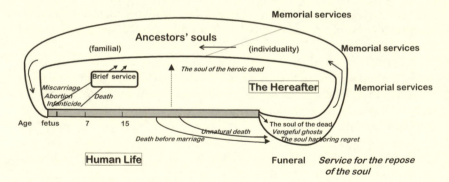

Figure 1. Traditional folk conception of human life and the hereafter in Japan.

These ideas of a transitional phase appeared in Buddhist beliefs that had developed in Tibet and been modified in China, as well as in indigenous Japanese beliefs. One specific influence from China that can be seen in Japanese notions of the hereafter has been traced by Teiser (1994). Around the tenth century, a specific concept of the afterlife emerged in China. However virtuous or vile one's moral behavior in this human life had been, one could be certain that a journey through the realm of purgatory awaited one after death. The deceased would be led through a series of ten tribunals, each under the direction of a king. In each court hall, the king and his assistants would review their records of the deceased in his or her lifetime. After leaving the final court, the deceased would be released to be reborn in a path determined by the moral balance of past deeds.

Theoretically there was no way to alter the balance of good and evil once one had died. Inevitably, however, this fatality had to be translated into funeral practices. And there, according to Teiser, the Chinese conceptualization was open to certain ritual manipulations. A particular class of mortuary rites performed by the living family members for 49 days after death was devised to circumvent the almost certain afterlife punishment under the control of the ten kings. Lack of posthumous family support would lead to increased suffering in the courts and also to rebirth in the bad paths of animals, hungry ghosts, and hell. Professional priests played a significant role in these funeral procedures, and so did descendants, who held memorial services for ancestors that extended over a long time, typically thirty-three years. We know from various records that these religious beliefs were prevalent in preindustrial Japan, and the essential part of them persists in present-day Japan.

Coexistent and partly mingled with these Buddhist notions was the commonsense indigenous belief in the continuity of the soul in human life and the hereafter. Many Japanese ethnologists (e.g., Makita 1990; Yanagita 1946) share the view that Japanese people believed that the souls of ancestors dwelled in the "other world" in the mountain area and continued to interact with the living family. For example, the souls of the dead were believed to visit and stay with the living family at the beginning of each year and at the Bon festival when feasts and prayers were offered to familial ancestors. It was and to some degree still is believed that improper or insufficient memorial services may cause illness and misfortune to the descendants (e.g., Takeda 1990). Only after many years of interaction does the soul lose its individuality and merge into the collective, familial ancestors' soul, which has spirituality and protects posterity.

The traditional Japanese also believed that babies came from the other world. In this connection it is of interest to note that many present-day Japanese junior high school girls, who apparently have no concept of purgatory or the endless transmigration of the soul, hold a naive idea of possible rebirth as a baby after their death. Equally striking is the recent finding by Amaya (2003) that more than half of seventh- to ninth-grade boys and girls reported that they had questioned the existence of the self. Among the questions they asked of themselves were some related to the concept of migration of the soul.

"Why have I selected this particular [i.e., my] body?" "Why was I born in Japan at this time rather than in another country in another time?" "Where have I come from?" In my view, these questions are constructed in a cultural milieu that still contains the folk concept of rebirth and continuity of human souls.

A related notion is also harbored by Japanese college students. According to recent research by Yamada and Kato (1998), a majority of Japanese college students believe in the existence of the other world and can pictorially represent relations between this world and that world. Generally speaking, they represent the two worlds as similar, continuous but separated. The other world is conceptualized as being neither transcendentally sacred nor fearfully tabooed. It is also of interest to note that the majority of students believe that communication between the two worlds runs only from that world to this, not in the opposite direction. It is the same with traditional folk beliefs on spiritualism. Female shamans call up the spirit of the dead and speak in the voice of the dead person.

To this point, I have treated the normative form of transmigration of life. In Figure 1, I also show four non-normative paths from human life to the hereafter. In the first, the case of unnatural death due to accident, murder, and the like, the soul of the dead was unable to make the journey to the next life and therefore influenced people as a vengeful ghost. Shinto or other religious services for the repose of the vengeful soul were required. From earlier times right up to the present day, rituals of this sort have been prevalent in Japan. Because this belief is still retained in some cultural forms that are accessible to youth such as comics, books, and movies, there have been occasions—rare but very shocking—when a suicide note by a victim of school bullying has expressed the dead youth's intention to take revenge on the bullies after his death.

In the second case, that of males and females who came of age and died without marrying, the soul might linger in a limbo-like state. A symbolic marriage for the soul was arranged by parents, and in some districts (Tohoku and Okinawa) it still is (Matsuzaki 1993). The procedure and the meaning of the practice are not the same among all east Asian cultures, but it has been practiced in a number of them, too (Matsuzaki 1993; Takeda 1990).

In the third case, that of children who died young, the soul was not believed to undergo long trials in purgatory. Infanticide in preindustrial Japan was rationalized by maintaining that the death of a newborn was not the extinction of a life but a return to the other world, allowing for the possibility of rebirth at a more favorable future time. From prehistoric times, the burial method for young children was different from that for older members of society. Even at the beginning of the nineteenth century, the mortuary procedure for a child under age seven was rather brief. Some evidence from family diaries and necrologies from Buddhist temples suggests that the mortuary procedure for young children in some districts began to move toward similarity to the practice for older people around the 1810s. The Japanese historian Ohta (1994) attributed this shift to the strict management of infants' death by the central government and also to changing sentiments in society. For the central and local feudal governments that mainly depended on rice production from their fiefs, maintenance of the peasant population was a matter of great concern.

Parents' deep grief for a lost child was recorded by some low-ranking warrior families in the 1830s and 1840s. One warrior who lost his only son to smallpox at two years of (real) age wrote many short poems of sorrow over a period of one hundred days. He also visited his son's grave frequently. Another warrior-class family lost an infant daughter to an influenza-like disease at just ten weeks. The father narrated in his diary his own deep sorrow and the grief of his wife and two siblings who had been attached to the baby. The infant was buried in a graveyard, following Buddhist rituals like those for adults. In my judgment, the sentiments of these families were essentially the same as those of families that lose a young child in modern Japan (Kojima 1987). Though the decline in the child mortality rate was still very gradual at that time, these adults no longer considered the death of a young son or daughter to be an unavoidable fate. They experienced it as a regrettable and sorrowful event (Ohta 1994).

In the fourth case, that of dead soldiers, especially those who died heroic deaths, the modern nation of Japan invented a special treatment for their souls. They were immediately enshrined as gods to defend the motherland.

In all these cases, three important features of Japanese views of human life appear. First, human life and the hereafter are continuous, and those in the two worlds continue to interact with each other. Second, family succession is very important, not only for property and as economic security for parents but also, and more important, for the souls of ancestors to attain spirituality and to merge into the collectivity of benevolent ancestor souls. Both these features, though changed historically, persist in present-day Japan. Third, children under age seven (by the former method of reckoning) were believed to have a somewhat different existence from their elders (Chen 1996; Hara and Minagawa 1986). This feature does not continue in contemporary Japan. Rather than endorsing the idea of "before seven, among the gods," present-day Japanese are more likely to turn to another early modern saying, "The mind of a three-year-old is maintained up to the age of one hundred." This adage roughly corresponds to the Western sense that "the child is father to the man." Keeping this background in mind, let us now compare the age-grading system in preindustrial and industrial Japan.

Childhood and Youth in the Age Grading System

The main issue in addressing the place of childhood and youth in the overall age grading systems of preindustrial and industrial Japan is continuity and change in the phases of life in the two periods.

THE PHASES OF LIFE IN PREINDUSTRIAL JAPAN

We can grasp the phases of life in preindustrial Japan by looking at the age-grading system prevalent at that time. Age-graded social groups were most typically found in villages, while age-graded rituals were more fully observed in urban districts. Age norms for group membership and rituals differed depending on social class, gender, district, and historical period. Figure 2 shows the typical norms in the eighteenth and early nineteenth century.

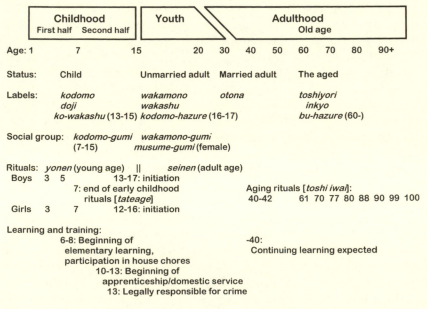

Figure 2. Phases of life in preindustrial Japan, eighteenth century to ca. 1870.

Several sources of information were used in constructing the figure. A 131-item questionnaire survey on annual events and customs was conducted in the 1810s, and copies of the reports from 22 districts have been found (Takeuchi, Harada, and Hirayama 1969). Travel writings in the late eighteenth century, family diaries in the early nineteenth century, surveys on civil customs conducted by the Ministry of Justice in the late nineteenth century (Shiho-sho 1877, 1880), and ethnological research conducted in the twentieth century that depended mainly on informants of an older generation also provide direct information on the practices that reflected the age norms of the society. More indirect information comes from childrearing manuals from the mid-seventeenth to mid-nineteenth centuries, health care books for adults and the elderly after the eighteenth century, social reform plans of the early nineteenth century, popular literature of the eighteenth and nineteenth centuries, and drawings of the life course in the early nineteenth century commissioned by Dutch collectors (Kagesato 1978; Rijksmuseum voor Volkenkunde 1987).

As is shown in Figure 2, the major generic terms to define people by age were *kodomo* or *doji* (child), *wakamono* or *wakashu* (youth), and *otona* (adult). *Toshiyori* (aged) and *inkyo* (retired) were part of the adult category. The boundary between child and youth was clearly distinguished, because youth had undergone an initiation and attained a more advanced status. The initiation consisted of a ceremony changing the child's hairstyle into an adult one and allowing the child to wear adult clothes, along with feasts given by family members and relatives. Boys in the last part of childhood were sometimes called *kowakashu* (minor youth), and those who had just entered youth were called *kodomo-hazure* (just off childhood). These special labels reflect people's realization that the transition from childhood to youth was a gradual one despite its ritual demarcation.

Children under seven. Though children before initiation were generically called *kodomo*, treatment of both boys and girls changed around the age of seven. Before then, adults celebrated a series of finely differentiated childrearing rituals in the first year of life. There were celebrations of first feeding, first bathing, first putting on baby clothes, naming, first visit to the tutelary shrine, first eating of solid food, first boys' and girls' festivals, and first birthday. Adults also celebrated rituals at the ages of three and five for boys and three and seven for girls. These rituals demarcated the shift to an age-appropriate hair style or to more adult-like clothes, and they were accompanied by feasts.

One meaning of the Japanese saying, "before seven, among the gods," is that children under seven were innocent like the gods, so their mischievous behavior would not be punished by the gods. As a matter of fact, a grandfather of the warrior class judged that the impurity of the firewood on which his grandson had intentionally urinated could be washed out by water because the boy was under seven years of age (Kojima 1986a). As far back as the eighth century, it was specified in Japanese law that offenses by those under seven (or over ninety) should not be punished.

Children over seven. Seven years of age marked the end of the early childhood rituals. After that, children belonged to an age group called *kodomo-gumi*. Their group membership became especially visible during festivals in the community. The daily life of children over seven still occurred in and around their homes. At about this age they began elementary intellectual learning, and some also participated in household chores. Between ten and fourteen, some children began an apprenticeship or engagement in domestic service outside their homes, but most children remained at home and in the community where they were born. The forces that detached youth in preindustrial England from home by age fourteen (Gillis 1981) did not prevail on a large scale in feudalistic Japan, which was more like the early modern Netherlands described by Kloek in Chapter 3. Economic factors did oblige some villagers to leave their native village for a certain period of time as servants, manual workers, or migrant workers, but such departures did not occur uniformly by age fifteen.

As I have explained elsewhere (e.g., 1986b, 1996a), a variety of manuals on childrearing and education in the preindustrial era were intended primarily for the parents, while a few were directly addressed to older children. In his book published in 1710, the Confucian Kaibara (1976) advised that formal teaching of children begin at age six or seven. After a few years of preliminary learning at home, children of ten should study under a teacher. The basic readings of the Chinese classics for seven years (ages eight to fourteen) would, according to Kaibara, build a solid base for advanced learning.

Youth. The initiation ritual for boys was carried out between thirteen and seventeen, and the ritual for girls between twelve and sixteen. After initiation youth attained adult status, but they were still not considered full adults until they married. The collection of civil customs by the Ministry of Justice (Shiho-sho 1877, 1880) officially recognized that initiation at fifteen was common. It also referred to a different treatment in one district, where people had to be twenty before they could dispose of their property without tutelage. In the Edo period it was typical that people became legally responsible for crimes at age thirteen.

Wakamono (youth) was a generic term for unmarried adults across social classes. Youth in general, and youth in villages in particular, belonged to groups called *wakamono-gumi* (male youth group) or *musume-gumi* (female youth group). Youth groups were most common among the farmer and peasant classes that were estimated to make up about 80 percent of the total population. They usually had a meeting place for their gatherings and common activities after work. Sometimes they had special lodging houses. Formalized rules for the conduct of group members were common. Youth undertook some responsibilities in the community, such as special roles at religious festivals, firefighting in the mountain area, or rescuing a wrecked ship, and attained autonomy from the adults. With regard to a marriage proposal, approval by the male youth group in a village often superseded the judgment of a girl's father.

Some youth of the townsmen class (merchants and artisans) participated in family businesses, while others served an apprenticeship. After the first term of an apprenticeship with a merchant, which typically lasted ten years, selected young men proceeded to a second ten-year term as clerks. Their coming of age was celebrated in their late teens, but their status as youth continued until they were married. When a clerk was set up in business by a shopkeeper, he became an independent merchant.

In the warrior class, a limited number of youths who inherited a family stipend performed roles in a feudal clan. Until they married, they were not considered to be fully grown-up; they were suspended in a moratorium-like status. Even after they married, they were expected to continue learning the Chinese classics and training in the martial arts until they reached about forty. In such arts as calligraphy, drawing, and poetry, it was assumed that a long time would pass before accomplishment was achieved. The majority of males, therefore, had a long period of youth that extended in some cases more than fifteen years. From the eighteenth century on, the tendency for male villagers to get married later became more prevalent in the western part of Japan. On the other hand, parents still expected their daughters to marry before they reached twenty. As a result, households where the husband was more than fifteen years older than the wife became more common in all social classes.

Adulthood. In sharp contrast with the frequent rituals of young childhood, there were few age-related rituals performed between initiation and forty-one years of age, when the aging rituals began. In some districts the first aging ritual was connected with an idea of the *yakudoshi*, typically at forty-two for males, when they were considered to be particularly subject to illness or misfortune. According to classical Chinese medical theories, biological aging began at the age of forty. The Chinese celebrated longevity at that age and at every tenth year thereafter. Japanese aging rituals began around forty-one and were followed by celebrations of longevity at the ages of sixty, seventy, seventy-seven, eighty-eight, ninety, ninety-nine, and one hundred for both males and females (Takeuchi, Harada, and Hirayama 1969). According to Kito (1983), the life expectancy of common people in nineteenth-century Japan was less than forty years. However, that number was affected markedly by high infant mortality. For those who survived the first five years of life, life expectancy was greater than fifty.

In eighteenth- and nineteenth-century Japan, longevity was highly valued. Many warriors over seventy-five were still in active service in the period of the Great Peace. In many feudal clans there was no mandatory retirement age. Each warrior individually tendered his resignation to the lord. It is therefore understandable that the Japanese celebrated longevity.

The Japanese interest in human growth and learning through the life phases is evident in manuals for the general public that were published in the eighteenth and early nineteenth centuries. Experts noticed that positive psychological and intellectual changes occurred after middle age (Kojima 1996a). The Confucian ethic of reverence for parents and the elderly compounded these rational accounts of the intellectual power of the elderly and the value to society of their accumulated experiences. These are certainly among the historical roots of the Japanese respect for elderly people that was still evident in the 1980s (Palmore and Maeda 1985).

A number of scenes in a series of drawings on the course of human life in the early nineteenth century (Kagesato 1978; Rijksmuseum voor Volkenkunde 1987) appear to reflect interest in age-related rituals in the initial and final periods of life. In addition to these, the artist depicted two important life course events in detail. He allotted many scenes to marriage and death, as if to zoom in on those events. The emphasis on these two events and their attendant rites is echoed in a detailed description of those rites in an ethnographic survey in the early nineteenth century (Takeuchi, Harada, and Hirayama 1969).

To summarize, the common ideas and customs of preindustrial Japan distinguished two phases of childhood and began the child's formal training in the second phase. After initiation there was a rather prolonged period of youth, at least for men. By marriage, young people attained socially independent adult status, though true social and personal maturity was attained later, between forty and sixty years of age.

Because preindustrial Japan was a socially stable but complex society, and a basic unit of the society was the small family where people grew up and aged, it is no wonder that the Japanese developed social systems and related ideas of human growth and learning that spanned the entire lifetime. Children and youth as well as the elderly were placed within this time perspective of human life. In a sense, a kind of historicism operated in Japanese thinking. The present state of a person was understood to be the outcome of preceding states and the precursor of states to come. This perspective is reflected in the ideas and practices concerning children that I discuss below.

STAGES OF LIFE IN INDUSTRIAL JAPAN

After the period from the 1850s to the 1870s, when Japan underwent rapid political and social change, the nation began concerted efforts to catch up with Western countries. Japan saw the maturation of its capitalistic economy and industrial revolution in the 1910s. The government had decided in 1875 that school age was between six and fourteen (real age), and by the 1910s a very high proportion of that age cohort attended elementary school. The rapid increase in attendance was noteworthy. Under 30 percent of six- to fourteen-year-olds were in school in the 1870s. By the turn of the century 50 percent attended, though girls were still underrepresented. Fully 90 percent attended during the 1910s and 1920s (Matsuno 1980).

Two conditions peculiar to Japan were involved here. First, the school attendance ratio in preindustrial Japan, especially in the nineteenth century, had been rather high (Dore 1965), though the majority of schools were private elementary schools for the general public. Second, industrialization in Japan was still in its rudimentary phase in 1872, when the government began its strong efforts to achieve a Western style of formal education. Industries that required a young work force got a late start in the tug of war between education and work. The lag helped Japan to enroll a large proportion of children in schools, at once achieving a major investment in education at the national level and avoiding the child labor problem in industry that plagued so many Western countries (Cunningham 1991). Of course industrialization and urbanization did cause problems in health and education for Japanese children, and the situation of children in impoverished rural districts was worse (Yokoyama 1985 [1898]). It was only around 1920 that infant mortality began to decrease, a demographic transition that came later in Japan than in such European countries as the United Kingdom, the Netherlands, and Germany (Mitchell 1980). In 1876 the first kindergarten was established in Japan. It was attached to the first normal school for women, and children of elite families in Tokyo attended.

Rapid economic and industrial development required highly trained manpower. The wages earned by employees differed enormously, depending on their level of education. The proportion of business leaders and bureaucrats with a higher educational background, and of those in the educational, medical, and legal professions, began to increase by the 1920s. The old middle class, consisting mainly of the privileged former warrior and landowning classes, sent some of their children to elite higher schools. For the emerging middle class that had no inherited property, the surest path to a higher socioeconomic status was through secondary and higher education. Thus the members of the new middle class invested in education for a smaller number of children beginning at the preschool or elementary levels and continuing to higher levels. Students of elite high schools and universities, some of whom lived with well-to-do families as student house boys, were typical middle-class adolescents of the time. Between 1910 and 1911 Ogai Mori wrote a novel entitled *Seinen (Adolescent)*, reflecting the social visibility of adolescents in Japan.

Figure 3 shows the life stages in industrialized Japan. The publication of translations of childrearing manuals for women since the 1870s, the child study movement since the 1890s, emphasis on the child's mind as a literary movement since the 1910s, and translations of Ellen Key's *Century of the Child* in 1906 and 1916 continued to stimulate people's interest in the child. Incidentally the most recent translation of *Century of the Child* into Japanese was published as late as 1979, for the first time from the original Swedish text (the third edition, 1927).

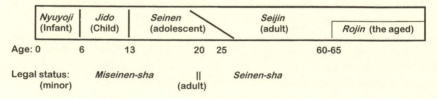

Figure 3. Stages of life in industrial Japan since the 1910s.

A young child was generically called *nyu-yoji* (infant), but *nyuji* (baby) and *yoji* (young child) were distinguished. These terms came from the science of pediatrics that was introduced from Europe. Compulsory education, beginning at six years of age, institutionalized the already existing differentiation of children before and after that age. Evolutionary views of human development introduced biological views of development and the concept of stage. On the one hand, social Darwinism attracted the attention of Japanese statesmen, some of whom actually had personal contacts with Herbert Spencer from the 1870s to the 1890s (Duncan 1908). On the other hand, in education and psychology, the theories and assumptions promulgated by Stanley Hall, especially recapitulation theory, were influential until the 1910s, fostering differential perception and treatment of children according to their developmental stage. Translations of Jean-Jacques Rousseau's *Le contrat social* were published continuously from the 1870s in connection with the civil rights movement in Japan, but *Emile* drew the attention mainly of educators. It should be noted that, according to Ida (1999), Nakae Chômin, who introduced *Le contrat social* to Japan, was very interested in *Emile*. As early as in 1873, *Emile* was among the subjects taught to senior students at Nakae's private school for adolescents. Still, though it has been translated repeatedly since the 1910s, *Emile*'s direct influence on the general public and on psychology in Japan has been limited.

It was true that initiation in preindustrial Japan signified entry only into the first stage of adulthood and that youth encompassed a long period of gradual attainment of true adulthood. Even so, the fact that the transition to youth was an entry to adulthood was socially visible to preindustrial children. Boys especially respected and were envious of youth, who enjoyed social privileges and autonomy from adult control that were not given to children. Thus to be a youth in the near future was important in a boy's personal timetable or life course perspective. In contrast, industrial Japanese children do not attain adulthood immediately after childhood. The courses of life to adulthood open to them and the kinds of life course events that awaited them were not easily comprehensible. This situation might have profound effects on the social definition of the self and the future perspectives held by older children.

A line of demarcation at the school entry age of six was evident. Even today, the Japanese conceive a child's entry into an elementary school as a very important life course event for both the child and its parents. Though the introduction of the Western concept of development and system of formal education provided a new framework for understanding childhood in Japan, the overall demarcation of childhood and people's interest in development has been consistent from preindustrial to industrial Japan.

A civil law enacted in 1898 defined majority as twenty years of age. The same law also declared the power of the patriarchal head of a household over the other members of the household. This law caused a drastic change for youth, who became more dependent on their fathers. At the same time, youth groups in the community were reorganized into young men's associations (*seinen-dan*) under the supervision of the central government. The government did not support the autonomous nature of community youth groups, their "immoral" sexual codes, or their other "uncivilized" customs.

At the informal level, however, social perception and some of the older norms of the community youth groups survived. Thomas Johnson (1975), who conducted participant observations of peer groups in rural Japan in the late 1960s, noticed a big difference among children in both their behavior and their verbal reports, depending on whether an adult (especially a teacher) was present. During his field work in 1971, Johnson noticed a remarkable change in the children's attitude to him once they knew that he was married. The differentiation between married and unmarried youth remained strong in rural Japan as late as the 1960s.

Let me briefly describe the Japanese situation regarding adolescents since then. First, the rapid economic growth that began in the late 1950s caused large-scale migration of young people to work places in urban districts. Then, as the proportion of adolescents who found employment after finishing their nine-year compulsory education dropped sharply, from 38.6 percent in 1960 to 3.9 percent in 1980, both the young men's associations in the communities and the educational and recreational classes for working adolescents in urban districts lost their functions. For a while, especially in the late 1960s and early 1970s, Japanese students were politically active. Nowadays, however, Japanese students in higher education, who make up 46 percent of the age bracket, apparently have no active roles in the society.

On the other hand, the age-related rituals and customs of young childhood as well as those of older age have generally continued from preindustrial Japan to the present time. As long as the basic interest in child development and the basically positive attitude to the elderly persist, the Japanese seem to find it appropriate to express their outlook in traditional ways of celebrating human development and aging. We have yet to see, however, what influence the recent rapid change in demography might have on people's conception of the various stages of life. The most notable demographic changes that Japan has witnessed in recent years are (1) a continuous decrease in the proportion of the population under the age of 15; (2) an increase in the percentage of elderly people over 65; and (3) an unprecedented pattern in which males typically have twenty and females thirty years left of their lives after the period of raising and supporting their children has ended. These changes, together with policy adapted to them, may certainly influence the value of children for the family and for society. They may also affect relations between the generations.

As I have explained, the first fourteen years of life in preindustrial Japan took place in a family setting. Parents were the principal caretakers, childraisers, and educators of the young, although school attendance gradually became common. This situation has not changed substantially in industrial Japan. Though formal schooling has expanded, parents have continued to be involved in childrearing and education and interested in child development. This active participation has been a consistent phenomenon from preindustrial to industrial Japan.

With regard to youth and adolescence, the picture is different. Though learning and character formation in youth were important issues in preindustrial Japan, the family was not directly involved in youth education and socialization. Youth belonged to more or less autonomous groups, and their socialization proceeded largely in community settings. The preindustrial Japanese neither developed nor transmitted theories of youth comparable to those they evolved for childhood. Thus the industrial Japanese were not ready to cope with emerging adolescents and their problems.

What filled this vacuum in adults' minds was Western psychology of adolescence. Stanley Hall and later Eduard Spranger and Karl Bühler were popular in the field of philosophy of education and psychology. Westernization brought the very idea of adolescence as well as its psychology. Therefore, historical research into the psychology of youth and adolescence shared by society in preindustrial and industrial Japan is simply not feasible. One remaining possibility is to study the everyday psychology by which youth understood themselves in different historical times. To my knowledge, this task has not been undertaken in Japan. Therefore I shall focus next on the construction of childrearing theories and practices in preindustrial and industrial Japan.

Construction of Theories and Practices on Childrearing: Four Related Roles

Four social roles can be identified with regard to ideas and practices of childrearing: layperson, practitioner, expert advisor, and academic researcher (see Figure 4). I once presented a model consisting of three roles, without the role of practitioner, but I now believe that a four-role model is more appropriate in discussing Japanese childrearing since the mid-seventeenth century.

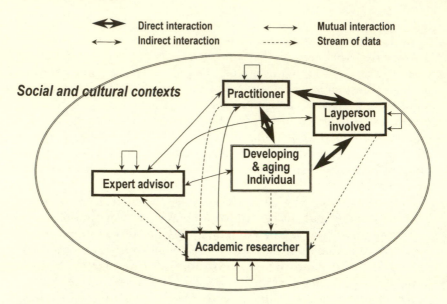

Figure 4. Relations among the four roles participating in the construction of theories and practices on human development. From Kojima (1998).

In the field of sociology of knowledge, Alfred Schutz (1964) distinguished the man on the street, the well-informed citizen, and the expert. These three represented *persons*, and an ascending order of levels of knowledge among them was assumed. When applied to certain realms such as computer technology, Schutz's model fits very well. No one would question the idea that an expert on computers knows most and that a well-informed citizen is more knowledgeable than the man in the street. With regard to childrearing, however, I believe that the distinction of *roles* without any assumed hierarchy among them is more useful, for two reasons. First, any complete technical innovation in childrearing is unlikely, due to the biological constraints on human development. Infants require a long period of time to reach maturity, under the protection, care, and guidance of nurturing adults who also serve the role of model for learning skills and social rules. Thus a common pool of ideas and skills for childrearing is not monopolized by a select few scientists or technocrats but is shared by many, from all ranks of society (Kojima 1996a). Therefore, grandmothers' wisdom can be more effective than professional practitioners' knowledge in solving children's problems. Second, it is not unusual for one person to fulfill more than one role with regard to childrearing. For example, it often happens that a person acts as an academic researcher, serves as an expert advisor, and is a father as well, with his own worries about his own son's problems.

My four-role, nonhierarchical model has grown out of my research in Japanese parental belief-value systems, and it is applicable to pre-industrial, industrial, and perhaps post-industrial Japan.

THE PREINDUSTRIAL PERIOD

In preindustrial Japan, various kinds of childrearing manuals were published by expert advisors (Kojima 1986b, 1996a). These publications systematically explicated three closely connected issues: the nature of the child and the developmental process, goals of childrearing and education, and methods of childrearing and education. The bottom line of all the advice was the third issue: straightforward advice on methods. However, in order to make such advice persuasive, the expert adviser had to construct a cohesive theory that addressed all three issues. The manuals were not published simply because their authors wished to enlighten people. They were not promoted by the government simply for the purpose of effective social engineering. Laypersons (e.g., parents, relatives, and peers), practitioners (e.g., teachers of the three Rs and family doctors), and developing individuals themselves needed these publications for ready reference as well as to construct their own implicit theories.

I have mentioned elsewhere (1986a, 1987, 1996b) how low-ranking warrior-class families in the nineteenth century were interested in the motor, social, cognitive, and language development of their children, shared their knowledge on milestones of early development, and communicated with each other on these matters. They had implicit theories, for example, to explain a child's pace of motor development that was slower than the norm. And their daily efforts to modify children's habitual behavior showed that they had developed some implicit theories on self-regulation of conduct.

While a developing individual, laypersons, and practitioners had direct mutual interactions with each other, as shown by thick bidirectional arrows in Figure 4, the interaction between expert advisors and their readers or audience was more indirect and sporadic. Still, the interaction between expert and audience was also bidirectional. Advisors influenced readers and took possible responses from the audience into account in formulating their advice (Kojima 1996a). The thin arrows that connect the expert advisor with the practitioner, layperson, and developing individual indicate the indirect nature of the interaction. Their unequal size pointers indicate the dominant direction of the flow of discourse, from expert advisor to audiences.

Who were the academic researchers whose theory and knowledge on childrearing were mediated by expert to practitioner and layperson? This role was enacted by medical scholars who conducted research on classic medical theory, tested its validity, and constructed their own theories. Confucians who inquired into human nature, goals of life, and ways of living and learning also took this role in preindustrial Japan. The theories of these scholars were referred to and quoted by expert advisors. At the same time, many scholars themselves also served in the role of expert advisor. Kaibara (1976 [1710]), a Confucian, physician, and naturalist in late seventeenth- and early eighteenth-century Japan, was a typical example of a person who served in both roles.

The preindustrial era was a time when no empirical research in the modern sense of the word was conducted on human development, so the stream of data from research subject to academic researcher shown in Figure 4 was not channeled. Still, expert advisors, practitioners, and laypersons developed their own more or less systematized theories and practices to serve their social roles. In addition to mutual interaction within the same role, direct and indirect interactions among the roles were pronounced in the realm of childrearing. In eighteenth-century Japan we can not only find fertile soil for modern developmental science but also clearly identify precursors of the science itself in specific social and cultural contexts.

THE INDUSTRIAL PERIOD

Figure 4 fully represents the modern scene, where professional academic research on child development and related domains emerged. The child study movement in Japan began around 1890. Depending on the Western framework of human development, Japanese academic researchers launched empirical studies of children. For a long time, they focused primarily on the development of the individual child, gathering data directly from children by observation, testing, and experimentation, or indirectly from parents and teachers by reports. Only rather recently did researchers begin to study social interactions involving the child, such as parent-child, teacher-child, peer, and sibling relations. Only in our own time did they try to understand naive psychology developed by laypersons (e.g., parental ideas and belief systems), practitioners (e.g., teachers' implicit theories), and children (e.g., theory of mind). So far as I know, research by developmentalists on expert advice and its changes over time dates back no further than the 1970s.

With the exception of the establishment of academic developmental psychology and the flow of newly produced data, the structural aspect of Figure 4 appears not to have changed much from preindustrial to industrial Japan. However, if we examine the content of the ideas, theories, and practices of the childrearers we find a few conspicuous changes.

The definition of the role of mother changed fundamentally from preindustrial to industrial Japan. Expert advisors in preindustrial Japan often referred to the strong, unintentional influence of mothers on their children. Some even referred to the transmission of incorrect upbringing across generations. It was, however, only after the 1870s that the expected maternal role in charge not only of caretaking but also of discipline and education of children began to be emphasized in Japan. Japanese leaders believed that women had to be educated to become good wives and wise mothers in order for the nation to catch up with Western countries. From the 1870s to the 1910s, a series of developments occurred that emphasized the maternal role. These included translations of American, German, and British manuals on childcare and education (Kojima 1989a, b), publication of manuals for mothers that combined Western methods with Japanese values, development of secondary education for women, and emphasis on the importance of maternal education conducted at home. In this period, a norm that made children objects of purposeful upbringing by mothers was invented by the middle class.

The Western concepts of evolution and progress—of the organism, of society, and of culture—were not introduced in preindustrial Japan. Neither had the Japanese developed such concepts indigenously. Though they did have notions such as the existence of civilized and barbarian countries, they had no unitary dimension on which to rank countries according to their progress in civilization. As was explicated above, they had a clear perspective on life phases from birth to old age, but they had no systems of meaning that inclined them to interpret age-related psychological change in terms of one-directional development followed by decline.

Thus far in this chapter, I have occasionally used the word "development" as if preindustrial Japan had a specific term corresponding to the Western concept of development for which we now equate the Japanese word *hattatsu*. Actually this is not correct. In preindustrial Japan, *hattatsu* meant primarily social success and prosperity, following one of its meanings in Chinese. Only in the 1870s did *hattatsu* begin to be used to indicate the Western concept of development, and only gradually afterward did the new meaning of the word replace the old one.

The introduction of the concepts of progress and development from the West necessarily introduced the antithetical concept of retardation. The preindustrial Japanese had noticed the small number of children whose pace of growth and learning was different from others', that is, fast and slow learners. However, they were able to accommodate the individual difference by adjusting the time at which the child began to learn and the level of attainment that was expected of the child, as well as the ways in which the child was taught. The introduction of Western concepts of human development, however, led the Japanese to categorize these different children as gifted, normal, and retarded.

In 1924, chairs for intelligence testing were created at the University of Tokyo. This was not unrelated to the fact that experiments in education for advantaged and gifted children appeared in the 1920s. Because Japanese primary education was generally egalitarian, the new middle-class family, with its strong motivation for upward mobility, was not satisfied with such education. According to Nakauchi (1998), the movement for new forms of education in the 1920s and 1930s was aimed essentially at the education of the advantaged and gifted and at the liberation of children from the oppression of the older educational system. Among the intellectual forces Nakauchi found in the movement were Malthusianism in education that was connected with social Darwinism, eugenics, and the birth control movement.

But the education-oriented urban family made up only a small proportion—less than 10 percent—of the whole population. After fourteen years of war from 1931 to 1945, and as many years of postwar restoration, Japan reached a new phase around 1960, when a majority of families embraced the idea of educational competition for their children (Kojima 1996a). The traditional egalitarian view of human learning potential and the belief in the importance of environmental stimulation from the earliest period of life (Kojima 1986b) were combined with an emphasis on competition from that early period. This combination has been a basic characteristic of Japanese ideas of child development for the past four decades. In its own way it has perpetuated the emphasis on the role of the mother as caretaker and educator that was first defined in the 1870s.

As involved laypersons (Figure 4) mothers have changed their ideas, theories, and skills on child development enormously over the past century. They have had increased access to information generated by others, and they have recurrently reconstructed their own role on the basis of their active involvement in the task of raising their children. On the other hand, present-day fathers in Japan appear to be less knowledgeable about child development than representative diarists of the early nineteenth century. Even if those child-oriented diarists were exceptional, we still need to understand the social and cultural conditions that produced a type of family living that supported the father's active participation in both the practice of childrearing and the theorization of child development.

Concluding Remarks

For some time I have been showing Figure 4 in my class on developmental psychology at Nagoya University and on my TV program on the University of the Air, with the following objectives in mind. First, I want to challenge my students' resignation to simple receptive learning of established psychology and to encourage their active engagement in constructing their own psychology of human development. I tell them that I am telling my scientific story of human development but that I am willing to listen to their story of development. Second, I try to emphasize the interdependency between the four roles and developing individuals. I tell them that, without it, developmental psychology as a scientific discipline could not function in society. Third, I try to widen my students' historical perspective. I tell them that since at least the mid-seventeenth century the Japanese have displayed a keen interest in the child, and indeed have developed a psychology of human development whose systems are similar to those they hold today. In a sense, we can recognize the precursors of the century of the child in the eighteenth and nineteenth centuries in Japan. Finally, I want to model an interrelationship between collective culture, intrapersonal culture, and individual actions so as to introduce my view that human development occurs within a cultural setting that I call an ethnopsychological pool of ideas (1996a).

Thus, by situating psychology within its cultural, social, and historical contexts, and by emphasizing the co-construction of psychology in the interaction among the four roles, I try to invite the active participation of students. This approach to developmental psychology is rather new, and it grew from my research experience in the field. Here I would like to tell a brief personal story.

My inquiry into human development in early modern Japan began two decades ago, when we witnessed a surge of historical studies on childhood, family living, and parent-child relations in Japan (1996a). I encountered these historical writings in 1976 and was amazed by the evidence of well-developed theories of child development and acute psychological insights from the middle of the seventeenth century, when Western influence in Japan was believed to be minimal (1986b, 1999). For example, the infant's competence in the sensory and cognitive domains, and the importance for later development of responsive caretaking of infants after two months of age, were clearly seen. At that time, my frame of reference for evaluation of those early works were the ideas of developmental psychology in the 1970s. Judged from that point of view, the descriptions and theories of preindustrial Japanese scholars and expert advisors were astonishing enough. As far as I know, no one to that point had ever noticed the intrinsic value of their writings from the viewpoint of developmental psychology. I therefore felt proud of my "discovery" and continued to express my admiration for the keen observation and insights of those earlier scholars. However, as I have admitted elsewhere (1997), I would probably not have been so appreciative if I had read those writings earlier, in, say, the late 1950s. Then I would probably have dismissed the observations and insights as unscientific superstition, because nothing in the mainstream of developmental psychology supported them and historical interest in childhood and family had not yet emerged.

In any case, more than ten years were to pass after 1976 before I began to rethink the fundamentals of our discipline. Because I have explained my thinking elsewhere (1997), I will not repeat myself. I will simply say that the rethinking led me to think of a diagram like Figure 4 to explain our discipline. Now I have come to think further that a historical view of the progress of developmental psychology itself should be reexamined. For that purpose, the Japanese case is worth further analysis, for the Japanese had developed theories of childrearing, at both the grassroots and expert levels, before the introduction of developmental science from the West. The modern developmental sciences in Japan have grown on the foundation of those earlier ideas. Needless to say, simply tracing historical change in Japan is not enough for a full understanding of the role of modern developmental sciences in the century of the child. We need, and will benefit greatly from, comparative and collaborative work on the history of human development research in several different societies.

For that purpose, the roles played by children in each society should be fully examined. In Japan, the reward that parents expect from having children has changed strikingly over time: from direct economic contribution to the family, through economic security in the parents' last years, to social support in their old age. Children continue to have an instrumental value for parents. Japanese families invest heavily in their children's education to raise the economic value of those children in the market, whether for the parents' or the children's sake.

In addition, as has been explained above, the Japanese have traditionally believed in the existence of the hereafter. They have considered family succession very important not only for preservation of property and the achievement of economic and emotional security in this world but also for provision of spiritual rest for ancestors in the next. Only an appropriate memorial service allowed the soul to attain spirituality and merge into the benevolent collectivity of familial ancestor souls. This concern about the hereafter led the Japanese to seek insurance in the hereafter mainly for their own descendants, and not for family surrogates such as social or religious guilds (Hanawalt 1986). Understanding of the roles of children in traditional—and contemporary—Japanese society is not complete unless it takes into account their life in the hereafter. Even today the hereafter is a matter of real concern for many Japanese. Childless families and families whose daughters all marry into other families simply do not have successors who will organize the memorial service for them. An only son of one family who marries an only daughter of another family cannot maintain the memorial service for both families. And of course those who remain single throughout life also have no one to provide their memorial service.

Some of these people may devise a surrogate family system. Others may change their religious beliefs. Still others may construct a solution based on the ethnopsychological pool of ideas of Japanese society or adopt new ideas developed in other cultures. We have yet to observe carefully what is occurring to Japanese concepts of the child, family life, and children's experience amid the rapid demographic changes and the increasing interrelations among cultures of recent years.

Chapter 8
Childhood, Formal Education, and Ideology in China, Then and Now

MICHAEL NYLAN

Perceptions about childhood in imperial China tend to be a function of our perceptions about childhood in China in the modern period. Our views of modern China, however, are often colored by our fundamental orientations toward domestic and international politics, no less than by our emotional responses to a number of highly controversial issues, such as gender inequality, infanticide, and abortion. Then, too, notions of childhood in China inevitably reflect ongoing debates inside and outside China over the very nature of modernity versus tradition, capitalism versus communism, and those "Asian values" defined in explicit opposition to the "universalist" notions of progress promoted by most Euro-American institutions (Han 1999; Nylan 2001).

The problems that beset the careful researcher who aims to disengage fact from fiction do not end there, of course. For however hard it is to present an abstract childhood for most eras, states, and peoples, it is obviously much harder to come up with accurate generalizations about "typical experiences" in the case of China. The very idea of a unified China, it need hardly be said, is an impressive construction of the modern nation-state, designed to bring disparate groups and autonomous regions into a single imagined community. Given the long history of the various cultures whose complex interactions have been conducted and recorded in Chinese script, the startlingly different patterns of social mobility within those cultures, the geographic size and population of the present-day People's Republic of China, and its regional and ethnic diversity, China appears as a monumental text writ with multiple grammars accommodating a number of distinct realities. Naturally enough, few students of China have been foolhardy enough to hazard comparisons over time and space. Fewer still have been trained to do so, since the discipline of Sinology has long divided China "experts" into two discrete groups: those concentrating on the pre-1949 past who rely on materials written in classical or semi-classical Chinese language, and social scientists concerned with the post-1949 era, who are usually unfamiliar with pre-modern grammar, vocabulary, and stylistic conventions. Add to this the academic time lag that marks a relatively conservative field shaped by Cold War concerns and it is hardly surprising that research on China in the two key areas of domestic life and children's history is in a quite preliminary stage.

Nevertheless, several considerations justify an attempt to provide a more comprehensive assessment of childhood in China at this point. To begin with, the Chinese themselves have recognized the special place of childhood since at least 1,300 B.C., though theirs has hardly been a child-centered culture. And though the "stagnant" or "ultrastable" nation of popular accounts hardly existed in the pre-modern era, the entities we now subsume under the term "pre-modern China" (excluding the Autonomous Regions) were in some ways impressively well integrated and durable, with people at every level of society having much in common. That means useful hypotheses can be proposed. We can say, for example, that some basic conceptions regarding the formative stages from childhood to adulthood stayed much the same for some two millennia (from 221 B.C., the start of the imperial period, to 1976, the year of Mao's death), despite foreign conquests, territorial shifts, drastic revisions to political paradigms, increasing urbanism, and exponential population growth. A broad overview, as a result, can serve to help us ascertain the degree to which longstanding beliefs in the fundamental importance of childhood education have been maintained or eroded in China during the post-Mao period. As sophisticated social historians understand, the difficulties of piecing together an accurate picture of the relation of past to present only increase over time, for in less than a single generation strikingly new ideas and new policies, aided by the mass media, can become naturalized ("the way it's always been"). Moreover, to postpone evaluations any longer may hamper the efforts of those hoping to build a kinder, gentler "century of the child" in the foreseeable future, for more than a nodding acquaintance with alternate ways of organizing humanity will be required if we are to accurately assess the relative successes and failures of capitalist modernity as dominant discourse.

This chapter will not offer a lengthy general description of the developmental stages prescribed for the Chinese child in pre-modern times; that sort of description would parallel accounts already included in this volume for the Japanese child as well as in two fine books (Kinney 1995; Saari 1990). Nor will it offer the expected contrast pitting the supposedly abysmal conditions of pre-modern China against the glorious achievements of the modern era, as revisionist historians decades ago had already traced the main features of that skewed portrayal to the initial encounters between "the sick man of Asia" and the imperialist powers at the turn of the last century (March 1974; Isaacs 1958; Appleton 1951). In its place, this chapter supplies a preliminary sketch of Chinese childhood that locates in post-Mao policies a wrenching break in age-old patterns of formal education. It focuses on formal education since the Chinese themselves from time immemorial have identified the formal education of the young as the best preparation for human moral and intellectual maturity and hence the most secure grounding for a strong Chinese state. Time and time again, therefore, as the standard histories attest, governments in China have made it their business to supervise the training of the young, lest the entire society eventually devolve into lamentable chaos. Thus a comparative study of this aspect of childhood in China, past and present, provides the single fairest test of the commitment of China's current leaders to the Asian values they officially espouse, a test that—if properly framed—avoids the imposition of extraneous foreign values on the Chinese context. And if the fate of "all-under-Heaven" indeed lies with the young, as so many slogans piously intone, then it behooves us to take up seriously the case of formal education for children in China then and now.

Critiques of Childhood and Childhood Education in Imperial China

In detailing Chinese ideas of childhood, until quite recently a remarkable continuity characterized the early received texts and modern anthropological reports (Saari 1990; Stafford 1995). Tradition envisions three stages of childhood: the first in the womb; the second from birth to seven or eight *sui* (six or seven years old by our reckoning), when the child first starts to *dongshi* ("understand things"); and the third, lasting until fifteen *sui*, during which time the child is "instructed" (*jiao*) in many cultural patterns (e.g., how to read and write Chinese characters, how to perform mathematical calculations, how to maintain constructive human relations). Once the child has internalized these patterns, it is ready to engage in that intensive "learning" (*xue*) process that is the chief business of adulthood (Ma 1936, 430). The ultimate goal is for the "realized person" to "become [truly] human" (*cheng ren*), with the greatly enhanced capacity for empathy that facilitates harmonious and reciprocal social relations.

During the first phase of existence, the unborn child is exposed to elements of high culture. For the fetus, classical music is played, canonical texts are read, and prescribed foods are consumed in accordance with cosmological theory. Following birth, in the second phase, the Chinese child is allowed a significant amount of freedom. So long as the child does no real harm to himself and others, he is generally left to explore his own world in his own way. As one early Western account put it, "Young Chang is very much indulged by his parents and does pretty much as he likes. He goes to bed when he likes and rises when he likes" (Helmer 1925, 51). No attempt is made to complete toilet training by a set time or—with few exceptions—to prescribe or enforce particular modes of conduct. During the third and final phase of childhood, however, "Young Chang" experiences a major departure: Whether in school or in an apprenticeship, he will spend long hours in arduous work, much of it repetitive (Davin 1991, 56). Ideally, this third phase represents the adults' ever-tighter imposition of *guan* ("oversight") on the child's activities, where *guan* implies governing, monitoring, controlling, loving, and caring for the child (Sing and Yeung 1996, chapter 2; Tobin, Wu, and Davidson 1989, 93).

Many trained in the modern Euro-American model have excoriated such traditional Chinese childrearing practices, no doubt because they reverse custom in giving progressively less freedom to the child as he or she grows older. The Chinese alternative is easily explained, however. In light of the high rates of infant mortality before the twentieth century (where one child in three died before age five), the Chinese sensibly regarded the passage from conception to puberty as a time fraught with peculiar dangers, external and internal. Frights, illnesses, hungry ghosts, and even an insufficient attachment to life itself could threaten the well-being of the child. The first task of all well-meaning adults was thus to build a sturdy mind and body in the vulnerable child. To this end, parents sought to stimulate the child's emotions and intellect through unregulated contact with the outside world, the better to bind the child more closely to earthly existence. The body could only benefit, it was thought, from such rough-and-tumble play. Meanwhile, prayer, taboos, and charms would tighten the child's bond with the living while averting a host of evils. (Healthy children were given derogatory names to render them odious to vengeful spirits, for instance.) From this standpoint, even that most straitlaced of neo-Confucian moralists, Zhu Xi (1130–1200), advised parents to urge all children below the age of seven or eight *sui* to make mischief (de Bary 1989; Saari 1990).

For those who passed that watershed successfully, a more serious course of study was in store—though this third phase of Chinese instruction was far less regimented in pre-industrial times than is usually thought. Simply put, children were now seen to be well enough prepared in mental, moral, and physical terms to familiarize themselves with the discerning ways of adult life. Through intensive immersion in a wide range of exemplary models (from Chinese written characters, the invention of the ancient sage-kings, to the personal characters of tutors), consistently enjoined by "mild yet firm" teachers and parents, the young child was to be alerted to his or her place within the evolving social fabric. As the child's innate ability to focus on the world around him expanded, so the child was to develop the concomitant capacity to move beyond mere desires for immediate gratification to a firmer grasp of larger realities and obligations. Play and fantasy then "naturally" would give way to a heightened awareness of self and society.

The theoretical literature of imperial China insists that each and every child, male or female, rich or poor, literate or illiterate, is endowed with the capacity to "become [truly] human." The inborn capacity must be enlarged (in the Chinese metaphors, "strengthened," "refined," or "polished"), however, through the appropriate modeling on the "natural" patterns pervading the triadic realms of heaven-earth-human, as presented in elementary and advanced education. As one primer put it, "If foolishly you do not study, how can you become human? The silkworm makes silk; the bee makes honey. The person who does not learn is not equal to the brutes. Learn while young, and when grown up apply what you have learned" (Giles 1910, 144).

But how did traditional pedagogical methods ever prepare young Chinese to take their place as socially responsible yet creative adults? Any honest answer to this apparently innocuous question must confront three cherished stereotypes about childhood in imperial China: first, that the great masses of children were illiterate; second, that traditional pedagogical methods were not only inefficient but counterproductive; and third, that gender inequality was more pronounced in China than in other pre-modern societies. Let us consider these propositions one by one.

A surprisingly high percentage of children in pre-modern China acquired "basic literacy" (defined by the acquisition of functional skills in reading and writing, rather than by an elite literary education) through a wide variety of educational opportunities, including home schooling, charity schools, and cheap "private schools" (*sishu*)—similar to our one-room schoolhouses—where two to twenty-five pupils at different levels trained under a single schoolmaster. Three standard primers were all that was needed to attain such literacy. The *Trimetrical Classic* (teaching some 1,200 characters), the rhyming *Thousand-Character Classic*, and the Hundred Names (supplying 400 family names) together taught about 2,000 characters. At the rate of ten new characters per day, the primers could be finished in less than a year, giving the child the necessary tools to read for content in advanced texts. (It was an added boon that the *Trimetrical Classic* encapsulated all Chinese cosmology, ethics, and history within its covers.) In defense of the old-style pedagogy, it must be noted that

to begin by teaching character recognition through complete sentences, thus improving the content of early lessons, would have exposed the child to many repetitions of characters but relatively few characters within a limited time span; at the same time, the content of the materials would have suffered from the restricted reading vocabulary the child had mastered . . . . Traditional methods [of instruction] . . . thus recognized certain problems inherent in the nature of the language and compensated by presenting materials in a sequence that shifted emphasis among the goals of reading, reading comprehension, and writing. (Rawski 1979, 48–49)

In traditional instruction, the tendency was—contrary to prevailing stereotypes—not to have the entire school chanting a single line of text, but to allow each student to progress at his own pace, a tendency made possible by the small size of the typical school (Borthwick 1983, 9). It was the Chinese, ironically, during their initial contacts with "West," who were startled to find the Euro-American system of "grades" based on the regulated factory or army model, for the Chinese never used to presume either (a) that at the exact same age all children can be counted on to be sufficiently socialized to engage with virtual strangers in a classroom or (b) that all children will advance in their subsequent studies at the same speed.

No less bizarre, really, are the charges—repeated ad nauseam in Western textbooks and by Western-trained teachers until many modern Chinese themselves have come to believe them—that traditional childrearing practices stifled autonomy, creativity, and individuality, in at least three interconnected ways: first, because rote memorization of a few textbooks (with children allegedly reciting each textbook "like a parrot, without having it explained") stifled the imagination (Helmer 1925, 60); second, because filial piety, continually endorsed in childhood training, kept the younger generation in perpetual bondage to parents, living and dead (Gernet 1996, 144; Wu 1921, 14–23; Louie 1980); and third, because infanticide was routine practice and corporal punishment more frequently applied in Chinese schools (vide "Farewell, My Concubine").

As mentioned above, memorization of three primers provided, in fact, the foundation for more advanced work in reading, writing, or arithmetic. But the most up-to-date analysis of traditional pedagogy flatly contradicts the received wisdom that ascribes great harm to rote learning. One expert writes:

In the West, the misconception has arisen that rote learning and meaningful learning are not complementary but mutually exclusive. . . . [Yet] repetition allows for contextualization. Repetition can reinforce meaning, . . . repetition creates understanding and is a precondition for . . . [thorough] understanding. There can be such a thing as "deep memorization": really learning a concept, and then committing it to memory so that both facts and deeper meaning can be called up. . . . The strategy of repetition is highly adaptive and sensible; it in no way preempts understanding. (Biggs 1996, 155–57)

Talk of the "lifelong burdens" of filial piety is equally unfounded, in part because it confuses moral prescriptions espoused in melodramatic Tales of Filial Piety with accurate historical depictions, thereby ignoring an abundance of counter-evidence drawn from history, in part because it discounts some undeniable benefits (including psychic security and the pleasures afforded by daily rituals) of "traditional" extended family life, naively asserting the post-industrial nuclear family to be "the best of all possible worlds" (Wolf 1985; White 1993; Lowe 1983; Erbaugh, ms.; Shek 1996). We lack firm data on infanticide, male or female, in imperial China, just as we have no adequate estimates for the frequency and severity of corporal punishment, but the available anecdotal evidence suggests that the traditional customs and law of China were no more repressive than those of its counterparts in Europe and America (Kinney 1993). On the supposed harshness of traditional Chinese education methods, one respected historian has remarked: "That the education was authoritarian, inculcated morality, and made surrogate parents of teachers need not be doubted. But neither are those exclusively Chinese characteristics. Has education . . . in modernized societies not . . . displayed similar characteristics?" (Mote 1973, 112).

Finally, there is the troubling charge of greater gender inequality leveled so often against imperial China. With every passing year, more and more studies in gender history dispute this charge (Holmgren 1981; Bray 1997; Mann 1997; Raphals 1998; Nylan, 2000). Yet students of China, whether Euro-American or Chinese, find that they cannot dismiss the powerful image of the little Chinese girl forced to undergo the painful footbinding process—nor should they. On the other hand, the same students often forget three relevant facts: (a) that Chinese girls did not undergo footbinding for most of China's history, since cloth bindings, originally designed to support the toes of professional dancers, were widely adopted by the upper classes first in the fourteenth century and by peasants in some areas of present-day China in the sixteenth; (b) that footbinding was a cultural marker, so the custom was not observed by many groups within China's borders, for example the Mongols, the Hakkas, and the Manchus, and was expressly forbidden by Manchu law in 1644 to non-Chinese; and (c) that Chinese reformers, whose anti-footbinding sentiments were registered long before the arrival of Western missionaries in China, also could not disguise their shock when they learned of the far more pernicious (to their minds) Western custom of binding the vital organs in tight corsets, which they rightly took to represent a far more serious health hazard to women (Gulik 1974, 222; Levy 1966). One sympathetic foreign observer summarized their views succinctly,

We find this deformity of the feet ridiculous, but it pleases the Chinese. What would we say in Europe if a society of celestials [= Chinese] made a campaign against the corset? Deformity for deformity, which is the more ridiculous: that which consequently produces a certain difficulty in walking, or that which, compressing the stomach, dislocating the kidneys, crushing the liver and constricting the heart, often prevents women from having fine children? (Matignon 1936, 236)

Reformers, such as Liang Qichao in an 1896 essay, tended to argue, quite rightly, that the record of China on the "woman question," however deplorable, was not all that unusual compared with the world at large.

Over the vast universe and down through the ages, . . . women were treated in one of two ways: they either were to fulfill their duties or to serve as playthings. They were reared like horses or dogs to satisfy the first need and adorned like flowers or birds to satisfy the second. These two methods of oppression gave rise to three types of punishment. In Africa and India, they pressed a stone against a woman's head to make it level, a punishment like our tattooing [for serious crimes]. In Europe, they wanted the woman to have a slender waist, and to accomplish this they punished her by pressing wood against her waist. In China, the woman had to have her feet bound, a punishment like cutting off the lower legs. These three punishments deformed women everywhere in the world. (Liang 1896)

Another satirical essay, entitled "In Praise of Footbinding" (Suh-ho 1915), emphasized the continuities between Chinese and Western gender practices: Western men denied their women the ballot, hamstrung their professional careers, belittled their intelligence, and minimized their value. But to be completely safe, the essay caustically commented, Western men had better take up the Chinese custom of binding the feet of their women, too.

In any case, footbinding, however debilitating, was never the whole story for girls in imperial China—and not only because the custom came very late in history. In assessing the lives of Chinese girls in imperial China, we must factor in the considerable ideological recognition accorded women's sexuality in imperial China and their economic contributions to the family, not to mention their undoubted cosmological significance (Black 1986; Bray 1997). Turning to the specific question of female education, studies compiled in the last decade have shown conclusively that it was first in the fifteenth century that debates over the propriety and content of female education erupted in China. Before then, girls shared the same classical curriculum with their brothers; and even after that time, families that could afford the luxury of private tutors for their children were apt to provide tutoring for their girls as well as boys (Holmgren 1981; Bray 1997; Mann 1997; Handlin 1975; Hawkes 1973). "Good" mothers in late imperial China, as in early China, were to teach their children to read the Classics at home, before they went either to school or to a formal tutor, as well as to expound the moral messages the texts contained. That gender inequality is not the inevitable outcome of a Confucian heritage is demonstrated by the case of Taiwan, which along with Norway, Peru, the Netherlands, and Canada, has implemented the lowest degree of gender differentiation in its treatment of children (Sing and Yeung 1996).

A monolithic China peopled by millions of ignorant and downtrodden beasts with no decent regard for human life—this is a stereotype that long predates the Cold War and the Cultural Revolution (1966–76). Conceived in the European culture wars of the eighteenth and nineteenth centuries (March 1974; Isaacs 1958), the idea gained greater currency when the vast majority of Western-language eyewitness accounts available for China came from a wartorn century (1840–1949) whose appalling conditions—some part of which had been occasioned by the imperialist incursions—seemed to confirm the imperialists' claims that the Orient would mightily benefit from "civilizing missions" led by representatives from "the West." Unlike earlier Jesuit reports extolling China's great peace and prosperity, these latter-day accounts depicted a body politic critically weakened by overpopulation, corruption, civil strife, and warlordism, unable to effectively resist its virtual dismemberment at the hands of the imperialist powers (Jochim 1995). Massive dislocations had by then forced local charitable institutions and academies to shut down. Curiously enough, while most readers today roundly reject the Social Darwinist doctrines that inspired such accounts of more than fifty years ago, they unwittingly accept their mistaken premises when they reckon that the deplorable conditions of the last, dying days of empire constituted the invariable norm prevailing throughout all history in China. The truth was that previous dynasties—and the early Qing itself—had overseen the production of great material wealth in a stable sociopolitical order, so much so that China by the late nineteenth century had become a victim in Malthusian terms of its own consistent and incredible success.

Not coincidentally, most of the negative accounts came from one of two groups, Western missionaries or the May Fourth "New Youth" educated in Western-style schools in the 1920s and 1930s. Members of both groups were, with notable exceptions, quite unfamiliar with even the rudiments of classical learning. Furthermore, missionary tracts composed for the sake of eliciting contributions for the Christian missions in China seldom resisted the temptation to dwell upon the worst possible scenes of degradation in the "heathen" land. This missionary disdain for "barbaric China" resonated with the naive New Youth in China, the generation which saw itself engaged in an epic struggle between the young (the modern, the vital) and the old (the decaying, the stagnant) over the fate of the nation. It was essentially from these two groups that the modern "experts" on China inherited as part of their professional stock-in-trade the tight analogy constructed between the supposed oppression of children within the family system and China's own vulnerability within the international structure (Pease 1995). As a result, reputable scholars could fall back upon a few overworked themes in their studies of childhood in imperial China. The purported lack of "healthy games" intended to toughen China's moral fiber (Helmer 1925, 61; Gernet 1996, 152) was one such theme, though numerous pieces of art and literature from the imperial era depict children playing all manner of boisterous games with marvelous penny-toys from the peddler's stock-in-trade, my own favorite being the ingenious "magic blocks" in sets of seven or fifteen designed to mimic any and all living forms.

This is not to say that all was rosy in pre-modern China. Poverty, ignorance, and inequity often ruled there, too—just as in our own society today. The foregoing remarks merely contend that further progress in the field of children's history will be impeded unless we set aside the invidious comparisons between an allegedly "advanced" West and a correspondingly "backward" China on which most prior studies have been premised. The comparisons are intellectually suspect, and they can have real consequences in the world beyond academia.

Formal Education in the Post-Mao Era:
A Test of Traditional Asian Values

Whenever Sinologists and politicians, in China and outside it, continue to pass off a sweeping cultural critique of imperial China as "common wisdom"—some out of genuine ignorance and some because they would cynically manipulate the past in order to maximize present power—they allow almost any unlikable feature of post-Mao China to be blamed on the damnable tenacity of recalcitrant "tradition," though many "ancient" traditions are of comparatively recent manufacture (Yang 1994, 36–39). In consequence, numerous authorities, in China and abroad, feel justified in absolving themselves of full responsibility for the continuing plight of children in China today. At the same time, almost any perceived innovation in childrearing practices, however minor or dubious, is hailed as a stunning victory over the drag of weighty tradition.

Such arguments form the subtext for the 1996 White Paper on Child Welfare (FBIS), where the PRC congratulates itself for its "earnest and responsible" leadership in matters of child survival, protection, and development. The White Paper lists an impressive series of achievements in child welfare in post-Mao China, including the following:

1. In China, the proportion of children who are underweight is just half that in other developing countries (17 versus 35 percent).
2. Since the 1970s, the mortality rate for children has steadily declined, except for infants less than a year old.
3. Ten-year plans have been formulated to reduce infant mortality and malnutrition further.
4. In 1991 China led the ratification efforts for the UN Convention on the Rights of the Child, which seeks to establish international standards for children's health and welfare.
5. Twice, in 1989 and again in 1996, China received formal commendations from the World Health Organization for its success in implementing its child immunization program.
6. China has recently undertaken to strengthen existing laws and devise new ones for the protection of children's rights and interests.

The list might look more impressive, were it not that it ignores earlier achievements of imperial China with respect to child welfare issues. Let us not forget that "The Chinese, without any influence from or association with Europeans, originated the biggest educational system ever made by non-Christian people" (Headland 1914), with the specific goal of comprehensive education (de Bary 1989, 9). Long before the late twentieth century, child immunization for smallpox was widespread in China; child orphanages existed, as did charity organizations to help poor mothers (Leung 1995) Frankly, with the imperial ideology from 135 B.C. on forging an absolute identity between good government and "cherishing the young" through education (with a degree of material security regarded as absolute precondition for that education), more appropriate standards of comparison for modern China might be located in the so-called "Confucian horizon" of East Asia (Taiwan, Korea, Japan, Vietnam, Singapore, and Hong Kong), rather than among the "developing nations" as a whole (a category that includes India and Africa, for example). After all, the East Asian states shared similar ideologies and institutions in the pre-modern era, and in the past few decades each has enjoyed comparable rates of economic growth—at least until the Asian stock market crash in the late 1980s. By East Asian standards, progress in the post-Mao era in China has been slow and spotty.

Certain "facts" about child welfare cited in the White Paper are almost certainly misrepresented. For example, the White Paper claims near-universal literacy (99 percent for boys and 94 percent for girls) for children in China today. But other available evidence directly contradicts that claim. A 1992 UNICEF report puts the basic literacy rate at 84 percent for males and 62 percent for females over fifteen (UNICEF), and those estimates tally with two in-house surveys prepared by party bureaucrats. (The White Paper's inflated statistics apparently derive from attendance reports compiled on the first day of school in the first grade.) Note also that the literacy rate is declining, especially among girls, the poor, and those in rural areas (Erbaugh 1990; Hooper 1985; Lewin et al. 1994; Epstein 1991; Wu and Daming 1995) (in synchrony with the situation in the United States).

More often, certain indicators that place the present-day People's Republic in a less favorable light are simply glossed over. For instance, China devotes a very small proportion of its national wealth to formal education. Throughout the 1980s, around 3 percent of the GNP and national income and less than 10 percent of total national expenditure were spent on schooling, whereas low-income countries around the world averaged 13.5 percent of national income, all countries averaged 15.2 percent, and Japan at one point went as high as 22.3 percent. The average public expenditure per youth has stayed for years around 60 RMB (U.S. $15), with expenditure on teaching materials less than 1 RMB—about 25 American cents—per primary school student (Lewin et al. 1994, chapter 2). In 1985, in fact, China ranked 149th among 150 countries in per capita expenditure on education

(Qian 1985); only Yemen, a country with quite a different tradition of schooling, ranked lower. In the 1990s China's investment in education failed to keep up with economic growth, inflation, or increased government expenditure, though every year propaganda claimed "that investment in education has increased in absolute terms" (He 1991, 157; cf. Ross 1991) And the situation is far worse than these figures suggest, because China spends a disproportionate amount on tertiary education (disproportionately allotted to the offspring of the political elite) while skimping on early education. For instance, in 1988, for every 100 RMB spent on a college student in China, less than 3 RMB went to primary school students (Hu, Jian, and Mao 1991, Table 9.6). By comparison, Japan allocated some 43 percent of its entire education budget for elementary schooling and only 13 percent to tertiary education; and in Western Europe (Britain, West Germany, and France), the ratio is roughly 50 percent to 10 percent (Pepper 1990, 144).

With reports showing child labor and dropout rates rising and literacy rates falling, prospects for future progress in combating illiteracy and gender inequality may well be receding. On average, people in China receive only 5.4 years of education, and by official count some 22 percent of persons over age fifteen are illiterate. Moreover, the latest major overhaul of the national educational system (the 1985 Educational Reform Act) will surely exacerbate, rather than ameliorate, inequalities in China. Because this Reform will shape the life of each Chinese child well into the twenty-first century, this chapter analyzes the main features of the Act.

On the surface, the 1985 Reform Act looks entirely laudable. For example, it urges local authorities to institute a nine-year cycle of "compulsory" education (primary school followed by junior high), to replace the former six-year system. Still, districts are free to implement the Reform when and how they choose. "In recognition of the varying economic and cultural conditions of the country," no target deadline has been set for any area by the government. As nine years of schooling is already the rule in China's four largest cities, the Reform merely acknowledges the status quo in this respect. However, some provisions of the Reform are bound to diminish the chances for a good education that the average school-age child enjoys in the People's Republic. The most fundamental problem, of course, is that the Reform operates in conjunction with the post-Mao economic reforms. For the average citizen, the introduction of the so-called "household responsibility system" and the concomitant dissolution of the urban work units and rural communes and collectives that once provided a range of benefits (daycare, education, health care, and old-age pensions, to name just a few) sharply escalates both the direct costs and the opportunity costs of keeping children—especially girls—in primary school. The children of high-level cadres have always—even at times of radical egalitarianism under Mao—enjoyed preferential access to good educations (Niu 1992; Hooper 1985).

In the Reform Act itself, potentially damaging reforms include the following: (1) the shut-down of local public schools judged "inferior," with a concomitant push for private schooling; (2) the "decentralization" of state control over education; (3) the abandonment of any state controls over job assignment; (4) the explicit calls for greater "flexibility" in pedagogical approaches, so that educational institutions may respond to "market demands" for trained workers; and (5) the ever greater concentration of scarce resources in highly selective "key-point" schools as well as in tertiary education. (Only one feature of the Reform Act, the "vigorous" promotion of technical and vocational schools, is likely to improve prospects for the average Chinese child. Unfortunately, the Chinese Communist Party to some extent has reinforced resistance to these schools among white-collar parents, since attendance at either type automatically disqualifies students from seeking admission to college.)

Let us examine each of these provisions briefly, in order to better understand the Reform Act's inherent problems. Massive school closures (almost all in rural areas), effected in the name of promoting quality, combined with the decision to withdraw financial and ideological support from the remaining rural schools, limit educational opportunities for the average Chinese child. (In a 1987 sample survey conducted by the State Statistical Bureau in nine provinces—Inner Mongolia, Heilongjiang, Zhejiang, Shandong, Hubei, Guangdong, Sichuan, Yunnan, and Liaoning—just over 63 percent of parents whose children were not in schools cited "schools located too far from home" as the chief cause for their children's truancy.) Nor can the rapid growth of private schools (often located in areas where public schools have decreased in number or declined in quality, due to inadequate state funding) make up the shortfall, since their higher tuition fees make them unavailable to poor children. In theory, "decentralization" offers local authorities and educational professionals—"free at last" from day-to-day micro-managing by the Party—far greater scope for educational innovation. In practice, decentralization signals "no more funding from the central government" for local schools outside the major urban areas. Public school administrators are known to rely upon charitable donations, individual "contributions" (in the form of high forced tuition of around 100 RMB per month per child, plus extra fees), and local surcharges (mostly head taxes and taxes on light industries) to make up the deficit, since relatively few collectives or communes (which are fewer and fewer in number these days, anyway) run onsite schools. Early education, undeniably cheap both in imperial China and during the Mao years, thus becomes too expensive for many in post-Mao China.

And while calls for "greater flexibility" to reorient schools toward "market demands" (seen in the abandonment of the job assignment system, in the retooling of the curriculum content, and in early tracking modes) sound sensible enough, they can ease the conversion of school grounds to virtual factory compounds, as muckraking reports by Chinese reporters show. Surely, they also work to disadvantage Chinese girls. Why? It's the same old story we often see in other countries: Employers are unwilling to hire girls, even girls who can boast higher academic qualifications than their male counterparts, because society reckons that girls are "inefficient" workers due to their heavier family obligations. As one employer put it, "We would rather take in a male hoodlum than a woman. A hoodlum can be reformed, but you cannot get a woman to give up childbearing" (Hooper 1985, 103). The Chinese curriculum has been revised accordingly. No longer are girls told to "hold up half the sky" as under Mao. Instead, their main sex education textbook, *Happily Accept Your Sex*, tells them that "natural" differences between boys and girls make boys the better workers (Ross 1991), which means in turn that fewer girls gain admission to secondary and tertiary schools than male counterparts with equal qualifications. Even the staunchest proponents of capitalism might think it premature to adjust educational goals to "market drives" in an oligopolistic environment lacking free circulation of capital and information. The current Chinese leaders, facing the twenty-first century, might have done better to sponsor massive mobilization efforts on the Maoist model to encourage higher enrollments in three target groups—the poor, girls, and minorities—since the People's Republic itself says that "governments have a responsibility to counterbalance the built-in tendency of free-market economic systems to favor the already advantaged" (Grant 1995, 43)

But it is the aspect of the 1985 Reform calling for the expansion of the keypoint school system (virtual at the primary level; actual at the secondary) and consequent diversion of scarce funds from ordinary schools that poses the largest threat to the average Chinese child. By law, keypoint schools, as the "main channel to university entrance," are "privileged institutions with unfair advantages over ordinary schools," absorbing an enormous share of the societal resources devoted to primary and secondary education (Lewin et al. 1994). By law, only keypoint schools may pick and choose their students from among a huge pool of applicants, with an eye to the job market and probable careers.

The vast majority of their students come from the cadre and professional classes. Keypoints get the lion's share of scarce state and local resources, so they can attract the best teachers and build the best facilities.

Official state support for keypoint schools exemplifies the strong rejection of the Maoist impulses toward egalitarianism in the decades after Mao's death in 1976. Above all, Deng Xiaoping wanted to create an elite track in order to train a small group of top-notch scientists capable of leading the Four Modernizations drive in technology, industry, agriculture, and the armed forces, so that China's might be restored to its "rightful place" as the dominant power in East Asia (Cumings 1999). To achieve his aim, Deng needed the support of China's senior educational experts. By and large, these intellectuals (many of whom had suffered, at first- or second-hand, persecution under Mao) were ready to subscribe to Deng's perspective, for their class had sharply resented the Maoist tendency to value "redness" (ideological loyalty) over "expertise," insofar as it seriously undercut their own standing in society (Wang 1996). Arguing that the rapid expansion of educational opportunities in China between 1949 and 1976 under the leadership of "anti-intellectuals" had had an adverse impact on the quality of schooling in all grades (despite the sharp reduction in illiteracy rates), the experts agreed with Deng that the chief goal in the post-Mao era should be to embrace the concept of "high quality" schooling throughout the country. In cooperation, then, top Party bureaucrats and their chosen "experts" contrived the following rationale for the preferential treatment accorded keypoint schools, often at rates two hundred times more favorable than for ordinary schools: given the current shortage of equipment, funds, and suitably trained teachers, China has to choose between equity and efficiency in training the young to lead the drive for economic growth. As Vice-Minister of Education Zhang Chengxian put it before the reforms were published:

China has a population of one billion; its economy is not advanced, and not balanced between different areas, so it is totally impossible to improve the educational quality in all schools and areas at the same time. For a time, we must recognize this imbalance and concentrate our energy on running keypoint schools well. . . . Only then . . . can institutions of higher education have highly qualified new students. (Lewin et al. 1994, 90)

To escape charges of elitism, the reformers uniformly stressed the "modeling" role that keypoint schools would have on other local schools, though such a role is at best an improbable fiction. First, keypoint schools cannot function as good "models" since no mechanism has been devised to foster professional exchanges between keypoint and non-keypoint schools. Second, the mere existence of keypoint schools hampers ordinary schools in attracting the best students, teachers, and resources. Third, with the overwhelming majority of keypoint schools located in cities and towns, the keypoint system further widens the urban/rural opportunity gap (Lewin et al. 1994, 90), a gap which had already grown under Mao (Kirkby 1985).

The keypoint system, like many provisions of the 1985 Education Reform Act, makes little sense in terms of current economic theory, which sees a need not only for better educated people but also for more educated people in any push toward a market-based economy (Bradsher 1995). As the reform largely seeks to grow a small pool of highly visible professionals who will serve as leaders of the future, it does little to supply society with workers who have acquired middle and high level skills. As early as 1980, scholarly articles in China began to warn that in the early twenty-first century half the cohort of young people aged six to eighteen would be either illiterate or semiliterate (Song 1991).

Inside and outside China, scholars tend to blame age-old traditions (dubbed "feudalism" in the Chinese Marxist lingo, though there has been no feudalism in China since 221 B.C.) for two of the most troubling aspects of post-reform education in China: its pronounced elitism and its strict regimentation of student activities (Lewin et al. 1994, chapter 2; Tobin, Wu, and Davidson 1989, chapter 3). But the 1985 reform, in presupposing the need to nurture especially talented children for the national benefit, smacks more of Social Darwinism and eugenics than of earlier traditions in the imperial era (Bennett 1996, 368ff). To be fair, Confucian tradition had insisted, first, that any individual committed to self-improvement could become a person capable of "influencing the sovereign above and benefiting the people below" (Giles 1910, 146-47); and second, that the main determinant of excellence in a field is hard work and self-discipline, not innate intelligence, let alone wealth or social connections. On the subject of regimentation, traditional pedagogy had children gradually undertake self-direction, without much adult interference (Hawkes 1973). Regimentation—the earlier the better—became desirable only in the industrial and "scientific" age, which was anxious to produce citizens whose "every action is like the rhythm of a machine, every move is like soldiers marching in step."

In one of the paradoxes of history, it was the "progressive" voices in Republican China, operating in the belief that China could only be rescued from utter ruin by legions of indefatigable workers and brave soldiers, who sought the best model for "new" education in the schools of prewar Japan, schools that were run with military drill, military-style uniforms, and severe discipline. Between World War I and World War II, even ardent members of the anti-Fascist resistance (for example, those in the Shaan-Gan-Ning border areas of China) found that the Japanese model held an undeniable cachet, for it managed to seem "scientific," aggressive, and distinctly East Asian all at the same time (Pepper 1990, 71; Tobin, Wu, and Davidson 1989, 116). Some senior "experts" in charge of China today knew this old Japanese model (not much in evidence in Japan today) from their own childhoods (Lewin et al. 1994, 3; White 1993; Nylan 2001), and it is this same model that enjoys a new lease on life in the People's Republic, rechristened as uniquely "Chinese Reforms" (Pepper 1990; Chen, Lee, and Stevenson 1996). Under the latest version of the Reforms, for instance, ultra-regimentation, whereby children at two or three *sui* are expected to perform like little adults (Tobin, Wu, and Davidson 1989, ch.3) in a dramatic compression of the three traditional stages of childhood, has become the norm, legitimated by the nation's pressing need for hyper-rapid modernization and its irrational fear of "only-child spoiling" (Wu 1996).

It was typical of Fascist education to merge the language of national citizen-making and the rhetoric of international conspiracy in its formal ethical training of small children. China's New Moral Curriculum, introduced in 1986, stresses patriotism, a blend of revolutionary and "Confucian" traditions, and a positive attitude to labor, in a mix familiar to us from Chiang Kai-shek's New Culture Movement in the 1930s (Dirlik 1975; Lewin et al. 1994; Kulander 1995; Thøgersen 1990, ch. 9) In support of that curriculum, state-sponsored publishing houses late in 1994 issued, in a revision of imperial culture, a brand new, beautifully illustrated *Trimetrical Classic* for use in China's primary schools. Composed of easy-to-remember rhymes—presumably to facilitate memorization by primary school students—the *New Trimetrical Classic* proudly proclaims China to be the "oldest continuous civilization," extols the "old Chinese virtues" (now sadly reduced to industry, thrift, and obedience), and exalts the usual roster of Communist Party heroes, including Liu Shaoqi, Zhou Enlai, Mao Zedong, and especially Deng Xiaoping (*Xin Sanzijing* 1995). But the primer does more. Whereas the old *Trimetrical Classic* of the pre-modern curriculum celebrated China's culture heroes in the civil arts, glorifying its classical heritage and educational system in the process, the new Trimetrical Classic focuses more on an extensive array of military heroes, "each cherishing the empire," who have had to rescue China from the machinations of its arch-enemies, including Taiwan (hence the placement of Deng Xiaoping against a background missile wreathed in white doves).

The publication of the hyper-nationalistic *New Trimetrical* primer should give us pause, particularly because the textbook's graphics are undeniably charming. Chinese children represent a quarter of the world's children, and a striking number of them may learn little about world relations except through the sort of pseudo-history this neo-classic provides. So long as the present government is resolved to "give moral education top priority in the educational work of the schools" (OPIN 1996), far too many youths, "eating bitterness" while "awaiting employment," may have to sustain their feelings of self-worth by ideology alone. As Americans, oblivious to the lessons taught by the Vietnam War, slide back into yet another Cold War, can we feel sure that China's youth will prove any less susceptible to such invented "traditions" of belligerence?

Conclusions

In certain crucial respects, children in imperial China were better off than is usually assumed. Children in the post-Deng era, on the other hand, are worse off than popular accounts would have us suppose. With recent educational reforms in China harking back to the elitist models of the 1930s and 1940s, is there no single straw of "common wisdom" about Chinese children that we can safely clutch? There is one: At all times, the Chinese government, like its principal rivals on the world scene, has longed for the ideological conformity of its inhabitants, believing the formal inculcation of "moral education" in its young to be vital to its own stability and prosperity. Still, agrarian-based, pre-industrial societies could not afford—and so they did not aspire to—direct administrative control over every subject; the late imperial state had the requisite funds to hire a single ill-paid magistrate for every 50,000 to 75,000 subjects on average. Therefore, the state in late imperial China contented itself with disseminating the sociopolitical virtues through the pull of the civil examination system, a formal system that proved of signal benefit to many of its subjects. (Davin 1991, 45; Lewis 1999, ch. 1-2) More recently, the Chinese state, in company with its counterparts elsewhere, has had a far grander array of tools at its command through which its bloated bureaucratic apparatus may shape the lives of its citizens, young and old.

Having reached the end of the so-called century of the child, we have been charged with the task of assessing from our vantage point in time the relative achievements and failures of powerful governments around the world in support of child welfare. In the case of the People's Republic of China, can we honestly report that more children now, in the wake of the concerted efforts of well-intentioned reformers throughout the last century, enjoy the type of protected learning environment that ensures that they will not be left behind by the country's current economic planning? I fear we cannot, nor am I alone in that fear. The internationally acclaimed director Zhang Yi-mou, in his 1999 movie *Not One Less* (*Yige dou bu neng shao*), gives audiences a glimpse of the conditions prevailing in the average rural school in China today. One piece of chalk for the entire one-room schoolhouse and a twelve-year-old girl asked to cope with the entire village's truancy and training—that says it all. Were he alive today, Lu Xun, China's greatest modern literary figure (d. 1936), would surely feel compelled to cry out, as he did in 1921, "Save the children!"

The Child in Developmental Psychology and Pedagogy

Chapter 9

On Infantilization and Participation
Pedagogical Lessons from the Century of the Child

MICHA DE WINTER

Like their counterparts in many western countries, Dutch citizens and politicians worry about the moral decay of children and youth, inspired by shocking—but scientifically disputable—measures of juvenile delinquency and nuisance appearing in the media. Many blame the family, concluding that parents have failed to impart moral education. Recently Dutch government officials asked us to advise them, therefore, on family policy. They particularly wanted to know what young people might think good family policy should be.

To develop an answer, we asked an ethnically diverse group of twenty-four vocational school students, ages fourteen and fifteen, to interview ten classmates each about the subject, and to discuss the results with us. Their findings were astonishing. The children, mostly from underprivileged neighborhoods, said that the problem was not so much inside the family as in the whole of their "educational" environment. Occasional family problems were "normal," they felt, but normal problems could get out of hand because of a "social education gap"—a gap between the care parents can provide and the invitations to adult responsibilities that young people seek from the rest of society.

Neither in their neighborhoods nor in the large, anonymous schools they attend do they find a sufficient number of adults who really care about them, see to their safety, and provide help and attractive activities. To the young people, the family and the outside world are connected. The absence of caring adults in their social world puts all the pressure on their families, an unfair burden that some parents cannot bear. The young people's principal advice to the Minister of Welfare therefore was: invest in educating adults, not in installing video monitoring in the schools. Children's participation—in this particular case through research and policy making—uncovered insights that policy-making adults had missed (de Winter and Kroneman 1998).

Why are children so seldom asked for insights about their own lives and needs? In this chapter we will try to find an answer to this question by connecting it to the history of the science of pedagogy as it developed during the century of the child. Pedagogical science has been assigned a significant but ambiguous role in encouraging the process of infantilization: the growing duration of childhood and the increasing distance between the world of children and that of adults (Koops 2000). Pedagogues who argued for child-centered upbringing and education (Vom Kinde aus) in particular have been blamed for both the growing "apartheid" of children in Western societies and for the allegedly negative individual and social effects of parental "permissiveness." However, the same pedagogues are credited with contributing to the emancipation of the child. Child-centered theories have increased awareness of developmental needs, supported the struggle against oppressive educational practices, and helped focus international attention on children's rights. In this sense pedagogy, as the science of childrearing and education, is clearly linked to historically changing conceptions of the child. As we will show, it may be considered as contributing to these changes and as being itself an expression of these changes.

Western children, as the Dutch educationalist Lea Dasberg wrote in 1975, have long been raised by keeping them "little." Ever since the Enlightenment, she claims, children have been increasingly confined to the hothouse of a special Youthland. In this land—or pedagogical province—the child was free to express its distinct nature unhindered and could find shelter from the perverting influences of the street, child labor, wars, and loose adult morals. This lengthening and shielding of childhood has undoubtedly had its merits. Exploitive child labor has become an exception in the West, very young people are seldom sent to fight as soldiers, and numerous measures have been taken to protect the young from maltreatment, abuse, and neglect. Moreover, the recognition of children's distinct nature has helped generate a great deal of knowledge on the upbringing, education, development, and health of young people. This psychological and social attentiveness to children as children first emerged among the upper middle classes. Only at the turn of the twentieth century did heightened prosperity, culminating in the emergence of the Western welfare states, establish the ideal that children have a right to protection and development as a social standard for all layers of the population (Schnabel 1992).

As a result, many Western countries have apparently turned into a child's paradise. Mean infant mortality rates have dropped from 10–25 percent around the beginning of the century to less than 1 percent in the late 1990s, mainly as a result of improved hygiene and nutrition, preventive health care, and the general spread of affluence (Corsini and Vazzo 1997, 13).

Though an enormous professional infrastructure of provisions for the education, welfare, and mental health of children has been created in the twentieth century, this special world of children has also come under attack. Infantilization has been blamed for an ever widening gap between the lives of adults and children, a gap that has seemed to undermine both child development and society itself. The social isolation of children was attacked for causing alienation between generations, child-rearing problems, learning disabilities, and adolescent psychological turmoil (Plessner 1946; van den Berg 1958).

Several twentieth-century pedagogical movements tried to bridge the gap between pedocentrism, an exaggerated child-centeredness, and the tendency to privilege adult interests above the needs of children. One proposal, which has gained ground recently among educators, stresses the importance of children's active involvement in their own educational process. Children are being (re)discovered as active participants in their own upbringing. Since the 1970s, Western parents have grown more willing to negotiate with their children rather than simply enforcing parental decisions on them. Pedagogy in the public domain follows that pattern, though at a somewhat slower pace. Proposals for educational reform, some of them dating from the first half of the twentieth century, are gradually gaining ground in present-day schools. Pupils are allowed some governance responsibilities through student councils, and they take a more active role in steering their own learning processes. The same is true for the area of child and youth care, where therapeutic programs are being discussed with young clients rather than being imposed. Client councils are emerging and protocols are being introduced that secure the client's rights. National and local governments have embraced "participation" as both a goal and a tool for youth policy. Many who work with young people have come to believe that actively involving youth in areas like neighborhood development, urban planning, and crime prevention helps them develop a firmer sense of democratic citizenship and strengthens the social fabric.

At first glance, the emergence of child and youth participation seems to offer a modern answer to some of the pitfalls of infantilization. Participation could help decrease the discontinuity in the process of socialization created by the social isolation of youth. Participatory education could be a new context that would help rather than hinder young people's development of the skills and attitudes necessary for democratic citizenship (Hart 1992; de Winter 1997). However, the concept of children's participation also raises a number of questions. Participation may risk saddling young people with responsibilities that actually should not be theirs, jeopardizing every child's need and right to be a child.

How, then, should this modern pedagogical discourse be interpreted? What kind of relationship does participation create between adults and children and between children and society? Should the inclusion of children in social decision-making be validated as an important sign of emancipation and democratization, in which hierarchical relations are eroding and the rights and needs of young people are gradually being recognized? Or is participatory learning, like so many earlier and contemporary innovations, just another instrument to discipline and manage youth?

Students of pedagogy disputed versions of that dilemma, directly or indirectly, throughout the twentieth century. Should pedagogy build on the natural development of the child, or should it be derived from the requirements of social life? Should childrearing and education serve personal development or the interests of the community? And should pedagogy be directed at assimilating children into the existing social order and ideology, or should it prepare children to be agents of social change? These debates have stimulated deep controversies, which have in turn encouraged a range of synthesizing theories and experiments. Therefore, this chapter will take a historical approach, looking to the development of twentieth-century pedagogical ideas and practices for the roots of a paradigm that privileges children's participation.

This chapter will try to throw some light on these present-day dilemmas, drawing lessons from twentieth-century pedagogical history. First, we will elaborate the concept of infantilization and explore its ambiguities, using the work of Ellen Key, who first labeled the twentieth century the century of the child. Then we will describe some of the major polarities in twentieth-century pedagogy, as well as some of the historical roots and dilemmas of a participatory pedagogy. Finally, building on these historical insights, we will suggest some principles and criteria for a viable, noninfantilizing, participatory pedagogy.

Ellen Key and the Two Faces of Infantilization

"Children should have the right to choose their own parents," the Swedish teacher and writer Ellen Key wrote in her book *The Century of the Child*, first published in 1900. Through this metaphor she expressed her strong conviction that children, as the torchbearers of civilization's future, deserved to be brought up in a loving, child-centered environment. Children should be raised by fully mature parents who have made a loving and rational choice to have them. By "rational" Key meant the use of scientific insights from both genetics and child psychology. For example, she favored "positive" eugenic measures, such as a marriage certificate certifying the medical fitness of both partners, in order to protect children from being born into unwelcoming and hazardous families (Noordman 1989).

When Key formulated her "revolutionary, romantic protest" against the "unnatural, authoritarian and oppressive pedagogy of her time," she most certainly intended to emancipate children. She criticized educators who "continued to educate children as if they believed still in the natural depravity of man, in original sin, which may be bridled, tamed, suppressed, but not changed." She characterized her new education as "the system of allowing nature quietly and slowly to help itself, taking care only that surrounding conditions help the work of nature" (Key 1909, 107). Children, therefore, were to be liberated from and protected against all expressions of physical and psychological violence, both within the family and at school. She strongly opposed rearing young children outside the family in daycare centers and kindergartens. There "children are handled in crowds from two and three years up, they are made to appear before the public in crowds, made to work on the one plan, made to do the same petty, idiotic and useless tasks." She believed that in this way these institutions were creating "units" rather than human beings. The preschool system, as "one of the most effective means to produce the weak dilettante and the self-satisfied average man," should be abandoned (235–37), along with elementary schools that force children to consume intellectual nourishment they neither want nor need (245).

In Key's opinion the most constructive element in child-rearing was the fixed, quiet order of the home, its peace and its beauty. In that natural environment, mothers should foster their children's social and inner life, laying the foundation for morality and spirituality. Tender rather than tyrannical fathers should strengthen the will of their children and open for them the doors to the outside world. Key accused the schools of her time of committing "soul murder": "the schools deal improperly with the mental powers of youth, through their lack of specializing, of concentration, in their depreciation of initiative, in their being out of touch with reality." She thought them to be absolutely destructive to the child's personality (229). By imposing early training on children, giving them untrue motives and half-true information, and threatening them with painful discipline, schooling corrupted children's identity from a very early age. Instead of suffering the oppression of their will, thoughts, and feelings, children should be "emancipated from the burden of learning by heart, from the forms of the system, from the pressure of the crowd, in those years while the quiet, secret work of the soul is as vital for them as the growing of the seed in the earth" (242).

High school and college education fared no better. Key fulminated against the worship of examinations and diplomas. These must be obliterated from the face of the earth because the aim of education should be "that the scholars themselves, at first hand, acquire their knowledge, get their impressions, form their opinions, work their way through to intellectual tastes, not as they now do, taking no trouble themselves, but being supposed to acquire these gifts through interesting lectures given by the teacher on five different subjects, heard every morning while the students are dozing, and soon forgotten" (230).

Key's pedagogical ideas were not at all politically neutral. She attacked the educational practices of her time not only because she believed them to be inhumane and unscientific but also because she was convinced that this oppressive pedagogy was one of the major causes of social and political evil. Key saw children who were drilled to obey, trained to deny their individual conscience, and made to follow the "collective laws of honor, collective patriotic feelings, and collective conceptions of duty" as ideal material for a system that "produces its Dreyfus Affairs and Transvaal Wars." German kindergarteners, she argued with chilling foresight, were already being drilled to wear uniforms.

Key's pedagogical ideals could be characterized as an important milestone in children's emancipation. She wanted children liberated from educational repression and parental discretion and given a measure of human rights. However, Key has drawn criticism for encouraging a kind of infantile regression in both youth and adults. In the tradition of Locke and Rousseau, she argued for a child-centered upbringing and education. She advised parents and teachers to "become like the child," so that by putting themselves in the position of a child adults would understand a child's feelings and needs. She envisioned a pedagogical province that sheltered children within a special, "natural" environment protected against the evil influences of industrialized and rationalized society. Key believed that such a sheltered, "natural" childhood would create productive, responsible, thoughtful adult citizens. But others disagreed.

Critiques of Infantile Regression

In 1946 the German/Dutch philosopher Helmuth Plessner was one of the first to argue explicitly that modern social life had an "infantilizing influence" on the population. According to Plessner, fast and fundamental social changes had changed the relationship between social life and education. Industrialization both caused and reflected scientific and technological developments in capitalist economies. Meanwhile, two devastating world wars eroded the general faith in human progress even as the spread of democracy increased individual rights and opportunities. Scientific and technological knowhow seemed to have outdistanced people's moral and emotional capacities. Plessner felt that this very disproportion inhibited and infantilized people, youth in particular. Continual confrontation with apparently insoluble social problems seduced youth into regressing to a "lower human level." Young people were accused of escapism, of reverting to playful irresponsibility. The older generation, their educators, showed the same regression by adopting an ideal of eternal youthfulness (as a symbol of progressiveness) and an indifferent attitude toward the wisdom of age. Plessner thought that Key's romantic child-centeredness, the art forms of Jugendstil, and the emergence of youth movements like the German Wandervogel signified a culture that idealized callow energy at the expense of the moral experience of age. By refusing to offer resistance to this growing cynicism and indifference to spiritual values, older generations unconsciously and unintentionally encouraged the "degeneration" of youth. Emancipated childhood, argued Plessner, led not to responsible adulthood but to the infantilization of the entire society. Through emancipation, childhood lost its fundamental transitional character. The "reifying" of youthfulness into an independent value system blocked the necessary exchange between generations, and this, Plessner feared, by undermining respect for the past and its values, could create a dangerous tendency toward nihilism.

It should be noticed that Plessner's critique of infantilization reached further than child-centered upbringing and education alone. To him infantilization seemed to be a general cultural phenomenon, extending over all age groups. The emergence of a Youthland, according to him, meant less an actual separation between children and adults than a generalized alienation between childish people and the serious realities of life.

In 1956 J. H. van den Berg published a daring study called *Metabletica* (English edition 1961), in which he also developed a culturally pessimistic outlook on infantilization. More explicitly than Plessner, van den Berg emphasized the negative social and psychological consequences of the lengthening youth phase and the growing separation between the lives of children and adults. Although van den Berg, like Plessner, thought that the impact of infantilization extended through childhood and adolescence into adulthood, he nevertheless observed a growing gap between generations that had far-reaching consequences.

At a psychological level he claimed that this gap was a major cause of frustration in both young people and adults. Ambivalent and even "dubious" relations between parents and children unable to bridge the gap often led to neuroses or aberrant behavior. He described how, since the eighteenth century, modernization had made adulthood increasingly complex, polyvalent, and invisible to children.

In the past, if a child walked through the streets of his town, he could see and hear around him how trades were practiced, one of which trades he would choose himself later on. The rope-maker, the smith, the brazier, the cooper, the carpenter, they all worked in places accessible to any child: in their houses, in work yards, or somewhere in the open. Today most trades are shut away in factories, where children are not allowed. How can a child know what happens there? (van den Berg 1961, 43)

Since children could not know adulthood by direct experience, the process of socialization needed to change:

Our adulthood has acquired such a peculiar shape that the child has to be childlike if he is ever to reach us; he has to get through a complicated period of psychic maturation before we adults can get the impression that he is really with us—that he really can take part in our complicated, inwardly contradictory but nonetheless, and even partly because of it, so delightful maturity. (72)

No wonder, said van den Berg, that scientific child studies (like developmental psychology and pedagogy) became necessary. These new sciences developed to compensate for the loss of inevitable and self-explanatory relations between the young and the old. When children still had free access to the world of adults, no scientific bridge of understanding was necessary (104).

The critiques formulated by Plessner and van den Berg fell somewhat silent during the 1960s and 1970s, while emancipation and democratization gained ground in the Western world, influencing the relations between generations. The 1960s culture of joint demonstrations of parents and children against nuclear missiles, along with joint patterns of consumption, sexuality, and fashion seemed to have built new links between youth and adults.

According to Dasberg (1975), however, the question is whether the apparent emancipation of children and youth really meant the end of infantilization and Youthland. Dasberg claimed that, although young people gained social attention and validation, they lost pedagogical consideration. When parents began questioning their pedagogical ideals and lost confidence in the future, they virtually ceased to educate their children, permitting children to withdraw from social life. In a similar way the German pedagogue Klaus Mollenhauer (1986) criticized the lack of cultural content in pedagogical thinking, leading, among other things, to antipedagogical attitudes in which "upbringing shriveled into a charitable contact with children." According to Dasberg, children and youth did the only thing they could do: through regression, nostalgia, and narcissism they turned away from a defaulting adult society that offered no guidance or perspective. They emerged from confinement in the special "waiting room" their parents had constructed to find themselves socially redundant. This redundancy was at least a provisional end of a lengthy process that had begun in the eighteenth century. Modernization first brought levels of economic prosperity that permitted extended childhood. Subsequently, the dominant pedagogical ideology barred children from entering the adult world. Ultimately, children ceased to want to become adults, and soon enough no one was even able to really "grow up" any more.

Pedagogy as the Bridge of Understanding?

Does pedagogical science, as van den Berg and others suggested, indeed owe its existence to the emergence of Youthland? Or could it be the other way around, namely, that the science itself has played an important constituting part in the growth of this pedagogical province and is therefore accountable for infantilization? Clearly, pedagogy has never existed independent of its sociocultural context. Child rearing and education have always been a theater where different ideologies and scientific approaches "compete," to put it delicately. As the Dutch pedagogue Johannes Hoogveld once put it, "whether one is a relativist or an absolutist, an empiricist or rationalist, a realist or an idealist, it is all reflected in pedagogy" (quoted in van der Velde 1975).

Historians and theorists of pedagogy have long sought a consistent and coherent framework in which all the different pedagogical schools and movements could be classified. As most of these classifications only evoke new controversies and new classifications, we will not try to repeat such an effort here. Instead, we seek, on the one hand, to clarify the tensions between pedagogy and infantilization. On the other hand, in our search for a workable participatory pedagogy we want to examine pedagogical theories that tried to avoid or resolve these tensions. Without pretending completeness, therefore, we will now look at some of the major controversies and synthesizing endeavors within twentieth-century pedagogy.

CALCULATION VERSUS CONSTRUCTION

Many modern pedagogical disputes actually date from the Enlightenment, from the confrontation of naturalistic ("reality-based") and metaphysical approaches to childrearing and education. Naturalistic pedagogy, or, as Jan Waterink named it in 1926, the *pedagogy of calculation*, is a generic term for theories based on observation and the systematic study of the biology and psychology of child development. Naturalistic pedagogues like Rousseau, Heinrich Pestalozzi, Friedrich Froebel, Friedrich Herbart, and Maria Montessori, and also Key, based their theories on principles of the "modern" natural sciences and the "scientific calculation of chains of causality." The child and the growth of its mental strength were the main object of study and pedagogical work. Naturalistic educators believed that pedagogy should take notice of the child's distinct needs and its "good" nature. The aim of all education was the full development of individual talent and potential. Childhood was to be considered and scientifically studied as a distinct phase of life, not to be measured by the dominant standards of adult culture. Schooling should respect the unique development of each child, and pupils should be allowed (limited) opportunities to follow their own interests.

The metaphysical approach, which Waterink called the *pedagogy of construction*, is based on a straightforward deduction of educational ideals, aims, and tools from predetermined philosophies of life, political ideology, or religion. Ancient Platonist pedagogy, which prepared children for a predetermined rank in the "polis," is a well-known example. Many political systems have followed that path, subordinating both the child and its education to political ideology.

The Christian dogma of original sin was also translated into a pedagogical formula. Christian pedagogues in the late nineteenth and early twentieth century developed biblically inspired doctrines of childrearing and education. The formation of civilized and faithful personalities required that education and discipline restrain the evil inclinations innately present in each child. Parents and educators had to do their utmost to help children master their dangerous natural drives and desires (Meijer 1996, 16). This Christian pedagogy strove to instill values like austerity, diligence, obedience, piety, and self-discipline in children and to enforce strict prescriptions and prohibitions designed to limit sexual and other temptations (Waterink 1956).

No strict polarity actually exists between calculation and construction, since naturalistic approaches are certainly inspired by ideological presuppositions. Rousseau, for example, clearly meant to teach, if not preach, a new morality, and Key also explicitly situated her pedagogy in a context of social reform, while constructive approaches can be refined by empirical study and experience. The distinction nevertheless clarifies a contemporary scientific debate. Should pedagogy be strictly empirical, leaving aside moral or ideological questions, or should these very questions be at the heart of every educational idea? Naturalism dominates modern pedagogy, which uses scientifically controlled investigation to test the effectiveness of pedagogical instruments. The goals of pedagogy, considered necessarily speculative or subjective, are explicitly excluded from scientific research. In his pedagogical metatheory, Wolfgang Brezinka argues for separating the domains of everyday practical pedagogy and philosophy of education (1978, 1981). His system "resolves"—or shall we say freezes—the schism between calculation and construction by formalizing it.

It would be tempting simply to ascribe infantilization to the emergence of naturalistic pedagogy. After all, the concept of child-centeredness developed in reaction to the dominance of "pedagogies of construction" shaped by the demands of adult society. However, naturalistic pedagogues themselves were divided on how to prepare children for adult social life. Although many naturalistic pedagogies were directed at individual development, naturalism as such did not necessarily exclude a more social orientation. A preference for individual versus social orientations not only distinguished the pedagogies of calculation and construction but also divided the naturalists among themselves.

INDIVIDUAL AND SOCIAL ORIENTATIONS

Devotion to the uniqueness of childhood certainly made pedocentric pedagogy vulnerable to the critics of infantilization. In different words, Plessner, van den Berg, and Dasberg all emphasized the negative effects of an emerging gap between education and social life. Most pedagogies of construction aimed to create (or force) the connection between children and the adult world, principally by subordinating individual development to the interests of the social or religious order.

Enlightenment individualism, meanwhile, guided and shaped scientific pedagogy. Immanuel Kant and Friedrich Herbart saw "moral perfection of the individual" and "mastery over the self" as the most important aims of education. The rational, free individual was the motor of economic, social, and cultural progress; knowledge and personal "civilization" were the keys to social success. The idea that education should serve individual happiness and the full development of the personality (at a safe distance from the evil adult world) meshed perfectly with the development of bourgeois culture in Western Europe, at least until the beginning of the twentieth century.

Around 1900, as Key was formulating her prototypically individualistic pedagogical program, a counter-movement, Sozialpädagogik, began to manifest itself, particularly in Germany. The new thinkers criticized traditional Individualpädagogik because it divorced human development from society. The philosopher Paul Natorp (1899), the godfather of Sozialpädagogik, argued that "Der Mensch wird zum Menschen allein durch menschliche Gemeinschaft" ("a human being only becomes human through human community life") (Coumou and van Stegeren 1987). According to Natorp, ethical principles like sincerity, justice, and social courage developed through taking part in social life, not in the seclusion of the relationship between educator and pupil. In his view, therefore, education was by definition a social matter: education and community could not exist independently of one another. With colleagues like Georg Kerschensteiner (1917), Natorp strongly opposed the authoritarian, class-bound Prussian system of education. Prussian education, in their view, preserved and celebrated enormous existing differences in social status between young people. Kerschensteiner and Natorp instead proposed educational reforms that would highlight and reward individual initiatives and social responsibility.

Social pedagogy takes on dramatically different meanings depending on how "social" is defined. If "community" is defined as a collection of free, independent individuals, then the differences between Sozial- and Individualpädagogik virtually disappear. If, however, community implies a collective ideal, social pedagogy can become an integration strategy as mild as voluntary youth welfare work or as rigorous as the compulsory strategies of Nazism and communism. Interestingly, both Nazism and communism embraced compulsory youth work in part because both regarded the family as unreliable. Through the Hitler-Jugend and the Komsomol, therefore, each tried to consolidate the grip of the state on socialization (Mennicke 1933).

Comparing individual to social orientations confirms that infantilizing elements are mainly to be found at the individualistic extreme. At the same time, precisely there also lies the greatest passion for the personal emancipation of the child. The most radical social approaches, by contrast, emphasize children's social integration and embeddedness, even if children are integrated by force and at the sacrifice of their individual needs and interests. The pedagogical controversy unmistakably reflects the sociopolitical cleavages of the twentieth century: liberalism versus socialism, religiosity versus secularism, and totalitarian (fascist and communist) reactions against Enlightenment ideas.

Many twentieth-century pedagogical reformers have tried to develop synthesizing approaches that connect the individual and the social. Imelman and Meijer (1986), for example, conclude that neither an individual pedagogy without regard for the influence of the community nor a communitarian pedagogy without regard for the role of the individual is in fact feasible. Their analysis of reform-pedagogical movements suggests that, although "personalistic" reformers like Montessori, Ovide Decroly, and Helen Parkhurst promoted empathy with the individual child, and social educators like Kerschensteiner, Dewey, Célestin Freinet, and Petersen argued for "empathy with the community," in practice their approaches often converged (1986, 65). However, the theoretical conflict remains in current pedagogical disputes, visible, for example, in different visions of State involvement in the moral and social education of children and young people.

ASSIMILATION VERSUS POLITICAL EMANCIPATION

The freedom and democracy movements of the 1960s and '70s stimulated a new polarity in pedagogy, over whether pedagogy was an instrument of social conservation or a tool for social change. "Critical" pedagogues began to attack the individualized concept of emancipation central to earlier naturalistic pedagogies. German scholars like Klaus Mollenhauer (1968) and Wolfgang Klafki (1976) claimed that "real" emancipation (for the child as an individual and as a social agent) could never be accomplished so long as the pedagogical relation functioned as a microcosm independent of social context. Drawing on the critical social theories of the Frankfurt School, these thinkers defined emancipation as a process of liberating children and adults from repressive social relations and structures, social inequality, and conflicts of power. These critics rejected as "idealistic" the pedagogies that separated childrearing and education from all contact with politics and power differentials. Through "idealistic" pedagogy, children were being taught, both implicitly and explicitly, to internalize the dominant social order. Through their learning, children maintained and renewed the existing structure of power and injustice by constantly repeating and enacting its priorities. In order to bring about social change, critical pedagogues proposed to emancipate pedagogy from responsibility for this kind of social reproduction.

While assimilationist thinkers derived their pedagogical theories and prescriptions from idealized models of society, culture, or religion, critical-emancipatory pedagogues sought to liberate children from the status quo. Emancipationist teaching therefore offered insight into the "ideologically obscured dependency-relations of society." Emancipationists argued that pedagogy should strive for autonomy from society and its institutions. According to Wolfgang Lempert (1971), critical methods in pedagogy should show children that societal relations themselves were manmade, and that phenomena like social injustice and inequality are therefore changeable.

The 1960s and '70s also stimulated the development of anti-authoritarian pedagogy and even objections to pedagogy itself. These movements considered pedagogy itself—whether critical or assimilationist—an essentially oppressive system (Görzen 1984; Miller 1984). They asserted that children and adults were equals, and thus the imbalance of power between them should be abolished. The adult's task in upbringing should be limited to "attending" to the child, respecting its rights and feelings, and tolerating its behavior. An educator should be a child's friend, "a nice person, spontaneously joining the child without falling back to one pedagogical theory or another" (Mollenhauer 1986).

Critical pedagogues differed from assimilationist thinkers over how much to involve children in shaping their own learning. Assimilationist pedagogies were explicitly aimed at conserving existing ideology and social relations, so assigning children an active, reflective role in this kind of education would have been a contradiction in terms. In contrast, the very aim of critical-emancipatory pedagogy was to encourage children to reflect critically on societal relations.

Critics of emancipationist pedagogy pointed out that the content of children's social reflection was predetermined by the adult teachers. But the emergence of emancipationist ideas raised its most serious questions about the relation between the social, cultural, and political goals of education on the one hand, and the child's own responsibility and autonomy on the other. The United Nations Convention on the Rights of the Child affirmed that children deserve to "have their own voice" in important decisions concerning their own lives. Would that mean that children should be allowed an independent say in the aims and methods of their upbringing and education? What if their opinions conflict with those of their educators? Anti-authoritarian pedagogy and anti-pedagogy, the uncrowned champions of children's voices, addressed this dilemma principally by denying it. They avoided important pedagogical dilemmas like the inescapable cultural content of education, the need to prepare children for life in a complex society, and the tricky business of transmitting adult experience to each new generation of kids without unfairly indoctrinating them (Mollenhauer 1986, 17-19). In order to overcome the pitfalls of infantilization, a pedagogy of participation has to permit and mediate conflicts of interest between generations, while honoring differences in educational backgrounds and competence. As we will show in the next section, different twentieth-century pedagogical "schools" have endeavored to find answers to these dilemmas.

Historical Openings for a Noninfantilizing, Participatory Pedagogy

Participatory pedagogy seeks to offer an alternative to the more or less polarized positions discussed above. Some new synthesizing approaches, sensitive to both the social and moral questions of childrearing and education, have tried to do justice to both the individual needs of children and the requirements of the community. Synthesizing thinkers have assigned children an active role in the pedagogical process without prescribing its outcome but also without denying children's need for guidance by experienced adults. The question here will be whether these synthesizing approaches contain useful building blocks for a viable pedagogy of participation.

PROGRESSIVE EDUCATION

Around the turn of the century, the American educator John Dewey proposed new content for and new ways of organizing schoolwork. Dewey argued that human beings are naturally active and social creatures who interact constantly with, and thus change, their environment. Individual and social growth are mutually dependent, both driven by the human need to interact.

Dewey believed that children are readily able to apply ideas learned in particular experiences to different, more general situations. All education is "self-education," so children should be challenged to explore and investigate their environment for its learning content. If parents and educators created adequate conditions for growth and development, carefully observed the child's potential, and offered purposeful learning possibilities (Biesta, Miedema, and Berding 1997, 331), children would develop the habit of learning through their own work.

By the same token, Dewey argued, the only way children could familiarize themselves with human culture and learn the cultural meaning of events and actions, was by active participation in social life. Dewey did not think of development as a natural process. Only through communication with other children and culturally-experienced adults would a child achieve the necessary experience to participate fully in society.

Dewey envisioned the "reconstruction of experience" as both the tool and aim of upbringing (Dewey 1938). School was to be a working social community where children as young scientists experimented with natural objects and production techniques. That way, students would experience the same development of knowledge that mankind more generally had experienced. Not until children themselves, working together, had experienced the evolution of knowledge and learned in stages how to apply it, would they adopt a positive, progress-oriented attitude toward learning and living.

Dewey rejected authoritarian teacher/student relations as inimical to this social laboratory situation. A democratic, fast-changing society could function only when its members had learned to take initiative and adapt to new circumstances on their own. Otherwise, they would be overwhelmed by changes in which they were caught and whose significance or connections they did not perceive. The result would be a confusion in which a few would appropriate to themselves the results of the blind and externally directed activities of others (Dewey 1923, 101, 102). School could only actually contribute to education for democracy if it challenged children to develop a sense of mutual interest, an active commitment to one another's work and to mutual communication. The essence of education, for Dewey, was to acquire the capability to freely, fully, and creatively participate in the democratic, developing community.

Children needed adult guidance to succeed in their inquiries. Without guidance children would have only random, accidental experiences to learn from, causing harmful discontinuities in their education: "There must be continuity, not a stab at one thing one day and a jab at another thing the next day" (Dewey 1938, quoted in Wielenga 1975, 325). Teachers should confront children with meaningful problems and stimulate them to be actively involved in a joint search for solutions. But they must avoid forcing themselves to the front by coercing "the" right solution.

Although Dewey's pedagogy depended crucially on the rational methods of the natural sciences (formulating hypotheses, experimenting, testing, and so on), he cannot be considered an objectivist in the mold of modern empirical-analytic pedagogues. He was closer to the social radicals, claiming that pedagogy was a science of social and moral progress aimed at "facing the great social and moral defects and troubles from which humanity suffers" (Dewey 1920, quoted in Wielenga 1975, 317). Although Dewey strongly dissociated himself from the sometimes exaggerated child-centeredness of progressive European reformers, some of their ideas on education were comparable

(Biesta 1995, 29). Two well-known Russian and Polish educators, Anton Semyonovich Makarenko and Janusz Korczak, experimented with various forms of self-government by children, although on the basis of very different ideologies and educational views. Makarenko worked with neglected and vagrant children in two Ukrainian communes between 1920 and 1935. Group responsibility here was seen as instrumental to the creation of collectivist ideas (Goodman 1949). Korczak, working with Jewish orphans in 1920s Warsaw, developed a children's court, children's parliament, and children's newspaper as components of an education based on equality and mutual respect between children and adults. In the Netherlands, the Werkplaats Kindergemeenschap (Workshop Children's Community), founded in 1926 by Kees Boeke, was a striking example of educational reform in which the pupils (workers) played an important part in the decision making of the school. As with other progressive reform-schools, learning by doing, self-motivation, and self-development of pupils as members of the school community were at the center of Boeke's educational philosophy and practice (Kuipers 1992).

Dewey and other progressive reformers were important "founding fathers" of a participatory pedagogy. By emphasizing how children grow in, through, and for the community, these reformers resisted infantilization even while they embraced the emancipation of pedagogy from authority and tradition. In contrast to progressive reform ideas, the current trend in educational sciences and schools toward limiting education to the transmission of existing "objective" knowledge is only the most modern version of an old habit of alienating children from relevant social experiences and disregarding their creative cultural and social potential (Biesta 1995, 32).

THE DIALECTICS OF PEDAGOGICAL RELATIONSHIPS

Proponents of Geisteswissenschaftliche Pädagogik, a German and Dutch pedagogical tradition, used social interaction within the pedagogical relationship to coordinate the individual and the social aspects of education. This tradition, predominant from the 1920s to the 1960s, was based on anti-materialistic and idealistic philosophies. Its theorists considered childrearing and education a distinct historical and cultural process that should be studied—and practiced—principally with reference to its own internal dynamics. Pedagogical norms and guidelines should be found within the pedagogical relationship as such (Meijer 1996, 34). Based on a "childworthy" anthropology of the child, which recognizes the unique properties of childhood, this pedagogy embeds itself in the actuality of development and the child's urge toward self-determination (Langeveld 1979; Beugelsdijk, Souverein, and Levering 1997, 31). The pedagogical process, aiming to guide children willingly toward their own emancipation, develops from a succession of *antinomies*: internal tensions and paradoxes (Hintjes 1981).

The first tension is that on the one hand children need and desire to develop their own (subjective) potentials, but on the other hand they have to be prepared to grow into the real (objective) world with its values and institutions already in place. A second antinomy demands that parents and educators continually balance the reality of a child at any given moment with the requirements of its future. Exaggerated concern with the future is too heavy a burden for a learning child. Too little attention to the future, however, can rob the growing process of exploration, tension, and the necessary developmental challenges they bring (Meijer 1996, 40). A third polarity, between bonding and freedom, means that adults have to find the ever changing balance between each child's need for help on the one hand and its desire to be an autonomous person on the other.

Geisteswissenschaftliche Pädagogik promoted a specific, active form of cultural transmission. The new generation should not learn to follow conventions, passively adopting the culture of their elders. Taught that way, culture would decay into meaninglessness. The adult's task was to engage children in *Bildung*, their initiation into culture, in ways that enabled the young to participate in culture and society in an independent, responsible, and constructive manner (Meijer 1996, 48). Rather than simply transmitting culture to children, parents and educators should mediate between the child and the culture. Childrearing thus becomes essentially dialectical, a process in which both children and educators are constantly entangled in paradoxical demands. Children alternate between an active, self-responsible role and a passive role as the recipient of education. In order to reach the stage of autonomy and emancipation, children accept the authority of the experienced adult, while the goal of the adult is precisely to surrender that authority in meaningful but gradual stages.

Critical pedagogues accused Geisteswissenschaftliche Pädagogik of isolating the communication within the pedagogical relationship from its social context (Lempert 1971; Heyting 1997). Critical pedagogy, in reaction, tried to "socialize" that communication by introducing Jürgen Habermas's concept of Diskursfähigkeit (communicative competency) (1981). Habermas believed that the differences in knowledge, skills, and values that necessarily exist between the educator and the child, had to be mediated by the adult. In order to produce Diskursfähigkeit, the educator should act "as if" children were already competent. If the educator communicated with children as if they were equal, even though they were not, they would learn by experience to participate in critical and rational communications. This view closely resembles the Soviet psychologist L. S. Vygotsky's concept of the zone of proximal development (1978). Vygotsky's concept refers to a range of developmental tasks that children at a given stage cannot yet perform independently but which they can perform successfully with the help of an adult or a classmate.

The emphasis on the dialectical and communicative character of upbringing is the key to a pedagogy of participation. The essential lesson is that children's participation itself should be considered as a dialectical process. Just "giving children a voice," assigning them adult responsibilities without the input of adult experience and guidance, would mean the end of the pedagogical process and would constitute a modern form of pedagogical neglect. The evident dialectics of upbringing require dialogue and deliberations between adults and children. In order to find a balance between children's needs and the requirements of culture and society, adults and children should collectively explore conflicts between personal interests and those of the social community, personal and social values, individual freedom and respect for others. The question is not whether participation saddles children with adult responsibilities but rather how children can become familiar with the inherent dilemmas of social citizenship in a pedagogical—thus adult-mediated—context.

The Rediscovery of the Participating Child

We began this chapter by noting that children and young people are gradually being rediscovered as active participants in their own upbringing and education. Our survey of twentieth-century pedagogical debates and syntheses has excavated some sources of participatory ideas in the history of pedagogical theory and educational practice. Thanks to its often explicit link to participatory democracy, however, participatory pedagogy was caught in, and its appeal limited by, the ideological and pedagogical controversies that polarized the twentieth-century West.

What, then, is the reason for the current revival? There is an idealistic and a cynical answer to this question. The first, idealistic reason could be that increases in children's active participation represent a growing embrace of democratic ideals of citizenship. Democracy remains controversial in many societies, but it is gaining ground in many European countries. The United Nations Convention on the Rights of the Child, ratified by most member nations since 1990, officially defined participation as a human right for children. Although in practice children's rights are still massively abused in many countries, the fact that most governments have recognized them at least in theory might indicate a gradual acceptance of egalitarian ideals. The question whether pedagogical science has actually contributed to this conceptual change is hard to answer unequivocally. In any case, the Convention embraces many notions that are also at the center of noninfantilizing, participatory pedagogical movements as described before (Veerman 1992). In its turn, however, the participatory pedagogical discourse and practice emerging in European youth policies, schools, and institutions have certainly been boosted by a general societal process of democratization and emancipation.

I have written elsewhere that the active involvement of children and young people in their own environment and decision making is "a basic right with beneficial effect" (de Winter 1997). Participation has two principal categories of benefit. A society that requires certain attitudes and competencies of adult citizens has a fundamental obligation to teach the necessary skills to the young. In a modern pluralistic democracy, citizens need, among other abilities, the capacity to negotiate, to form independent, critical opinions about social issues, to act in socially responsible ways, to respect other people with different backgrounds, opinions, and interests, and to show solidarity and community spirit. Since democratic values and skills are not developed in theory but have to be learned in practice, all citizens, young and old, require practice and room to gain experience.

Participation, besides nourishing the skills of citizenship, also fosters children's psychological well-being. A society committed to children's participation will also maintain a developmental environment that satisfies basic human needs for social attachment and solidarity. By giving young people a chance to make their own contributions and feel they are valued members of society or of a community, in short, social as well as individual purposes are served.

A second, more cynical reason for the rediscovery of children's participation emphasizes its disciplinary and indeed its repressive potentials. Participation as a mainstream pedagogical device has emerged in the late twentieth century, just as Western societies have grown concerned about social cohesion. Burgeoning cultural, ethnic, religious, and moral diversity strains the capacities of individualistic societies, producing an urge for self-discipline and social control. Self-control becomes the major vehicle for maintaining social order whenever social relations are egalitarian (van Daalen and de Regt 1997). Children's and young people's participation in this sense could be explained as a "smart trick." Assigning them the responsibility for their own behavior and environment suggests that they are to be taken seriously, disciplining them in a more or less attractive way. Michel Foucault himself could not have invented anything cleverer!

Certainly idealistic and cynical pedagogical motives can and do exist side by side, particularly when adults deploy children's participation as an instrument of problem solving. When Moroccan school children in Amsterdam are trained to be peer-educators for friends at risk for criminal behavior, or when New York City teenagers are asked to design a preventive strategy for truancy, both perspectives become visible. The participants certainly are being highly validated, and they almost certainly learn a lot. At the same time, they are part of a carefully planned strategy of normalization: the organizers hope that peers might be able to achieve what adults alone cannot.

Conclusion: Toward a Pedagogy of Participation

By engaging in serious dialogue with young people about the problems they experience, adults communicate positive respect, a far better message than the persistent demonization that young people hear from the "man in the street," the press, and the policy makers. However, children's participation matters for much more than prevention and behavioral management. Developed as a central concept of modern pedagogy, participation could avoid the historical, social, and personal pitfalls of infantilization. Participation bridges the gap between Youthland and the rest of society, while still respecting children's distinct individual and social needs.

Contemporary society seems to threaten childhood in a paradoxical way. Children can be held apart through sentimental infantilization (Zelizer 1985) or isolated in a "virtual" world (Gillis, Chapter 5). At the same time, the pressure cooker of societal expectations hurries them prematurely into adulthood and consumerism (Postman 1982; Elkind 1981). And that may be the best case. At worst, considerable numbers of marginalized young people are left without any affirmative social bonds at all (de Winter and Kroneman 1998).

Contemporary children and young people are growing up in a world of contradictory demands and expectations. They are urged to "live their lives their own individual way" *and* to "take the interests of others into account." They learn to revel in the pleasures of consumption, with the ethic of ecology in their other ear. Adults all around them search for unambiguous social norms and values while requiring openness and tolerance in a society of cultural differences. Childrearing and education thus inherently feature paradox, as *geisteswissenschaftliche* pedagogues argued with their dialectics. But there should be an intermediate pedagogical activity, a kind of teaching that neither throws children unguided into the depths of adult contradictions nor protects children falsely behind a veil of sentimental simplifications.

Participatory pedagogy is aimed at the triangular relation between a child, a responsible adult, and the social world. After all, the "social world" is not an alien, static entity for which children should be prepared in advance, but a dynamic system in which they themselves, together with adults, are important actors and agents of change. Therefore, in a participatory pedagogy, while an adult mediates between the child and the social world, the social world itself—consisting of both children and adults—mediates the interactions of teacher and learner.

For example, a participatory school would not view itself as a safe haven for children moving from a state of social incompetence toward the full demands of mature citizenship. Rather, it would be organized as a social training ground in which children's active involvement—in their own learning process and as organizers of school life—is both an instrument and a goal of education. The curriculum would not be mediated by educators dedicated to filling pupils with "objective" knowledge and shared values. A participatory curriculum would provide children instead with the opportunity to experience and address everyday social dilemmas in a context rich in guidance and support. The key to participatory pedagogy thus is that people learn through interactive experience and communication. Social knowledge and values are not simply transferred from an active educator to a passive recipient. In Dewey's terms, knowledge and values grow in a well-coordinated joint action. Children are neither shielded from social reality nor left to unguided exposure. The "social world" is created jointly as children and adults interact as fully responsible subjects, in a context that considers such exchange one of its main pedagogical tasks. Within the triangle of children, adults, and social context, whether in schools, families, or neighborhoods, adults are irreplaceable, not because they represent the outside social world *to* children in the classical sense, but because they are responsible for introducing children to the mutuality of social processes. Therefore the adult's task is to unpack and interpret the social dilemmas of everyday life, to help children to acquire the necessary communication skills, and to structure an effective process of mutual interaction and problem solving.

Educators should take differences among children into account. Children grow up in rather different circumstances that by early childhood have already created large differences in their participatory

skills and attitudes. Denying those differences will only enlarge the social distance between children and turn participation into another tool
reserved for an already privileged elite.

Engaging children in social participation naturally requires a loving,
caring, and respectful pedagogical environment. By exhibiting and
modeling these attitudes, adults can provide children with the sense of
trust and safety necessary for the give-and-take of participation. Caring respect, however, is not the same as the kind of equality between
children and adults sought by anti-authoritarian pedagogy. Pedagogical relationships between adults and children are by definition unequal in knowledge, social experience, and responsibility. This very
inequality, however, could be the starting point for participatory
learning. Habermas argued as much in his critical theory of communication, as did Dewey in his concept of the "reconstruction of experience." The maturation of knowledge and values through joint action
often requires the more experienced, coordinating, helping, and
sometimes provoking hand of the educator.

Children's participation, like participatory pedagogy, is an ambivalent
concept. On the one hand, the active social involvement of children
helps materially to connect them to the community. Emile Durkheim
argued that connectedness, mutual dependency, and a sense of lasting, serious responsibility for others are essential to human well-being
and happiness. In this sense a participatory pedagogy can counterbalance the excesses of modern individualism and challenge the presumption that, whatever the cost, self-interest should prevail over
cooperation and solidarity.

On the other hand, children's and young people's participation is a
kind of social gunpowder, a powerful vehicle susceptible to all sorts of
social and political usages. Misused, a participatory pedagogy can become just a new, modern cover for the same old pedagogical process
of imposing social standards and values on children and youth. The
distinguishing criterion, however, is that participatory pedagogy practices the very democracy it preaches. By recognizing that, as developing fellow-citizens, children have the right to be actively engaged in
shaping pedagogical goals and methods, teachers invite and instruct
them to take joint responsibility for their own environments. The
goals of democratic upbringing, actually reflected in pedagogical action, become real in children's experience.

It is almost self-evident that in extremely individualistic societies,
such as the United States, a participatory paradigm of education will
elicit much resentment or anxiety. A culture consecrated to the interests of the individual will undoubtedly be inclined to suspect that by
emphasizing the social nature of education, participation could be

used to indoctrinate the children. Participatory pedagogy already finds a warmer reception in democracies with a more social orientation, such as the Dutch, British and Scandinavian. Like many other Western societies, these countries include increasing numbers of people with different interests, cultural backgrounds, economic resources, values, lifestyles, and ideologies. Within this context, participation is expected to strengthen or maintain social cohesion, an issue of major political concern. Showing diversity to children, instead of alienating them from it by adopting a false neutrality, could enable them to develop their own autonomous social identity and teach them to handle diversity in a socially responsible way.

The history of pedagogical science during the century of the child shows that neither exaggerated child-centeredness nor giving priority to adult interests above the needs of children does justice to the social nature of childhood. In a society committed to universal justice and the development of human potential, children's participation is no longer just another visionary pedagogical scheme but a serious attempt to align social education with the ideals of democratic citizenship. Children need it, and so does a civilized, civil society.

Chapter 10

The Nephew of an Experimentalist
Ambivalences in Developmental Thinking

GERRIT BREEUWSMA

> *When parents told me that their babies could reach soon after birth, for years my reaction was to pat them on the head (metaphorically in most cases) and say, "Yes, your baby is wonderful!"*
>
> *I was so convinced that the textbooks were right and that reaching began at about five months—not five days—that I simply paid no attention to such reports. I was finally convinced that they had some substance when I saw my own nephew display this behavior at three weeks of age; and again when a child of a colleague (not about to be put off by polite skepticism) also did so at the age of only one week. It was only after these parents had alerted me to this behavior that I even noticed it, despite the fact that I had been working intensively with babies in this age range for several years. (Bower 1989, 14)*
>
> —*T. G. R. Bower,* The Rational Infant *(1989)*

At first sight one might be inclined toward feelings of sympathy when an important and established scientist like T. G. R. Bower has the courage to change his point of view on important matters like those mentioned above. According to the classical assumptions of developmental thinking, the newborn child was a primitive creature: an instinctive animal, with a very limited repertoire of reflexive behaviors, in almost every way dependent on the protection of his or her caretakers. Psychological development had to take place on a minimal basis of reflexive behavior, while the distance between baby and adult functioning was assumed to be maximal.

Modern research in developmental psychology has undermined this point of view completely. In examining the behavior of infants more precisely, the "little animal" turns out to be well equipped with behavioral tools. Even though physical appearance still suggests the contrary, the baby can now in many ways be considered psychologically the same as an adult.

We may believe this to be the major contribution of developmental psychology to the understanding of human behavior and even to the understanding of man—and many developmentalists actually do believe so—but this should not keep us from the opportunity to pose a few critical and even skeptical questions about the successes of developmental psychology in the twentieth century. To a certain extent, one could say, developmental psychology managed to close the gap— the gap between children and adults—that was made by developmental thinking in the first place. And although breaking down a thing and then repairing it—as boys often do with their mopeds and girls with their friendships—is sometimes the best way to understand its functioning, you cannot say after repairing it that you made the thing yourself. But let us not dwell too long on the self-proclaimed successes of developmental psychology.

Bower's seeming open-mindedness reveals at the same time some professional arrogance. Even though he presents this anecdote about his nephew as an argument for a new look at development, with new insights into the infant's capacities, it may make us wonder about the reliability of some of his other observations. What else has he overlooked and for what particular reasons? Why is someone who has, year after year, chosen to disregard the observations of other people— parents—suddenly convinced to overturn his former beliefs after just one or two of his own observations? And whose nephew is next in line to turn developmental thinking upside down?

I am not in a position to predict the future, but in this chapter I will say a few words about the relatively short history of developmental psychology. I will focus on early development—roughly speaking, the child's first three years—because developmental thinking has in many ways been shaped by its treatment of these so-called formative years. However, much of what I have to say could also easily be applied to older children or even to adolescents.

Compared to a century ago—a time that might be considered the infancy of experimental developmental psychology—we have learned a great deal about the infant and about child behavior. When Ellen Key (1900) proclaimed the century of the child, she had high expectations of the then young discipline of developmental psychology. It would be unfair to ourselves to say that none of these expectations have been fulfilled in the past century. We have, indeed, learned a lot about the child and its behavior. Still, many authors have questioned the power and the claims of developmental thinking (Bradley 1989; Kagan 1984; Morss 1996; Nossent 1994). Bower himself noted that, "in looking at infant behavior, scientists, as much as anyone else, tend to be blinded by their preconceptions about what the organism can and cannot do. They look for what they expect to see, rather than looking straightforwardly at what the organism actually does" (1989, 14). And Kagan states: "The behavior of the infant is so ambiguous it is easy for the culture's beliefs about human nature to influence observers' interpretations of what they think they see" (1984, 27). Bradley (1989), among others, goes one step further and questions the possibility of finding definite truth about children.

Many researchers may make the mistake of thinking that the use of objective methods automatically leads to objective knowledge. This, of course, is not always the case. If, for instance, a developmentalist believes that driving a car is the ultimate goal of human development and if, as a researcher, he decides to study all human behavior from that point of view, then, although his scientific methods may be very adequate, his assumptions are not. Ordinary people could have told him from their common sense that he was wrong a long time ago, but sometimes it takes an authority like Bower to make him see. Still, there is, of course, the possibility that we will have learned something about driving a car after all.

In this chapter, I cannot discuss all the flaws in developmental thinking or, for that matter, praise all its many successes. Indeed, I will not even speak of a great deal of what has been going on in developmental psychology. I will not, to take the most obvious example, go into the work of Piaget, though he is perhaps responsible for 90 percent of what is now happening in developmental psychology. It is only out of politeness that I briefly mention his name here (and again near the end). I have no particular reason to question his great enterprise. That has been done elsewhere, and far more extensively than I could do here. (The results of that inquest are far from conclusive; against any presumption that Piaget is passé, see Lourenço and Machado 1996.) The point I want to make can be made without extensive references to the work of Piaget.

According to Bradley, "Scientific questions about babies [and, I might add, about children and even human beings in general] always emerge from particular circumstances for particular reasons" (1989, 180). In this chapter I would like to focus on one of these "particular reasons," the one already implicit in Bower's metaphorical "patting on the head" of parents. I want to examine the delicate relationship between developmentalists and parents.

Developmentalists are always, in one way or another, dependent on parents as the "producers" of babies and children. But as far as child-rearing and child care are concerned, parents are also "consumers" of scientific knowledge about children. Developmentalists and parents are, so to speak, two of a kind. They are sometimes even united in one and the same person. And still they are rivals. As is clear in Bower's remarks at the beginning of this chapter, they are competitive in their search for "true" knowledge about the child and in their concern with the well-being of their children. Following Bower, one might be drawn to the conclusion that, after a century of developmental research, experimentalists have finally been persuaded to see babies as their parents see them: as wonderful creatures. However, I will try to make clear that, even in contemporary research, the relationship between developmentalists and parents remains very ambivalent.

I will start with a short overview of the (pre)history of developmental thinking and will show that experimentalists initially needed parents to make their arguments acceptable. In subsequent sections, I will focus in more detail on the "particular circumstances" under which the ambivalences in developmental thinking become manifest. Although much developmental research has taken place in an environment that differs greatly from everyday life—the laboratory—its results have implications for or are legitimized by their relevance for childrearing practices. For that reason I will use a broad definition of developmentalism and will not confine myself to those experimentalists who spend their working days within the confines of their research institute. In all this I hope to clarify how developmental thinking mingles with childrearing practices and how it tries to define both child and parental behavior. Parents will appear in my account not only as *subjects* of developmental research but also as *collaborators* of developmental psychologists.

A Short History of Developmental Thinking

I think we know more about rats than we know about children. I have never read a treatise on "the child" that I haven't furiously thrown away in a corner halfway through, for it never seemed to be about the child I was or the children in which I projected my prejudices. (Kuijer 1980, 118)

Historically, the rise of developmental psychology as an empirical science is closely related to a growing interest in the so-called baby biographies. *A Biographical Sketch of an Infant* by Charles Darwin (1877) and *Die Seele des Kindes* by Wilhelm Preyer (1882) are often considered to play a key role in this respect. However, almost a century before the publication of these two studies, many writers on the topic of childrearing and child care already were convinced that a meticulous observation of babies and children could make an important contribution to the description and explanation of human development. The diary of the German philosopher Dietrich Tiedemann (1787) was probably the first scientific baby biography, and it has in many ways served as a standard for subsequent diaries.

Tiedemann observed his son closely for 31 months, starting with his birth in 1781. In his description of his child's behavior, he introduced many important topics of developmental psychology, from instinctive behavior to language development. Tiedemann considered the observation of babies a matter of great importance. He hoped to lay bare the development of the mental faculties of the child and even of man, and in that endeavor he needed observations made by other people:

What has here been observed cannot be taken as a general law, since children, just like adults, progress variously, the one with speed, the other more slowly; but at least it informs us of *one* among the possible rates of progress, and allows us to put some determination upon the previously indefinite subject. When we shall have several such records it will be possible by means of comparison to strike an average for the common order of nature. (quoted in Murchison and Langer 1927, 206)

From that time on, scientists and parents were encouraged to keep a diary of their baby. Up until the twentieth century, baby biographies played a major role in developmental psychology, albeit not always for the same reason or with the same purpose. While parents expected practical advice about their children, scientists aimed for a higher, more general goal and therefore needed a more objective approach than parents could provide. Eventually it became obvious that this objectivity could not reliably be reached in diaries. Scientists took up a search for new methods.

In the United States, Granville Stanley Hall gave an important impulse to the scientific study of the child. With the emerging Child Study Movement he tried to provide developmental psychology with an empirical basis. Hall and his followers developed a set of questionnaires and sent them to parents and teachers. The questionnaires enabled their informants to observe and report about the everyday behavior of their children in a more structured way. Hall's studies dealt with all kinds of behavior, from simple automatisms to church processes and practices (White 1994). He published the results of his questionnaire studies in the *Pedagogical Seminary*, which he founded in 1891 and which still exists as the *Journal of Genetic Psychology*.

During the early years of developmental psychology, the role assigned to parents as observers was striking. Mothers in particular had the opportunity to follow their child's development very closely. It seemed only sensible to draw on knowledge about the child's everyday life. For some time Preyer's *Die Seele des Kindes,* introduced to the United States by Hall, was seen as a directive for daily observations:

It was felt that a careful reading of Preyer's "Mind of the Child" should render an intelligent woman capable of following in his footsteps and of recording from day to day observations that would bring their reward to her in the pleasure of their revelations of her baby's growth, and which she could contribute as an offering to the vast sum total of observations needed to trace out laws of development. (Barus 1894, 996)

So, initially, parents and developmentalists were seen as "collaborators," more or less working on the same project. Each could learn from the other and profit from their collaboration in observing babies. Mothers could not only learn but also obtain more pleasure from their child's development, while researchers could extrapolate the laws of development from the accumulated observations (Wallace, Franklin, and Keegan 1994).

However, the romance between parents and developmentalists did not last long, for the lovers had different intentions and expectations. With the propagation of the importance of objectivity, researchers began to doubt the value of the contribution of parents and in particular of mothers. Mothers were too sentimental and involved with their offspring to guarantee an objective and rational "scientific eye" (Sully 1881). A scientific approach required a more detached attitude. In a word, it required masculinity (Burman 1994). The importance of parent observations receded more and more into the background of the scientific scene.

In fact, the first signs of this devaluation were already clear with the standardization of observations in Hall's questionnaires. Hall designed them in an effort to systematize the enormous amount of data on child behavior. But the task was beyond him. Many researchers criticized his messy use of the questionnaires and his arbitrary interpretation of his results, and one can say that after the first period of the Child Study Movement there was an unmistakable tendency toward a more rigorous rationalization of the methods of investigation (White 1994).

Initially, however, the Child Study Movement was considered an essential step toward the improvement of child welfare. Indeed, it was seen in many ways as a reform movement. Developmental researchers were financially supported by reformers, sometimes private individuals, sometimes institutions concerned with the child. According to Cravens (1987), they had hardly any resources and depended heavily on reformers. In fact, in those early years, reformers founded many of the child research institutions, since the scientists did not yet have any real authority or professional expertise. It was only by making their way of working more specialized and thereby less transparent and accessible to lay persons that they managed to establish developmental psychology as a scientific enterprise.

The establishment of the laboratory as the proper domain of investigation played an important role in this respect. In the laboratory it became possible to organize experiments in a more structured way. This made possible the posing of more specialized and abstract questions about development. In the Child Study Movement many questions about child development were concerned with the health and well-being of the child. Research was closely connected with child care and education and with problems related to the child's everyday life. From 1920 onward, developmental psychology focused more on general characteristics and mechanisms of psychological change instead of aiming at practical solutions for practical problems. The use and possibilities of statistical methods also changed the scope of the research. The population rather than the individual child became the center of scientific interest. Ideas about actual behavior were transformed into predictions about future behavior, on the basis of the characteristics of the group—the population—to which the child belonged (Cravens 1987). The child became a statistical child, a subject that only existed within the domain of a specific research question in an experimental laboratory that became the scene of action (Cahan, Sutton-Smith, and White 1993). And in many cases the experimenter did not even need children for his investigations. He could stick to his rats or ducklings, which were much easier to handle, and make extrapolations from animal behavior to child behavior.

In short, a host of things that have happened in developmental research since the 1920s have had hardly any direct relationship to the public interest. Some professionals did reach out to a larger public, offering their expertise on the rearing and education of children, but it is a long way from the laboratory to practical advice. Within the field of developmental psychology, practitioners and researchers went their own way and created their own lines of work. They also found their own means of financial support. For experimentalists, the university, more or less independent of the practical demands of child welfare, became the place to be.

The result is that experimentalists have grown reluctant to speak about a particular child. They prefer to speak about a population and its members. This might be one of the reasons parents recognize themselves in the quotation at the beginning of this section. Quite often there seems to be an enormous gap between the children we know (and have been) and the little statistical rat that is called "the child" in the textbooks on developmental psychology.

One can say that initially scientists needed the interest and support of parents but that part of the emancipation of developmental psychology as an empirical science depended on a more detached attitude among its researchers. Parents did not fit into the image of developmental psychology as an objective science. While they started as allies, they changed into competitors of the experimentalists, in a game they were bound to lose. It is only quite recently that the importance of parents for our knowledge of children and their development has been rediscovered.

In summary, the sources of the ambivalence toward parents that marks modern developmental psychology can be traced back to the early years of the discipline as an empirical science. In the next sections I will focus on some more detailed exemplifications of this ambivalence. My approach is loosely chronological. I follow the "development" of developmental psychology as a scientific enterprise, starting with the behavioristic turn in child psychology.

The Importance of Being Earnest

Give me a dozen healthy infants, well-formed, and my own specified world to bring them up in and I'll guarantee to take any one at random and train him to become any type of specialist I might select—doctor, lawyer, artist, merchant—chief and, yes, even beggar-man and thief, regardless of his talents, penchants, tendencies, abilities, vocations, and race of his ancestors. (Watson 1970, 104)

Before the First World War the Child Study Movement had been repeatedly criticized for its lack of scientific rigor (Cunningham 1991). As a consequence the work of Stanley Hall lost much of its authority, the demands of "science" came to be taken far more seriously, and the role of parents as intermediaries in the study of children became increasingly problematic. In particular the contribution of mothers was questioned. As early as 1881, Sully wrote that a mother's "way of looking at babies unfits her from entering very cordially into the scientific vein" (546). With the rise of behaviorism after the First World War, Sully's "way of looking at mothers" became fashionable. Behaviorism made an unambiguous plea for objectivity in the approach to children and questioned the value of parental intuitions. Child care and pedagogy had to become sciences, based on the insights of psychological research.

Even though it would be wrong to call John Broadus Watson a developmental psychologist, according to Gardner Murphy he was "the most important single influence in child psychology from the period of the First World War until the thirties" (quoted in Senn 1975, 26). Watson (1878–1958) was in many ways extreme in his ideas. He met a lot of opposition in his own time, and even today many psychologists feel uncomfortable with the implications of his work. According to a survey done by Frances Degen Horowitz, contemporary developmentalists often consider Watson's contribution to developmental psychology "an embarrassment," "harmful," or "very important, but mostly a negative influence" (1994, 233).

According to Watson, the child is shaped entirely by his environment or, to be more precise, by learning. Watson saw learning as the major mechanism for explaining behavior and development, and so with behaviorism the idea of the child as a tabula rasa was revived. The newborn baby is nothing more than a "lively squirming bit of flesh, capable of making a few simple responses" (Watson 1928, 46). This situation places an enormous responsibility on parents, a responsibility that is very hard to handle. And, according to Watson, parents, following their parental intuitions, are inclined to make the wrong decisions. Emphasizing learning as he did, Watson insisted that parents should consider their roles as teachers before all else. They had to approach their children as pupils. They had to set the agenda for the child's development, and they had to do it in a rational way (Maccoby 1994).

Watson insisted on objective and impersonal management of children. He detested mawkish sentimentality and needless affection:

There is a sensible way of treating children. Treat them as though they were young adults. Dress them, bathe them with care and circumspection. Let your behavior always be objective and kindly firm. Never hug and kiss them, never let them sit in your lap. If you must, kiss them once on the forehead when they say good night. Shake hands with them in the morning. Give them a pat on the head if they have made an extraordinarily good job of a difficult task. Try it out. In a week's time you will find how easy it is to be perfectly objective with your child and at the same time kindly. You will be utterly ashamed of the mawkish, sentimental way you have been handling it. (1928, 81–82)

Apart from its disclosure that psychologists have a peculiar urge to pat people on the head, the most remarkable thing about this quotation is that it leads parents away from everything that is, in our eyes, normal and natural in parenting. To educate your children in terms of Watson's behaviorism is a serious undertaking. It requires an earnest mind. Parents have not only to control their children but also to control themselves. They must refrain from the immediate pleasure-seeking tendencies so common in human beings and wait for the reward that is located somewhere in the future. There is an element in Watson's ideas that is attractive: the promise that, if you try hard enough, you can make of your child whatever you like (Scarr 1984). But of course there is an element that is dangerous as well: the threat that if you fail you have no one else to blame but yourself.

One of the major problems with Watson is that the polemical tone of much of his writing obscures the meaning of his work. One could call him bold in his claims, but reckless might be a better characterization. Still, it would be wrong to think of him as a fool. The comment at the beginning of this section, for example, was followed by another: "I am going beyond my facts and I admit it, but so have the advocates of the contrary and they have been doing it for many thousands of years" (104). Even though here again he exaggerates with his "many thousands of years," he acknowledges that many of his claims are in fact hypotheses and should be subjected to careful investigation (Horowitz 1994).

Nevertheless, there is a disproportionally large gap between Watson's claims and the actual substance of his research. To frighten an eleven-month-old boy with rats and noisy bangs, and to make him a doctor or a lawyer, are quite different things. And although Watson taught us something about learning mechanisms, he failed, in the long run, to persuade parents and teachers about the rearing of children.

Dangerous Intuitions

Thus far I may have given the impression that developmentalists only talk *with* parents about their children. However, they also talk *to* them and ultimately talk *about* them and their influence on their children. That is where the parent's role changes from collaborator into subject of scientific scrutiny. This, of course, complicates the relationship between the two parties.

During the first decades of this century, there was little empirical research on the relevance of parental influence on children's development. There was no lack of ideas and opinions on "how to raise your children," but these ideas and opinions were usually derived from the morality of the time. Some of them were inherited from the good old days of the nineteenth century; others were tuned to the new scientific approach of child psychology. Most had to wait another ten or twenty years before they could be empirically tested and falsified. Still, there must have been a great felt need for a (pseudo)scientific approach to childrearing and education, for many of the loosely formulated ideas found their way into the home.

While it may be hard for us to experience the attraction of Watson's ideas, his *Psychological Care of the Infant and Child* (1928) sold many copies. But Watson did not have a monopoly on child care advice. A second major approach concerning child care came from Freud's psychoanalysis, in its many elaborated forms. Most of us are inclined to think of psychoanalysis as quite the opposite of behaviorism, and with good reason. Though Watson himself believed that psychoanalytic concepts could be translated in terms of learning mechanisms and though, ultimately, through the work of Miller and Dollard, a marriage between behaviorism and psychoanalytical ideas did take place (Horowitz 1994), the differences between the two disciplines are more numerous than the similarities, regarding their approach to children and the role that they attribute to parents in facilitating child development.

Freud's child differed in many ways from Watson's. Watson pictured the child as an empty vessel that had to be filled with experiences. Freud's picture of the child was of one stuffed with intrapsychic forces of a dangerous kind: sexuality and aggression. It has to go through a series of qualitatively different stages of development, each defined by an experience of intense conflicts. As Sandra Scarr put it, "Freud's child is a surging mass of conflicts set in time-bombs" (1984, 68). Freud gave the Romantic notion of the "innocent child" a death blow and came up with a new interpretation of parental responsibilities.

The child may be born as a creature whose behavior is controlled by its instincts, but the quality of the parents' practices determines the quality of the child's experiences. Experiences change with each stage of development and are crucial in determining the future development of the child. Psychoanalysis stressed the importance of the first five years of the child's life. Everything that went wrong during those years could be devastating for life. Parents had to attune themselves to the experiences of the infant and young child, but here they were to encounter a real difficulty, for in adult life most of our childhood experiences are not directly accessible. Compared to behaviorism, Freud's theory appealed more to parental intuitions about childrearing, but Freud did not make it easy for parents. Where Watson defended strict discipline toward children, psychoanalysis taught parents that they had to be neither too harsh nor too soft. According to Freud, both harsh discipline and lack of discipline could be the source of personality disorders, neuroses, and so on (Scarr 1984).

Much of what Freud had to say about child development was not directly meant for the practice of childrearing. In many ways it was unsuitable for direct application in everyday life. Sometimes Freud's work is interpreted in the light of his Viennese and Victorian cultural background. His work was certainly not appealing to Americans. In fact, many of his ideas reached a larger public only through his followers, mostly in a weakened version (Scarr 1984).

Perhaps the greatest influence of Freud on parents has been through the work of Doctor Spock and his world-famous book on child-rearing, *The Common Sense Book of Baby and Child Care*, published first in 1946 and subsequently in many editions in many different languages. In this book, Spock converted psychoanalytic theory into everyday language. He made it understandable for ordinary people, and at first sight he seemed to make it easy to apply. In comparison with the strict regime that Watson prescribed to parents, or the world full of conflict and turmoil that Freud pictured, Spock portrayed childrearing and parenting as something nice and warm. The title of the book immediately made clear that childrearing was, in the first place, a matter of *common sense*. His point of view became even more explicit at the beginning of the book, where he wrote, "Trust yourself," and invited parents to rely on their instinctual adequacy (Zuckerman 1993a). With the words "What good mothers and fathers instinctively feel like doing for their babies is usually best," Spock seemed to put the expertise in the hands of parents.

But there are a few weak spots in his sunny, unproblematic world, and we could have guessed that when he spoke of "good mothers and fathers" and "usually best," because it is not easy to say what "good" means in this case or under what conditions good mothers and fathers might not be able to do the best for their children. In an eloquent analysis of Spock's smash hit, Zuckerman makes clear that the book is not only a "contradiction in terms"—why teach people something they instinctively already know and do?—but also full of contradictions. In their childrearing practices, parents have to rely on Mother Nature and enjoy parenting, but at the same time Spock "orchestrates" parents' actions in detail. Even the simple procedure of taking the child's temperature takes up five pages of "painfully detailed description" (Zuckerman 1993a, 269). Also, as everyone knows, a lot of things can go wrong with a child. When they do, according to Spock, parents are always to blame. They pressed the child too much or encouraged him too little, they did not recognize his natural needs or overdid the whole thing, and so on. They could, in fact, damage the child's development with their mistakes, not only for a while but for years or even forever, which is a long time indeed. Such a specter could make "good mothers and fathers" rather uncertain about their practices. It could give them good reason to doubt their own instincts (if that is ever possible).

With Spock, of course, we have strayed from developmental psychology as an empirical discipline. But much of the ambiguity and ambivalence in his book goes beyond childrearing practice as such, to leave its trace in the minds of experimentalists. Zuckerman thinks of *The Common Sense Book of Baby and Child Care* as "an embodiment of its culture" (271), by which he means American culture. But in the years since the Second World War American culture has spread over the Western world. As far as psychology is concerned, its premises have become standard for empirical research. To take just one example, much of the attachment research tradition is saddled with the same ambivalence: the importance of parents is recognized, but this very recognition makes them vulnerable as individuals and makes their actions questionable. In the next-to-last section, I will try to make clear how psychology tries to get rid of this ambivalence by redefining the role of the parents in practice and theory, but first we have to spend a few words on another question.

Who Cares?

Up until now we have been talking about parents as if they exist as a clear-cut entity in developmental psychology. But that would suppose that fathers exist, and that is hardly the case in developmental psychology. There is, of course, a respectable body of literature on the role of the father (Lamb 1981; Parke 1981, 1995). But I would argue that such studies are the exception to the rule. Much of the ambivalence toward parents is, in the first place, focused on the mother, not because developmentalists have made her unimportant, but because they have made her presence essential. They have suggested over and over again that "only the biological mother is capable of providing the emotional satisfaction and stimulation that is necessary for personality and intellectual development" (Wortis 1974, 360). And where developmental psychology is usually very cautious about its conclusions, it is quite definite about the role of the mother. When she is not available for the child, her absence is at the expense of the child. "Dire consequences must follow from any separation of the child from its mother, even if only for part of the day" (Wortis 1974, 360).

Ironically enough, developmental psychology has been concerned with the absence of the father too, but only to propagandize the intact nuclear family. The father had to be there; he was the breadwinner, the support of the family, its model for identification and sex-role differentiation. In spite of the importance of the mother, developmentalists made clear that she could not make it on her own. Their research "proved" that single parents put children at a disadvantage (Burman 1994). Not until quite recently did developmentalists attribute a more substantial role to fathers and expect them too to contribute (in a

more active way) to their children's development. However, the paternal role is still limited and concerned with the "fun part" of development. According to Clarke-Stewart, "the father is more likely to be a
playmate who engages in exciting, physical games and active rough
and tumble play." But we should not forget that his contribution is
marginal rather than essential: "he provides psychological support to
the mother and affects the child's development indirectly through
her" (1982, 93–94).

Although developmentalists have a lot to say about the mother, they
do not always feel comfortable with her. This was already evident in
Sully's observation that women lack a "scientific eye." And it is evident
as well in the discomfort expressed by many experimentalists with the
idea that developmental psychology could very well be a domain in
which women might play a major role:

Many experimental psychologists continue to look upon the field of child psychology as a proper field of research for women and for men whose experimental masculinity is not of the maximum. This attitude of patronage is based
almost entirely upon a blissful ignorance of what is going on in the tremen-
dously virile field of child behavior. (Murchison 1933, x; quoted in Burman
1994, 9)

Women should stick to what they are most suited to: motherhood.
"Alongside the child, developmental psychology constituted the woman
as mother as its object of concern and intervention" (Burman 1994, 94).
Just as such, the discipline tried to restrict her conduct to child care.

This is very much the case within the tradition of attachment research. Covered by evolutionary thinking and psychoanalysis, attachment theory tries to prove how Mother Nature has provided us with a
natural mother. The "strange situation" experiment—in which a child
is left in an unfamiliar context, with an unknown person, and in which
the reaction of the child after the mother's return is taken as a measure of the quality of its attachment to the mother—is taken as the
litmus test. The theory purports to measure the quality of the relationship between mother and child, but it also functions as a measure of
the quality of a woman's mothering. It is true that attachment theory
no longer devotes itself principally to the mother, but the main part of
the research has focused on the role of the mother.

Attachment theory has been used many times to prove that mothers
should not leave their children in the hands of babysitters or daycare
centers and should not have a career outside the home (Rapoport,
Rapoport, and Strelitz 1977; Scarr 1984). But one of the few sensible
things one can say about the "strange situation" experiment is that it is

indeed a strange situation: "in real-life caregiving contexts . . . children are generally left with caregivers with whom they have some familiarity and in contexts to which they have become accustomed" (Burman 1994, 83). There are, in fact, indications that children may profit from visiting daycare centers and that growing up in an extended network of caregivers may enhance their development (Goossens 1986).

Even when the mother is constantly available for her children, this cannot guarantee that she is a good mother. A lot of things can still go wrong. She can be manipulative, overprotective, interfering, excessively indulgent, unduly dominant, and so much more. It seems almost impossible to do the right thing. Blaming the mother has been quite a popular sport for some time, resulting in more or less serious publications such as *Momism: The Silent Disease of America* (Sebald 1976).

Only recently has developmental psychology tried to be more realistic, and I would say less tense, in its attempts to account for the role of parents, both mother and father, in the development of their children. However it will take some time before this new attitude becomes "normal science" and finds its way into the social institutions that support development.

Self-Fulfilling Theories

"Parenting is a complex, real-life phenomenon," wrote Valsiner and Litvinovic (1996, 56) in the opening sentence of their chapter on "parental reasoning." There are, of course, many real-life phenomena—breathing, for one—but developmentalists must have come very far if they think they have to remind their readers of something so obvious. Maybe they have to remind themselves, because within developmental psychology things are not always what they seem to be.

It is not my intention to make a laughingstock out of developmentalists, although it is rather strange that they have taken so long to grasp the importance of parenting for development. It is tempting to say "the importance of parenting for the *development of children*," but in that case I would be making a classic mistake of treating parents and children as if they are distinct entities.

Many debates in developmental psychology are organized around the dichotomy of nature versus nurture, nativism versus environmentalism, or any of the other names by which the dichotomy is called. The environmentalists assign more substance to the role of learning and experience than the nativists do, but both parties acknowledge the importance of parenting influences. The differences between them are quantitative, not qualitative. It would of course be very difficult for developmentalists to reach children without maintaining a more or less friendly relationship with their parents.

During the years of the Child Study Movement, researchers hoped that their expert knowledge concerning the development of children would inform parents and thereby change the experiences of their children (Senn 1975; Young 1990). Those early developmentalists trusted that the benefits of scientific knowledge would be unequivocally beneficial in improving childrearing practices. They also trusted that influence on development went unidirectionally from parents to children. This view was dominant for a long time. And even now, when hardly anybody subscribes to this view, it is actually quite difficult to go beyond their paradigm.

Unidirectional studies often treat the socialization of children as the major goal of parenting and try to make clear how parents achieve this goal. The observation of interactions between parents and their children is the most obvious way to study this question (Stafford and Bayer 1993). But it is difficult to get a reliable picture of parental behavior. According to Lewis (1982), for instance, parents' behavior is influenced by what they think the investigation is all about. If they think the research is on play, they play more with the child; if they think it is on language, they talk more to the child (see also Burman 1994). However, in many cases it is not really possible to distill the parental influence from the interaction pattern. It is not always easy to say where parental influence stops and the effect on the child begins. Even more important, it is usually difficult to say what the particular role of the child itself might be.

This issue is in fact the main motivation behind the turn to bidirectional studies of parent-child interactions. The study of language development and of turn-taking in language and other parent-child interactions have played a major role here (Bruner et al. 1966). These studies made it obvious that parents influenced their children's behavior, and, the other way around, that children influenced their parents (Bell and Harper 1977). Parents home in to the child, but children, even very young infants, also home in to parents. In their play with parents, for instance, children do not wait patiently for the next action to come. They take the initiative, introduce new elements, or ask for the repetition of older ones. According to Schaffer (1992), much of what is taking place in development is in fact the result of "joint involvement episodes" and highlights the reciprocity of development.

From this reciprocal view on development it is only a small step to what is often called a systems framework for development and for parent-child interaction. This approach goes beyond the bidirectional approach in at least two ways. First, it expands theoretical conceptualizations beyond the dyad and tries to account for the relationship of parent-child interactions with other social and cultural influences (see, for instance, Bronfenbrenner 1989). Second, it treats development not as something that takes place *within* the child or the parent-child interaction but as something that *emerges* out of specific child-parent context constellations and is shaped by the participants in those constellations. As Lerner and Busch-Rossnagel (1981) put it, "individuals are producers of their own development."

The systems approach coincides with a new appraisal of the parental role in terms of "parental belief systems" (Sigel 1985; Harkness and Super 1996). Parents are recognized as producers of ideas about children and the way they develop. They do not merely react to their offspring's doings. They also have expectations, anticipate possible developmental trajectories, and attune their actions to specific courses of development. According to Cruts (1991), parental beliefs and actions can work as self-fulfilling prophecies, in which parents help to shape the development they expect and, most of the time, prefer.

The recognition that developmentalists are not alone in their attention to children's development is an important advantage of the systems approach. Parents, social institutions that have to do with children, and society itself all contribute to psychological development and developmental thinking. Still, this should not leave us with the impression that, for the first time in this century, developmentalists have managed to give an unambiguous account of the parental role in psychological development. After all, much of the content of parental beliefs is formed from ideas borrowed from developmental psychology itself, and vice versa.

Developmentalists want to study child development as separate from the knowledge that their studies produce. But such separation cannot be sustained. Developmental psychology, on the one hand, actively influences everyday beliefs about development through the dissemination of its knowledge in manuals, magazines, institutions, and practices. Parents, on the other hand, redefine ideas about development in their behavior. This is already the case when parents attune their behavior to the expectations they have about the research topic. More generally, parents will quite often try to interpret empirical findings on child development in terms of practical consequences for their own children. Developmentalists have to account for that.

The relationship between developmentalists and parents becomes more complicated when research procedures are used as a standard for normal or adequate behavior. The importance of the mother-child relationship, for instance, is again and again reproduced in developmental studies, just by constructing experimental settings in which maternal care comes to the fore (Burman 1994). Parents have expectations about their children's development which are, at least in part, derived from developmental thinking, and developmentalists are in turn sensitive to those elements that fit in with their theories.

Even with more abstract matters such as these studied by Piaget, developmental psychology reproduces its own findings. Piaget tried to get a grip on the mental development of children. To that end, he designed research procedures that confronted children with intellectual problems at once appropriate for a certain level of development and abstract and quite remote from everyday practices. The main reason for this remoteness was that Piaget was primarily interested in the development of knowledge, not in the learning capacity of children. However, his procedures did not remain remote for long. The child care manuals and magazines on childrearing soon took them up. "Piagetian tasks employed by psychologists were communicated to parents as activities to do with the infant" (Young 1990, 25), with explicit suggestions that children's development would benefit from learning the Piagetian tasks. The instruments to measure development were, at the same time, used to enhance development.

One could conclude that, within the systems framework, parents are recognized as very important contributors to and producers of development. But we should not overestimate the significance of this recognition, because developmentalists also look for parental ideas that reproduce developmental thinking. This might seem one of the great successes of developmental thinking, but I would consider it more a societal than a scientific merit.

Conclusion: Back to the Future

"The study of the child from the standpoint of the scientific interpretation of mind and its making is a new science—but it is here to stay." So said an Illinois school official in 1916 (Cunningham 1995, 204), and so thought many others. The first decades of the twentieth century were characterized by an unequivocal enthusiasm for child psychology, and, like Ellen Key (1900), many people in and outside the scientific community expected that the best was yet to come (Cunningham 1991). An almost unconditional belief in the powers of knowledge prevailed. One of the leading ideas in the Child Study Movement was the expectation that informing parents about child development would ultimately change the experiences of children for the better (Young 1990, 25).

The role attributed to parents by developmental scientists has changed over the past century, and in this chapter I have tried to focus on some of these changes. I think they provide insight into the "development of developmental thinking." Developmental psychology has tried to establish itself as a discipline within the universities and within the schools, the health care system, and the nursery as well. However, parents are always the first who have to be convinced of the blessings of a scientific approach to *their* children. Let me try to recapitulate the major changes in the relationship between parents and developmentalists.

Initially, parents were approached as important allies in the quest for scientific knowledge about the child. Parents could actively participate in and contribute to this quest as collaborators of the scientist, in the first place by keeping a diary of their child. Wallace, Franklin, and Keegan (1994) distinguish between *domestic* and *scientific* diaries, but they conclude that "the practice of domestic diary-keeping was drawn on in order to "advance" scientific understanding and pedagogical theory as well as practice" (3).

After their first enthusiasm for this collaboration, developmentalists began to rationalize their approach to children. They confined the contribution of parents more narrowly to the role of teacher (with the child as pupil). They came to doubt the scientific rigor of the mother in particular. Their rationalization of the parental role was carried to an extreme in behaviorism, when parental sentiments were considered to be unfavorable and even harmful to the child's development. Parents could still gain from scientific insights, but their own contribution became negligible. Developmentalists had little to learn from parents. Parents had to learn from experimentalists.

With psychoanalysis, and all developmental theories and childrearing practices based upon it, the importance of the parental role was revived. Parental instincts and intuitions about the handling of the child were seen as crucial but at the same time dangerous. Psychoanalysts took a tremendous interest in everything that could go wrong; and when things went wrong, parents—in particular, mothers—were the first suspects.

In recent developmental research there has been a shift from a unidirectional approach to a bidirectional one, and quite recently to a systemic approach. From contributors to development—for better or worse—parents have been transformed into producers of development. In a systemic approach parental beliefs, expectations, and actions are now considered to have a great impact on the emergence of development.

When its history is told along these lines, we can easily get the impression that developmental psychology has finally managed to estimate the real value of the parental role in child development and now knows how to deal with it. But such an impression would be misleading. Much of the ambivalence of the discipline's early years is still with us today, although it appears in much more sophisticated form.

Up until now, developmentalists—with the exception of those of a behaviorist conviction—have tried to persuade parents that *they* (parents) know best. Nevertheless, it seems to be necessary to tell them time and again *what* they know best. In a bestselling childrearing advice book in the Netherlands, which claims to be based on the latest insights in developmental research, the authors begin their introduction with the statement that parents, mothers in particular, know instinctively how to handle their children. For one reason or another, many parents have lost track of their own instincts, but fortunately the authors are prepared to bring them in contact again with those instincts (van de Rijt and Plooij 1992).

The ambivalence becomes even more explicit when advice books devalue oral traditions in childrearing practices and caution women not to rely on their relatives, neighbors, and old wives' tales (van de Rijt and Plooij 1992; see also Burman 1994). With these maneuvers, the experts isolate women from their social context. Though they give their readers a bookshelf full of advice books, they leave them, in the end, alone with the responsibility for the upbringing of their children.

Developmentalists have made a point of controlling their observations with the utmost care. They trusted that this would ensure the objectivity of their findings, to the benefit of both children and parents. However, in their attempts to describe and explain development, they also created potential problems. Children's development, for instance, ought to reach certain levels at certain ages; if it does not, there is reason to get worried. And developmentalists strengthen this worry by stimulating parents to maximize and speed up development. They demand that parents cooperate in this stimulation of their children's development, and they label parents' behavior "good" or "bad" on the basis of such cooperation. For instance, "a mother who 'orders her child around' is seen as being 'intrusive,' whereas a mother who insists on her child answering a long series of 'What's that?' questions is not" (Pine 1992, quoted in Burman 1994, 129). Being intrusive is not regarded highly because it does not fit in with our ideal of an autonomous child (though I can hardly think of anything more intrusive than subjecting children to developmental investigation). Furthermore, when things go wrong in development they easily become stigmatized as "abnormal," whereas it may be more realistic and appropriate to treat "going wrong" as one of the most normal things in development.

I must repeat that developmental psychology has brought us many new insights into the behavior of infants and children. However, I must also insist that it gives us a very particular picture, a picture of what Bradley called "infancy as paradise" rather than the struggle that it is in many ways for infant and parents. Developmentalists have burdened parents and their children with the idea of progressive change, while many things in everyday life are not easy to classify under that optimistic view. As developmentalists we should take more seriously these discrepancies between how development should be, according to our theories, and how it quite often is. We should try to recognize and account for our ambivalent relationship with parents. If we do not, we may all end up with Burman (1994), who dedicated her book on *Deconstructing Developmental Psychology* "to my nieces and nephews, . . . in the hope that its contents will one day be irrelevant to them." In the long run, much of what we are doing will be irrelevant anyhow, but it would be very peculiar if that became the main motivation behind developmental thinking.

Chapter 11

Developmental Psychology in a World of Designed Institutions

SHELDON H. WHITE

A designed social institution is a pattern of human activity put together by conscious and deliberate human thought, designed to serve human purposes and governed by rules of human design. The institution is designed to be a stable part of the social environment, though it generally changes over longer periods of time, being reengineered in some large or small way to fit changing circumstances and changing human needs. Examples of designed human institutions are the Society for Research in Child Development, a school, a hospital, a kindergarten, a store, a corporation, a hotel, a railroad, or a railroad station. People in modern societies live among hundreds of designed institutions, serving with traditional institutions to provide systems of cooperative activity—what Barker and Wright (1954) would call "behavior settings"—in their local community. Local designed institutions are often connected from place to place to form higher-order designed institutions to provide systems of cooperation and governance across local communities (Bronfenbrenner 1979). Developmental psychology, I believe, came into existence when people began to live in societies composed of a myriad designed institutions, when people needed to think about human motives and abilities and needs in order to create the institutions, and when individuals living in these new and slowly changing societies confronted historically new responsibilities for designing their own and their children's development.

It is generally understood that in the nineteenth century there was a great growth of science and technology. Thousands of large and small inventions changed the way in which people lived, farmed, made things, thought and planned together, and did business. The big inventions were those that dramatically changed forms of human work: the harvester, the cotton gin, railroads, the telegraph, sewing machines, elevators, typewriters, and so forth. There were also many small inventions, and there was a spirit of invention addressed to all aspects of human life. We remember Herbert Spencer today as a philosopher and a significant ancestor of developmental psychology, but Spencer was a railroad engineer before he was a philosopher. In his autobiography, written near the end of his life, Spencer (1904) recalls the inventions of his youth—a watch, a printing press, type, a survey instrument, a "cephalograph" (a device for phrenological measurements), a "binding pin" (something like a paper clip), a color-naming scheme, a planing machine, and some preliminary efforts toward an airplane. Most likely, Spencer did not see his synthetic philosophy as something completely apart from his engineering. In the spirit of the Enlightenment, he saw his philosophy as a vehicle for informed, intelligent social design.

Human lives were changed in the nineteenth century by new science and technology, and to a degree the creations of science and technology were drawn forth by changes in the way people worked and lived. In his history of American business, Alfred D. Chandler, Jr. (1977) has argued that most of the inventions that changed nineteenth-century American businesses drew on science and technology that had been available well before that century. There was a *managerial revolution* that allowed a subset of American corporations to organize themselves so as to become very large, productive, and efficient and there had to be new technologies to permit those businesses to operate at a new speed and scale. Ripple effects spread out from this managerial revolution to produce a substantial number of social changes, some benign, some problematic (e.g., Veblen 1973 [1899]; Wiebe 1967; Braverman 1974). Much of the social work, social policy, and politics emerging near the end of the nineteenth century represented an effort to deal with such ripple effects.

The nineteenth century was also a time of many social inventions. Alexis de Tocqueville, visiting the United States to explore what happens to people in democracy, commented on the extraordinary tendency of Americans to form voluntary associations:

The political associations that exist in the United States are only a single feature in the midst of the immense assemblage of associations in that country. Americans of all ages, all conditions, and all dispositions constantly form associations. . . . Thus the most democratic nation on the face of the earth is that in which men have, in our time, carried to the highest perfection the art of pursuing in common the object of their common desires and have applied this new science to the greatest number of purposes. (de Tocqueville 1981 [1840], 403–5)

The rising tide of social inventions of the nineteenth century had much to do with the growth of a discipline of developmental psychology in the twentieth century. In this chapter, I propose to consider social inventions of three kinds.

I would like to discuss, first, a number of enlarging, elaborating streams of institutional inventions for children and families in the nineteenth century, looking at the growth of *kindergartens* as a concrete case and then briefly describing a broader pattern of institutional growth and development that seems to apply to organizations other than kindergartens. As these social inventions grew in number and kind, second-order professional and political institutions were created. A web of new social and political arrangements came into being, imposing new demands on the way in which children grew up, parents took responsibility for their children, and diverse institutions and "whole-child professionals" situated within the web had to perform. Child study emerged as a natural, necessary, and diversified activity of a number of the actors situated in the web. After a time, an organized and systematic form of child study appeared, situated within universities, that we know as developmental psychology.

Second, I will discuss the growth of developmental psychology as a cooperative human enterprise in the twentieth century. This new enterprise would, on the one side, elaborate methods and ideas that would help in the building of the web and, on the other, help individuals— parents, teachers, assorted professionals—to contend with the strange new freedoms and necessities to be faced in the designed world in which they lived.

Finally, I will suggest some social inventions we need in the present. Developmental psychology is an invention of a modern society; only in a modern society do parents need to read books to rear children. For one or two generations in American psychology, graduate students have been introduced to the meaning and mission of their field through courses on the history of psychology and philosophy of science. I will propose that we reinvent the traditional history and systems course and that we introduce young graduate students to the politics of their young science, to developmental psychology as a human enterprise.

The Growth of the Kindergarten

How do ideas about human development become embodied in a set of social practices? We have a well-documented study of such an embodiment in accounts of the nineteenth century invention of the kindergarten (e.g., Blow 1895; Church and Sedlak 1879; Shapiro 1983; Beatty 1995; Brosterman 1997; Rubin, ms.).

Friedrich Froebel, born in 1782, was the son of a Lutheran minister. He studied briefly at Jena, Göttingen, and Berlin, where, deeply influenced by the writings of Fichte and of the nature philosophers

Schelling, Novalis, and Carus, he arrived at a vision of a natural path of child development (Blow 1895). In an autobiographical essay, he wrote:

Man is compelled not only to recognise Nature in her manifold forms and appearances, but also to understand her in the unity of her inner working, of her effective force. Therefore he himself follows Nature's methods in the course of his own development and culture, and in his games he imitates Nature at her work of creation. . . .
  I regard the simple course of development, proceeding from analysis to synthesis, which characterizes pure reasoned thought, as also the natural course of the development of every human being. (Froebel 1879, 76, 118)

Froebel's writings have a lofty, mystical quality, but Froebel had gifts for down-to-earth scientific work and, later, for the invention of toys and activities that appealed to children. Between 1811 and 1816, Froebel worked with one of Europe's great crystallographers and at the end of that time he was offered a professorship of mineralogy in Sweden. He declined, choosing instead to pursue his vision of an education based on the child's "self-activity." Froebel believed in the kind of intellectual growth that is possible for the spontaneous, unhurried child. He chose to work with children in the preschool years, before they started schooling and became too intellectually rigid to be able to pursue the growth that play might bring them.[1] In 1837, he opened his first Kindergarten (garden of children), in Blankenburg, Germany. At the heart of the kindergarten were some toys stuffed with philosophy that Miller (1991) has described in these terms:

Between 1835 and 1850 Froebel worked on his "Gifts and Occupations"—a set of geometric blocks (Gifts) and basic craft activities (Occupations), that would become the centerpiece of his pedagogical theory. The Gifts and Occupations were introduced in a highly ordered sequence , which began in the child's second month and concluded in the last year of kindergarten at the age of six. The sequence was intended to mirror the child's physical and mental development: the malleable, brightly colored spheres from the first gift are followed by a hard, wooden sphere in the second gift, conveying a tactile, material "progression"; the second gift of the wooden sphere, cube, and cylinder encouraged an understanding of the cylinder as a combination of sphere (motion) and cube (stability). The fourth gift, a cube divided into eight smaller blocks, would teach the relationship of the whole to its parts. Gifts three through six divide the cube into smaller, increasingly complex geometries, forming a progressively finer vocabulary of elements. This vocabulary would, in Froebel's plan, become rich and various enough to enable the child to form representations of the surrounding world. (Miller 1991, 10)[2]

  The kindergarten's activities would help children to see complicated objects as constructions made out of simple forms. There were ideas taken from Froebel's crystallography in the design of his Gifts and Occupations (Rubin 1999). Froebel had other ideas, social ideas. He saw his kindergarten as a vehicle for an emancipation of German women that would come through training in childrearing and early education, not through politics.

Froebel's kindergarten went well, and he and his followers pushed for more kindergartens For a time they were successful against opposition. Men did the teaching in Germany, and conservative educators objected to the kindergartens' female teachers and administrators, one of them remarking, "I have a horror of philosophical women!" (Allen 1982, 324). In the end, the Prussian government, alarmed by the political upheavals of 1848, banned kindergartens as socialist institutions. (This might be, conceivably, the earliest social policy for early education on record.) German liberals, emigrating from Germany in reaction to the repressions that followed 1848, brought the kindergarten with them to other countries.[3]

The first American kindergarten was opened by Margarethe Meyer Schurz in Watertown, Wisconsin in 1856. She saw this as a way of offering some of her German heritage to her children. A number of German-speaking kindergartens were opened in the United States, probably for similar reasons. Beside them, there began to be English-speaking kindergartens.

Stimulated by the leadership of Elizabeth Palmer Peabody in Boston, English-speaking kindergartens were begun by upper-middle-class women. Froebelian methods and philosophy were espoused, though it is not clear that the philosophy was either expressed clearly or understood well by adherents. The kindergartens were seen as freer and more open environments at a time when public schools were regimented and rulebound. Encouraged by Peabody, Milton Bradley began to manufacture the gifts and occupations and to publish Froebel's writings, and books by kindergarteners describing exercises and activities to be used with the materials (Beatty 1995, 57ff).

A rapid expansion and Americanization of the kindergarten movement began in Saint Louis after 1873, under William Torrey Harris as Superintendent of Schools and Susan Blow, a local convert to Froebelianism. William Torrey Harris was a remarkable man who appears again and again at the margins of early developmental psychology in this country. He was an able educational administrator who, after leaving the St. Louis schools, would become U.S. Commissioner of Education. He founded the Saint Louis Philosophical Society in 1866, began editing America's first philosophy journal, the *Journal of Speculative Philosophy*, in 1867, and was for a time the leader of the "St. Louis Hegelians."[4] What led Harris toward kindergartening were data for

the St. Louis school system revealing inequalities, educational deficiencies, and early school leaving for poor children. Harris and Blow
believed that kindergartens could help with these problems.[5] The St.
Louis schools began to offer kindergartens while, as a practical school
administrator, Harris addressed budget questions—the need to offer
kindergartens at costs that were tolerable for public education, legal
questions—the question whether money taxed for compulsory education over age six could be used to support programs for children under six, and a political question—an undercurrent of public concern
about bringing a German method into American schools.

During the next thirty years there was a substantial growth of
kindergartening in the United States, driven largely by an interest in
using kindergartens to aid in the education and Americanization of
poor, immigrant children.[6] But the traditional kindergarten designed
by Froebel had to change—to accommodate it to poor children and
subsequently, when kindergartens began to be absorbed into the public schools in large numbers, to bring it into consistency with the
resources, mission, and espoused aims of public education.[7]

Toward the end of the nineteenth century, early American psychologists appeared on the scene, at first expressing sensitivity to the problems of the traditional kindergarten and subsequently offering ideas
and principles of human development around which other forms of
kindergartening were designed. G. Stanley Hall, from the perspective
of child study, criticized the Froebelian kindergartens because (1) they
did not adjust their methods to evidence about the nature of the child;
(2) they presented toddlers with exercises requiring fine-muscle control at a time when this was just beginning to be developed; (3) they
had small children work in highly regulated ways, when they should
be moving freely; (4) they paid too much attention to intellect, when
children from four to eight were at a stage where feelings and emotions were most important. Hall brought those objections to an 1895
meeting of the International Kindergarten Union in Chicago; 33 of
the 35 kindergarteners in his audience walked out on him (Shapiro
1983, 119). Between 1894 and 1899 there were repeated political
showdowns between Froebelian kindergarteners and advocates of
child study.

John Dewey disagreed with the kindergarten people in another
way, feeling that the kindergarten should stress social development.
Dewey wanted his developing child to get a sense of himself or herself
as a social being, and to exercise intelligence to solve problems that
grew out of the classroom's community environment. Dewey once
said that his Laboratory School at the University of Chicago was a reconstruction of the kindergarten, preserving what was right about

Froebel's invention but redirecting the educational scheme toward a more meaningful path of human development (see Dewey 1976 [1899], chapter 6).

Neither Hall nor Dewey changed kindergartening, but they provided ammunition for individuals within the kindergarten movement, "radical Froebelians," who were advocates for change. Kindergartening came into American schools in a big way. In 1910, the U.S. Census counted 396,431 children under the age of six attending school (Beatty 1995, 252). Then substantially new forms of kindergartening were put forward. The ideas around which they were built were quite often notions of human learning and development put forward by early developmental and educational psychologists: G. Stanley Hall and some of his students, John Dewey, Edward L. Thorndike, and William Heard Kilpatrick.

The growth of kindergartens in the nineteenth century resembles the growth patterns of a number of social inventions for children in that century. If we look at the lives of American children and families as they are reflected in Robert Bremner's (1971) remarkable documentary history, we encounter a rising tide of new institutions and institutional arrangements for children and families—infant schools, kindergartens, settlement houses, orphan asylums, freedmen's schools (for the education of former slaves after the Civil War), homes for the deaf, schools for the blind, institutions for feebleminded children, infant asylums, children's hospitals, visiting nurses, school physicians, school nurses, juvenile reformatories, municipal milk stations, juvenile courts, schools for tuberculous children, orphan trains, fresh air or outdoor schools, programs of compulsory physical education, associations for the aid of crippled children, hospitals and schools for crippled children, mental hygiene clinics, programs of compulsory birth registration, child guidance clinics, nursery schools, publicly supported high schools, humane societies and societies for the prevention of cruelty to children, compulsory education laws, provisions for adoption and foster care, foster homes, and so on.[8] Amid this sea of institutional inventions, there was a tidal growth of public schooling set in motion by compulsory education laws and, in following waves, growth of secondary and higher education.

If we look one by one at the growth of the social inventions of the nineteenth century, we find examples again and again of what looks like a main sequence of institutional growth.

1. There is a nuclear invention embodying some conception of human development. Charles Cofer (1986) has pointed out how in past centuries social inventions have been designed on the basis of particu-

lar conceptions of human capacities, motives, and abilities to learn. A social invention for children, similarly, must entail some nuclear conception of the possibilities of human development. In the eighteenth or nineteenth centuries, this nuclear conception would often be associated with the ideas of mental philosophers or moral philosophers—individuals we commonly recognize as actors in psychology's long past.

2. If the new practice is successful, others like it appear in one city or county after another. Sometimes there are parallel lines of growth set up by different religious groups.

3. As there begin to be more and more instances of the new practice and more and more people with common interests in it, higher order organizations appear—professional associations, journals, training and certifying institutions, and organizations concerned with fundraising and political advocacy. A species of child study writings begins to appear, allowing practitioners to share experiences, talk about practical and political decisions, and discuss the possibilities and limitations of their work. Much but by no means all of this writing is down-to-earth and practical. There is apocalyptic and utopian writing. There are writings aimed at stirring up sentiments and attitudes, feelings of solidarity, and morale.

4. As the organization of the new practice becomes very large, there are movements toward coordination with other services and toward policy. As with kindergartens, we see again and again in the nineteenth century a movement away from private or religious systems of support toward public support. The larger picture we are considering, of course, is the interweaving of "island communities" to become components of the interconnected local, state, and federal governmental systems characteristic of the late twentieth century (Wiebe 1967). In this hierarchical arrangement, there are "distal bureaucrats" who deal not so much with flesh-and-blood children, families, or practitioners as with symbolic representations of large numbers of them. An important role of developmental psychologists, among other social scientists, is to participate in the creation of the symbolic world used by such higher order management and to give it semblances of life and meaning (Siegel and White 1962; White 1978).

5. Over time, and as the institutional growth processes that I have been describing take place, the philosophy of the nuclear practice that starts the sequence usually will not be sufficient for the purposes of later descendants. As happened in the case of kindergartening, new inventions, reconstructions, and reengineerings of the nuclear practice will be found necessary. As we move into the twentieth century, more and more of these reconstructions will involve ideas taken from developmental psychology.

Up to this point I have tried to characterize the cultural and historical world within which developmental psychology was born and some
of the activities of developmental psychologists in that modern world.
Developmental psychology as a cooperative research enterprise is an
invention of the twentieth century, not of all but of some societies in the
twentieth century. Why did developmental psychology emerge in just
the times and places it did? I would like to set forth three arguments:

1. Developmental psychology as a cooperative human activity is a
useful component of a modern society, since much of that society is
made up of a web of designed social institutions and practices dealing
with human health, education, and welfare. Developmental psychology participates in the perennial design processes and reconstructions
that maintain the ability of that society to address the needs of children and families.

2. In contemporary society, developmental psychologists help with
the establishment and management of social programs through work
on *representation*—offering indications of the conditions of children
and families in American society; *demonstration*—designing programs
to explore the possibilities of constructive action; *idealization*—offering
ideas about how programs might influence human development; and
evaluation—designing studies and collecting data to indicate the effects
of social programs and policies. These four functions have been reasonably clear in the course of developmental psychologists' sustained
involvement with Head Start (White and Phillips 2001).

3. Not only institutions but individual lives must be designed in a
modern society. Parents in one way, and children in another, are faced
with a disconcerting openness, set of options, and choices of the possible paths a child might take toward adulthood. There are not strong traditions to restrict and guide them. Parents are responsible for complex
and poorly understood negotiations and coordinations with professionals in their upbringing of children. Parents are expected somehow to
find "optimal child development" and a career line for the child in a
"world of work" holding out some 40,000 occupations. Children are
faced with school tasks whose significance, they are told, is very large
but whose human meaning is not always completely clear. A substantial part of the work of contemporary developmental psychologists has
been to contribute to psychological testing, counseling and guidance,
and assorted remedial and clinical services in support of a child's complex task of finding his or her way toward adulthood. We assign a
quasi-medical, or "mental health" interpretation to much of this work,
but that designation is wearing thin and we badly need to reconstrue
the nature and meaning of such work at this time (White 1996). But

the contributions of developmental psychology toward the design of individual lives is, I have little doubt, quite real and quite necessary in a modern society.

Three Waves of Developmental Psychology

Given a limited place in the early years of the growth of the modern university, developmental psychology has struggled to come to terms with questions about its scientific status and practical value. Can one create a shared empiricism about children? What can a university-based science of childhood tell us about rearing and educating children? At the very first, easily and spontaneously, biological science began to send messages about how children develop. Charles Darwin's writings led him into an evolutionary account of human development, in books like *The Descent of Man* (1871) and *Expression of the Emotions in Man and Animals* (1872). George Romanes picked up some of Darwin's notes and followed through on his ideas with books like *Animal Intelligence* (1883), *Mental Evolution in Animals* (1884), and *Mental Evolution in Man* (1889). Postulations about stages of human intellectual development flowed directly and easily from this evolutionary perspective (White 1983). Textbooks of what people of the nineteenth century called the "new psychology," scientific psychology, recognized the study of children as part of one of the three or four basic methods. John Dewey's textbook described the comparative method in these terms: "Mind, as existing in the average human adult, may be compared with the consciousness (1) of animals, (2) of children in various stages, (3) of defective and disordered minds, (4) or mind as it appears in the various conditions of race, nationality, etc." (1967 [1887], 15).

Three years later William James described the comparative method in somewhat more pungent terms:

So it has come to pass that instincts of animals are ransacked to throw light on our own; and that the reasoning faculties of bees and ants, the minds of savages and infants, madmen, idiots, the deaf and blind, criminals, and eccentrics, are all invoked in support of this or that special theory about some part of our own mental life. . . . There are great sources of error in the comparative method. The interpretation of the "psychoses" of animals, savages, and infants is necessarily wild work, in which the personal equation of the investigator has things very much its own way. A savage will be reported to have no moral or religious feeling if his actions shock the observer unduly. A child will be assumed without self-consciousness because he talks of himself in the third person, etc., etc. No rules can be laid down in advance . . . the only thing then is to use as much sagacity as you possess, and to be as candid as you can. (1890, 194)

What Dewey and James recognized in their textbooks was an evolutionary perspective on child development and heterogeneous writings about children distributed through scientific, philosophical, and medical literatures. Toward the end of the nineteenth century, a programmatic inquiry appeared. A cooperative, systematic, university-based study of human development has grown up in three waves. From 1894 to 1904 there was a small body of questionnaire studies generally known as the Child Study Movement. This died off before World War I. A second, differently organized and substantially larger body of cooperative research work known as the Child Development Movement began in 1917 and lasted until 1950, when it was substantially moribund. Its peak period was between 1924 and 1934. Beginning in 1960, a third program appeared, Developmental Psychology, much larger, continuing with some vitality into the present.[9]

G. Stanley Hall's program of questionnaire studies, initiated in 1894, began a program of systematic naturalistic inquiry into child development (White 1990). Most likely, Hall did not see the questionnaires as methods that would be the basis for a differentiated subdiscipline of developmental psychology. His use of the questionnaire data in his 1904 *Adolescence* indicates that he saw such data as elaborating an evolutionary account of human development grounded on the scientific work of a number of disciplines. What would be the practical value of this cross-disciplinary inquiry? It would elaborate a biological-social vision of child development: the child, as he or she grows up, becomes able to participate in more and more complex forms of social organization. The discussions and numerous practical recommendations in Hall's *Adolescence* were based on the premise that this evolutionary picture of children's development could offer scientifically based guidance to individuals concerned with the upbringing and education of children (White 1991, 1992).

Phenomena of Religious Conversion

Hall's questionnaire studies are not very compelling methodologically to modern eyes. Nevertheless, we can trace the influence of one of Hall's questionnaires forward toward a significant contemporary group of human services. In February 1896, Hall and a graduate student named Edwin Diller Starbuck sent out a questionnaire called "Religious Experience." Starbuck (1897, 1888, 1899) would eventually publish two papers and a book on the findings of his questionnaire studies of religious conversion. William James wrote an approving preface to Starbuck's book and a few years later drew on his work in his own *Varieties of Religious Experience* (1902).

Some thirty years later, William Griffiths (Bill) Wilson, an alcoholic at a time when many regarded alcoholism as a hopeless and deadly addiction, came to the belief that only through a full-blown conversion experience could the alcoholic save himself. Someone put into his hands James's *Varieties of Religious Experience*, and he saw described there in some detail the conversion experience he had been thinking about:

Spiritual experiences, James thought, could have objective reality; almost like gifts from the blue, they could transform people. Some were sudden brilliant illuminations; others came on very gradually. Some flowed out of religious channels; others did not. But nearly all had the great common denominators of pain, suffering, calamity. Complete hopelessness and deflation at depth were almost always required to make the recipient ready. The significance of all this burst upon me. *Deflation at depth*—yes, that was *it*. Exactly that had happened to me. (1942)

Bill W. used William James's thought and his name in the establishment of Alcoholics Anonymous. Wilson extracted from him the importance of hopelessness as a first stage. He drew on James's discussion of the *varieties* of religious experience to argue that there was no one religious form necessary for participation in AA.

Wilson formulated twelve steps that would have to be taken for an alcoholic to recover. The success of Alcoholics Anonymous has led to imitations. At present there are over one hundred twelve-step programs in the United States directed toward a number of addictions and dependencies. It is not unreasonable to look at these twelve-step schemes as elements of a procedure through which individuals might be led through the kind of developmental sequence delineated in Starbuck's questionnaire studies.[10]

THE CHILD DEVELOPMENT MOVEMENT

A second establishment of developmental psychology began in the 1920s, when a number of multidisciplinary institutes and centers directed toward the study of child development were established. Funding from the Laura Spelman Rockefeller Foundation, offered through a program administered by Lawrence K. Frank, made possible the development of this movement while at the same time offering serious constraints to the directions in which it might develop. At the center of the movement were normative and psychometric studies directed toward exact scientific descriptions of norms and standards of child development (White 1995).

The movement did not have a full-blooded scientific program

including a cumulative line of research and theories meaningfully connected to the research. Lawrence K. Frank, after, in my opinion, organizing and constraining the institutes and centers so that they could not form such a program, ultimately would complain that it was uninteresting and lacked theory. But the program he sponsored directed the centers toward research and outreach efforts to support a more scientifically based parent education. Such education, Frank believed, would offer a "preventive politics," acting against those problems in child development that tend to produce problems in American society. Frank had been a cost accountant in his early years and his vision of science-based guidance for parents amounted to a scheme for scientific management. Papers published in the first years of *Child Development* do not make clear that the researchers of the institutes and centers were all captured by this vision. But the papers one finds in the journal are quite conservative, oriented toward norms and psychometrics.

The Child Development Movement is generally recognized as part of the main line of growth in developmental psychology from G. Stanley Hall to the present. But the study of children in the 1920s and 1930s, like mainstream psychology at just this time, was becoming pluralistic and multiparadigmatic. In the heyday of the Child Development Movement—that is, roughly, from 1924 to 1934—there were a number of parallel research programs:

- A traditional body of research in comparative psychology, studies of perception and learning in animals and children, published in the pages of the *Pedagogical Seminary*, now changing its name to become the *Journal of Genetic Psychology*.
- Educational psychology, research programs building on the design set forth by Thorndike, established as a staple requirement of teacher training in the United States, including work on tests and measurements and on experimental studies of human learning.
- The psychoanalytic study of the child, just beginning to emerge in the 1920s.
- The work of the Child Guidance Movement, growing rapidly in the 1930s, organized under the American Orthopsychiatric Association. Papers of this movement were published in the *American Journal of Orthopsychiatry*, founded in the same year as *Child Development*.

Most of these bodies of inquiry were practice-centered. With one or two notable exceptions such as the research of Myrtle McGraw (1943), the work of the Child Development Movement was not about theory.

Nor was it about the creation of services for children and families. It was about providing tools and standards for the management of the twentieth-century architecture of programs and policies for children and their families. Thorndike's educational psychology set the pattern. There were several visions of what psychology might offer education at the beginning of this century—Hall's developmental vision, Thorndike's engineering vision, and Dewey's reconstructive vision (White 1991). All had some validity in the long run, but it was Thorndike's engineering approach that set the pattern for the immediate future. Abilities tests, achievement tests, "child accounting," descriptive statistics, tests and measurements—these were instruments of scientific management. Educational psychologists brought them into schools, and the aim of the Child Development Movement was to provide such tools for parents and for professionals dealing with children and families.

On the American scene, an important part of the scientific structure of developmental psychology as we know it today was missing, the theories of development. Curiously, at just this time, a brilliant group of developmental theories was flowering in Europe. Heinz Werner, in Hamburg, published the first edition of his *Comparative Psychology of Mental Development* in 1926. Jean Piaget, in Geneva, published the first five books of his theory, sometimes called "the famous five," between 1923 and 1932. Lev S. Vygotsky, in Moscow, completed almost all the corpus of work for which he is known today between 1924 and 1934, when he died of tuberculosis. It is remarkable that these theorists, who formed so important a part of the intellectual leadership of developmental psychology after 1960, should have been so little recognized and dealt with in the American Child Development Movement of their own time.

DEVELOPMENTAL PSYCHOLOGY

Developmental psychology in something like its contemporary form began to emerge in American psychology in the 1960s. The Child Development Movement was clearly moribund by the early 1950s; reviews of the time clearly said this was so (White 1991a). Research work with children began to be aligned with the theoretical interests of mainstream American psychology—for instance, in Robert Sears's antecedent-consequent analyses of the development of dependency and aggression in children (Sears, Maccoby, and Levin 1957) and, subsequently, in the work of experimental child psychology directed toward behavior theory and behavior engineering. But the large movement in the renaissance of developmental psychology was toward the study of cognitive development. Some dramatic social issues pulled developmental psychologists in this direction. The initial success of the Russian satellite program, the launching of Sputnik, led some to argue that the United States was falling behind in science. Leading American scientists participated in a number of projects intended to build new and state-of-the-art school curricula in science education. Not long after, in the mid-1960s, the War on Poverty was launched. A prominent and popular part of the War on Poverty were programs such as Head Start, Follow Through, and the Title I programs of the Elementary and Secondary Education Act, intended to stimulate the cognitive development and improve the education of disadvantaged children. In psychology at large, the "Age of Theory" was coming to an end and the "Cognitive Revolution" was beginning. These factors, all together, pulled the theory and research program of Jean Piaget across the water and gave them a prominent place—indeed, a central, organizing place—in American developmental psychology of the 1960s and 1970s (White 1991a).

During the 1960s, individuals coming from a fully developed and complex set of research programs in developmental psychology were brought into involvement with social programs and policies designed at the federal level and requiring programmatic inventions and creations at the local level. The best-known example of this is the creation of Head Start in the 1960s. I have said above that in contemporary society developmental psychologists help with the establishment and management of social programs through work on representation, demonstration, idealization, and evaluation (White and Phillips 2001). Something much more complicated is going on in the contemporary world than simply spinning out an idea about human development in one place that becomes the nucleus of an invention in another. It will take serious study of how questions, ideas, methods, and findings move among researchers, professionals, practitioners, and policy makers to fully understand the scientific meaning of a field like developmental psychology. Such studies ought to be undertaken.

Reconstructing the History and Systems Course

I propose that developmental psychologists give some serious consideration to the systematic reconstruction of the "history and systems" course that once was a staple of graduate training in psychology in this country.

John Dewey in his *Reconstruction in Philosophy* (1950 [1920]) argued that it is the eternal task of philosophers (including us) to reach into the human institutions of the past, to pull forth the values embedded in and governing those institutions, and to re-embody those values in institutions of the future. Human institutions keep changing. Schools, courts, universities, factories, institutions like marriage and childrearing, government agencies—all these keep changing over time, and we are all involved in processes of reinvention, reconstruction, and reengineering. John Dewey's analysis is one cornerstone of the approach I have taken in this chapter. It is a pleasure to acknowledge this debt. It is also a pleasure to acknowledge my debt to Donald Campbell (1988) and his postulations about the growth of human knowledge through evolutionary epistemology and the deployment of scientific methods and findings for society's benefit through "the experimenting society."

Let me suggest a small item of reengineering that is, to my mind, fundamentally necessary for the well-being of developmental psychology. When I was a graduate student, two of the foundational courses in psychologists' graduate education were the history and systems course and the philosophy of science course. The history and systems course, usually based on Edwin G. Boring's (1950) *A History of Experimental Psychology*, told students where the psychology they were entering into had come from. When I took my first job in the Psychology Department of the University of Chicago, the chairman of the department met me at the door. "The man who has been teaching our history and systems course has just left. You'll be happy to teach history and systems for us, won't you?"

"Yes, sir," I said, and for seven years I taught the history of psychology at Chicago. I taught Boring's *History* like Billy Graham's Bible, cover to cover, and I thoroughly enjoyed it.

The science of psychology, Boring said, had been created by a fusion of two traditions, two centuries of epistemological inquiry moving from Empiricism into Associationism, brought together with scientific procedures developed in nineteenth-century laboratories of physics, astronomy, physiology, and medicine. The marriage of these two traditions had taken place in Wilhelm Wundt's Leipzig Laboratory in 1879, and from that laboratory there emerged a scientific psychology. By tracing a path from the past into the present, this kind of course suggested a path stretching toward the future. This psychology you are entering into, it said, is an empirical epistemology. Its "destiny," so to speak, is to confront the problem of knowledge.

The traditional philosophy of science course was based on the systematic writings of a philosophical group espousing a position called logical positivism. What it offered students was a general thesis about the nature of scientific psychology and, based on that thesis, specifications for what a properly scientific concept, law, and theory ought to look like. Newtonian physics was taken to be a model for properly scientific work, and under the doctrine of unity of science psychology could be characterized as an "immature physics." The traditional philosophy of science taught in American graduate education interdigitated reasonably well with the history and systems course, and both together gave students a sense of the purposes and nature of the scientific enterprise they were joining. Histories can have this power. They can organize and make coherent the flux of the present (White 1978).

Neither of these traditional courses is taught regularly any more. There are small and large problems with Boring's history, and philosophers and physicists alike challenge many of the basic presuppositions of logical positivism. For developmental psychologists, this is good news and bad news. The time has passed when a majority of the pluralistic community of American psychology can live comfortably with the idea that their tradition can be fitted within a history of experimental psychology. Developmental psychology did not come out of Leipzig. G. Stanley Hall went to Leipzig but he took his Ph.D. at Harvard under James and Bowditch. The questionnaire studies that were the core of his research program were extensions of questionnaire studies done earlier by German schoolteachers. If we look for a reasonably appropriate and meaningful history of the full array of Hall's early child study work, I believe we arrive at the mixture of social and scientific history I have been sketching out here.

I would recommend that graduate students in developmental psychology be taught to understand exactly such a mixture of social and scientific history as part of the introduction to their field. It will give them an intelligent sense of the traditions, meaning, and everyday utility of the community of inquiry they are entering.

Rather than teaching graduate students that developmental psychology is a science just like any other, it would be useful to consider in a very fresh and open way what is possible to a collectivity of observers seeking to share observations and understandings of children's behavior. Part of an appropriate history course for developmental psychologists would entail some kind of consideration of the philosophy of science they are picking up. The most reasonable construal of the scientific meaning of developmental psychology available within the framework of the old-time philosophy would be that it stands as an immature aspect of a discipline that is itself an immature physics. But perhaps there is a more fundamental problem. Developmental psychology just doesn't look and feel like physics. There may be a few optimistic members of our field who feel that, somewhere off in the distance, they can detect the possibilities of mathematical laws and theories of human development. There is no way to prove that such formulations *won't* come, but I'm skeptical.

What if developmental psychology is not an immature natural science but an adolescent human science? Emily Cahan and I reviewed a 200-year-old series of arguments that there ought really to be two psychologies, a bottom-up science in which reasonably simple aspects of mind and behavior are synthesized from constituent elements—the familiar psychology that everybody talks about most of the time—and a second psychology, not so familiar, through which the more complex aspects of mind and behavior are understood in a top-down fashion, as aspects of the mind formed by the language, myth, and culture within which people live (Cahan and White 1992). I believe this is an appropriate way to understand a good deal of what is most salient and meaningful about developmental psychology today.

Why should we characterize the enterprise as adolescent?

It is half-grown. One of the problems of the traditional "immature physics" story of my generation is that it left a good many psychologists with a more-or-less quiet feeling of despair. I've heard the despair in talks with friends. "When if ever is this field going to be a *science*?" "Is this discipline ever going to be a science?" Yet I believe that if you look in the right directions you will find interesting ideas, insights, patterns in the phenomena of human development that are intriguing and worth thinking about. Our inquiries have brought them forward. And our work has been useful. Throughout this chapter, I have pointed toward work on human development that has found its way into real changes in social practices. I do not wish to exaggerate for a moment the power or the necessity or the all-goodness of developmental psychology for modern life. I believe that, on balance, it has been useful, and that if you look in the right places you can see that.

It has an identity problem. A problem for developmental psychology is that, as it defines good science, it often has trouble measuring up. There was an attempt, near the turn of the last century, to begin to set forth notions of methodology and procedure appropriate for a human science. One of the great strengths of Vygotsky's approach, Cahan and I have argued (Cahan and White 1992), is that he recognized the necessity of a second psychology and deliberately set out to find procedures, concepts, and methodological ideas appropriate for such an enterprise. Today, with growing bodies of interest in discourse-processing, in the case study method, in cultural psychology, and in qualitative research methods, the hunt seems to be on for a basic understanding of the discipline appropriate to its work and its needs.

It is clumsy. Finally, there is a third way in which developmental psychology has features of adolescence. It enters into social practices and policies, but it has a distressing tendency to bump into the furniture.

Without a clear sense of what the nature of their own knowledge is, of the social and political world to which they relate, and of their own efficacy, developmental psychologists stand in an uneasy relationship to the practitioners with whom they deal.

Future Steps

I have proposed that we revive at least one of the traditional staples of graduate education, the history and systems course, but that we reinvent the course to try to give a richer and more adequate picture of developmental psychologists as a community of investigators, related in real and meaningful ways to the people and the life of the designed human society in which they function. Without such a course, without an understanding of where their enterprise stands in the scheme of human events, graduate students become simply craftsmen learning to put together a well-formed study. I have every respect for well-formed studies, but I believe that scientists who are going to do meaningful work need more intellectual tools.

A few new inquiries would help us to understand better the situation of developmental psychology in the modern world.

We need to explore more carefully the threads of method and ideas that move into and out of developmental psychology in connection with various forms of practice. It is not easy work, but it is interesting work, to try to trace the movements of knowledge, ideas, and intuitions back and forth between individuals situated in the "ivory tower" and the "real world." Here, I have written briefly about kindergartens, Alcoholics Anonymous, and Head Start. Research-based knowledge has also been used in the creation of *Sesame Street*, the Boy Scouts, IQ testing, Margaret McMillan's nursery school, Maria Montessori's Children's Houses, and contemporary Piaget-based forms of preschooling. We could well use more detailed tracing.

We need to explore more carefully some further aspects of the ecology of developmental psychology itself. What is there about life in a modern society that leads parents to want to read books about parenting, teachers to study teaching, and one and all to consume the variety of literatures that make up popular child psychology? Developmental psychology has a "double" or, better, a crowd of doubles. When Hall was initiating his program of child study in Clark University, Louis N. Wilson, Clark's librarian, began to collect bibliographies of miscellaneous writings about children, and over a ten-year period arrived at 4,427 items (Wilson 1975). It is easy to show that there was far more writing than Wilson counted at the time. A very small part of the stream was made up of university-based child study. What were the purposes served by the other writings? Look outside the walls of the contemporary university, and it is easy to see that the stream goes on. Why is this so? I think we have to begin with the manifold purposes and needs that people in our modern society have for the understanding of children and for the understanding of their own agency as parents or professionals. We have to understand what aspects of those needs our collective science is able to address. Then we can begin to arrive at a more complete understanding of the role of developmental psychology in a world of designed institutions.

Epilogue
The Millennium of Childhood That Stretches Before Us

Michael Zuckerman

It was about time. A century was ending. A new millennium was upon us. It was a time to think about time. Time past, time to come. Where have we been? Where might we be going? And ours are studies of time. History is nothing if not a meditation on time. Developmental psychology is the one branch of psychology that pries into change over time.

And it was about time. Considering their convergences and complementarities in sensibility and subject matter, historians and developmental psychologists should have been collaborators from the first. Both try to trace the crystallization of character. Both think it matters in the evolution of humankind. And each supplies the deficiencies of the other: history over-attentive as it is to particularity, developmental psychology to pattern.

And it was about time, within each discipline, to take another look at the discipline itself as it bore specifically on the study of childhood. History and developmental psychology are, today, the two great domains of scholarly inquiry devoted to that study. Both fields found their current form a generation ago, history on the inspiration of Philippe Ariès, developmental psychology on the paradigm propounded by Jean Piaget. Recent work in both fields has begun to challenge Ariesian and Piagetian assumptions alike.

And it was about time, beyond the bounds of these scholarly disciplines, to assess the experience of children in the century that was expiring. A hundred years before, in a bestseller that swept the Western world, Ellen Key had implored a "century of the child." At the end of the twentieth century, it seemed worth asking whether we had actually enjoyed (or suffered) such a century, and it seemed worth wondering what the evidence of the century past portended of the century to come.

A Century of the Child?

When Willem Koops and I solicited these papers from these distinguished scholars and scientists, we had only a vague anticipation of what they might say. I think that I thought that they would look back on the past in the light of Ariès and forward to the future in the dim and distorting refraction of linear extrapolation. I distinctly remember dreading that people would look back on our predictions, fifteen years later, and laugh.

As things have turned out, very few of the participants in this enterprise have worried much—or at all—about forecasting the future. (A pity, even if it does absolve us of embarrassment in time to come.) At the same time, quite a number of them have looked at the past and found very little to sustain a premise of a century of the child.

Barbara Hanawalt insists that there was no conspicuous absence of awareness of or concern for children in the late Middle Ages and so no subsequent emergence of the child in the modern era; in her twentieth century, we have a century of the child only in the sense that all centuries are centuries of the child. Els Kloek sees in the Netherlands of the seventeenth century the great age of Dutch child-centeredness; in her eighteenth century we have a retreat from such fond focus rather than its ever-augmenting elaboration.

Karin Calvert finds that in America adults have always set their own obsessions ahead of the needs of the newborn and the young; in her account, we have centuries of the parent, not of the child. John Gillis suggests that, in Victorian Anglo-America and ever since, men and women have preferred their fantasies of childhood to any substantial encounter with its realities; on his interpretation, children are depositories for their elders' anxieties, in a century of the evaporation of the child into virtuality. Peter Stearns maintains that, in modern America, men and women have put their own pleasures before those of their children; in his view, we have had a century of hedonic indulgence that leaves the young too often to their own devices.

Gerrit Breeuwsma observes that developmental psychologists attend to children only when they happen to notice a newborn nephew; otherwise, they pass their professional lives in a nearly principled indifference to actual children and a barely disguised antagonism toward actual mothers. Sheldon White inadvertently confirms Breeuwsma's mordant observation, writing of a century of developmental psychologists rather than of the childhood they study and writing of those developmentalists as "distal bureaucrats" who deal less with "flesh-and-blood children" than with "representations" of real children designed to "provide tools" for parents and for "higher order management."

And that is just the tally from the West. When we turn to the East, these proliferous problems compound themselves. Hideo Kojima assumes a long perspective in which the novelties of the nineteenth and twentieth centuries, after the Meiji restoration, pale beside the persistences of a folk psychology that goes back centuries in Japan. Michael Nylan takes an even longer view in which the deliberate policies of the late twentieth century, after the death of Mao, diminish the numbers of children and deny the resources for their development as traditional regimes never did in China. What can it mean to speak of the century of the child when, for the fifth of the population of the planet that live in that one country alone, the regime is willfully making things worse for children?

All the same, I would propose that these debunkings and devastations of our premised century of the child end up, in an intriguing way, affirming it. Each of them finds its force precisely *as* a debunking or a devastation *of* that premise. Each would have a very different import, or no import at all, if we did not cling so fervently to child-centered assumptions. Each would carry very different significances, or no significance at all, outside those assumptions.

If we simply took for granted, as people did until recently, that the young should do the bidding of their elders and that parents would put themselves before their children, then we would not be surprised, disturbed, and even offended by the findings and the implications of the papers we have to consider here.

We are unsettled by the evidence of so many of these studies because we are the parents whom Philippe Ariès postulated in 1960, heirs of an early modern ethical revolution that set the child at the moral center of our existence. At the dawn of the twenty-first century, Ariès's insistence on the emergence of the child as the fulcrum of the family and of modern middle class culture still frames our discussion. No matter how powerful the demolitions and denunciations, his formulation still controls our conversation. Perhaps precisely because it is as imprecise and elusive as Els Kloek says, it is one of the seminal historical theorizations of our time. Perhaps precisely because it is as poetic and polemic as she argues, it promises to go on provoking us—as, say, the Weber thesis has gone on provoking us—long after being "disproven" dozens of times over.

Progress?

But we would do better to begin at the beginning of this century, with Ellen Key, than in medias res, with Ariès. Her book, *The Century of the Child* (1900), was the unlikeliest of international bestsellers. She herself was an open adherent of paganism and an explicit enemy of Christianity. She spoke out stridently against industrialism and indeed against capitalism itself. She proclaimed herself an unabashed feminist. And if her feminism sought to keep women out of the workplace and in the home, raising children, it openly avowed its eagerness to raise those children as Nietzschean supermen.

Key never thought her century of the child a plausible prospect. Her appeal for such a century was a cri de coeur, and an anguished one at that. Like Rousseau, she sought to preserve a "natural" child against pressures to precocious sophistication in an ever more disciplined society. Like him, she beseeched a "religion of development" (Key 1909, 183, quoted in Macleod 1998, 52). And like him, too, she recognized all too clearly, even presciently, the forces arrayed against the sort of childhood she sought to promote. For every youngster afforded the sheltered childhood she idealized, there were dozens growing up in a poverty that precluded it. Her summons to a century of the child arose out of anxiety and urgency more than out of any conviction that it would be heeded.

Her American contemporaries exceeded, if anything, her keenness to protect children from the demands of modern adult life. Early twentieth-century child welfare workers in the United States took up the title of her book and, with obtuse optimism, changed it from a summons to a slogan. Savants such as G. Stanley Hall set out to scientize the romantic idea of "development." On the basis of a prodigious collection of questionnaire responses that defied all systematic analysis, Hall insisted that his data demonstrated stages of youth, each qualitatively different from adulthood. On the basis of his own will to believe, he proclaimed childhood "the paradise of the race" (Macleod 1998, 52).

Even at the time, it was clear that only parents in the upper reaches of the middle class could preserve their children from precocity as the reformers required. At the time, it was not as clear as it is now that efforts to avert youthful independence entailed paradoxes all their own. The self-styled progressivism of the Child Study Movement impelled increasingly strict scheduling and increasingly minute age-grading. It authorized increasingly severe anxieties about the pace at which youngsters crossed developmental thresholds. Middle-class reformers never did succeed in controlling the poor, but they controlled their own offspring, in everything from bottle-feeding to schooling, with an intensity never known or imagined on such a scale before. Their determination to dominate their young was as explicit before World War I as after, in L. Emmett Holt as much as in John Watson (Macleod 1998).

By the 1920s, as Ann Hulbert says, "bullying behaviorists had taken over." Psychologists disparaged parents who expressed love for their little ones, warning that overt displays "bred unwholesome dependence." And psychologically inclined pediatricians patronized mothers who hesitated to impose the fierce "regularity" the doctors demanded. The progressives' century of the child was compatible with a good deal of brutality toward children (Hulbert 1996, 82).

John Watson was an equal-opportunity brutalizer. He meant to subject parents as much as children to his punishing regimes. He made explicit his scorn for all who lavished undisciplined affection on children. And he made plain that mothers were the worst offenders. It was not just that they were "overwrought cuddlers and clingers." It was that they failed to appreciate their power to shape their offspring. They had to be remade into cool trainers who could treat children "as though they were young adults" (Hulbert 1996).

Today, developmental psychology seems to be returning in this regard to Watson. Sophisticated work in the field now offers some empirical warrant for believing what the first behaviorists took for granted: that the child mind is much more like the young adult mind than unique unto itself. Contemporary research challenges the Piagetian premise that children develop through a succession of incommensurable organizations of cognition. It calls into question Key's insistence, and Rousseau's before her, that the young pass through psychic stages that demand deference to their distinctiveness (Koops, Chapter 1).

In short, it looks as if we have been before where we are going now. At least among psychologists, the century of the child has ended very nearly as it began. One does not associate such circularity with the normal course of science.

Science?

One does associate such circularity—such premiums on revisionism, such cycling and periodic freshening of a relatively restricted stock of interpretive alternatives, such going around in circles—with history. And it is fair to say that many of the developmental psychologists among the contributors to this collection would concur with the historians that the study of childhood is inherently a historical study. Indeed, it is striking how many of the developmental psychologists among our contributors have in some measure made themselves over into historians of impressive ingenuity and integrity.

At least one or two of our developmental psychologists very nearly suggest that their discipline cannot be in any old-fashioned sense a scientific one. Most of the rest are adamant that, as Hideo Kojima puts it, "childhood is not an isolated phase or stage of life" (Kojima, Chapter 7). It can only be comprehended in context. And the study of childhood cannot situate itself outside our common life, in rarefied scientific detachment. As Sheldon White argues so eloquently, developmental psychology must position itself in a world of designed institutions. A crucial part of the context that White and our other psychologists implore is historical, in both the broad sense in which ordinary readers use the term and the more specialized sense in which developmentalists speak of the life course.

In asserting the indispensability of historical context to the interpretation of childhood, it is not necessary to follow Kojima into the most fascinating aspect of his argument: the demonstration that in traditional Japan those stages and phases bent time as we in the West understand it. The Japanese life course has extended, and to this day extends, beyond death and before birth. It takes in, consequentially, both the hereafter and what we might call the "foretime." (If that seems exotic, consider the notions of child competence and character held by successive cohorts of Americans, as Karin Calvert reviews them in Chapter 4.) It is merely necessary to affirm that the demarcation and characterization of childhood in a culture depends in part on the demarcation and characterization of other phases and stages. It is merely necessary to observe that neither children nor childhood can be disentangled from adults and their assumptions, aspirations, and anxieties.

That is crucial, because the single proposition that is asserted, implied, denied, and contested more than any other in the essays in this collection is the proposition that modern youngsters live in an isolated enclave unto themselves. Most of our authors worry that modern youngsters are set apart to come of age alone. On such analyses, young people find themselves growing up in a veritable kindergarten. They evolve autonomous cultures even as they remain innocent of the adult world and unprepared for citizenship in it.

The postulation and problematization of this "youthland" seem to derive in their contemporary conceptualization from Ariès. And the Frenchman did undeniably forge the discourse that has dominated the last four decades. But Ariès did not invent the elements of that discourse and indeed could not have done so. He could hardly have been the historian of infantilization if he had been the first to speak of it. His precise point was that he was far from the first. Notions of an isolated, innocent childhood appeared in Western Europe at least as early as the fifteenth century. Such notions were normative if not normal by the nineteenth century, when loving surveillance of vulnerable youth came to define respectable middle-class standing among the Victorians. They became inescapable in the twentieth century, when the G. Stanley Halls and the turn-of-the-century child savers, the Erik Eriksons and the Doctor Spocks and the legions of *New York Times Magazine* writers elaborated them as the moral Muzak of our time.

Yet Ariès cannot so clearly stand as the avatar of this new and unprecedented pedagogic province. He did, to be sure, describe the isolation of the young in increasingly age-graded precincts of their own. But he also described those precincts as increasingly subject to adult oversight. Indeed, he insisted that the only real independence that the young in the West ever enjoyed appeared in the only configuration he actually admired: the brutal and exploitative but self-governing youth cohorts of the Middle Ages. His account of modern child life is an account of children hovered over by doting parents and infantilized by the fond supervision of anxious adults.

Infantilization?

Certainly the accounts we have here do not demonstrate the isolation of the young that their authors sometimes purport. If anything, these essays suggest the impossibility of an authentic child culture, disconnected from the culture of the elders. Even the most striking and strident arguments for such a disjunction that we have here admit of other readings.

Take Micha de Winter's marvelous reconnaissance of reform pedagogy in the twentieth-century West. It is full of the ideas of a remarkable array of critics of conventional educational practice. But it is almost empty of the industrial economy that produced the public schooling systems that the reformers assailed and of the conventional pedagogy that has prevailed and still prevails in virtually every one of those systems.

Whether or not the twentieth century was the century of the child, it was assuredly the century of universal public education, in the West and in many other parts of the world as well. And everywhere those new schools of the state sought to produce youth who would be serviceable to the state and to its economy.

Exactly insofar as those schools embraced mass education in order to educate the masses, they disdained to shelter students in a pedagogical province. Insofar as they taught standardized curricula to increasingly age-graded, regimented children, they disdained to create isolated and infantilizing youthlands. On the contrary, they promoted the very practices against which Key, Ariès, and other reformers railed. In the name of the child, for the sake of her protection and his development, they achieved an extraordinary augmentation of surveillance, punishment, and repression.

Precisely by offering the mass, impersonal education they did, the schools of the twentieth century assured the connectedness of the young to the mass, impersonal social order of their elders. Precisely by teaching standardization and regimentation, obedience and punctuality, and conformity to fixed rules, the schools taught the work-discipline—and the disempowerment—at the center of modern citizenship.

Even Winter concedes that the fashioning of children into "economically profitable and socially well-adjusted" men and women has been the "dominant" aim of normal pedagogy (Chapter 9). In that sense as in many others, conventional schools have prepared their pupils for adulthood rather than detaching them from it. And if, in our own time, schools do not seek such adjustment as strenuously as they once did—if now they seek to instill in their students the acquisitiveness, the insecurity, and the disposition to derive a sense of self from the possession of commodities that a consumer society requires—that testifies less to an abandonment of the determination to fit children to adult reality than to the transformation of adult reality.

From the dawn of universal public education to this day, conventional educators have tried to ready children for adult responsibilities. Progressive educators may have promoted the emancipation of the young, but pedagogues in the mainstream never did. They knew very well the industrial and financial masters whom they served and whom their students would one day serve.

Even the reformers on whom Winter dwells were unable to construct an age-based apartheid for their charges. Their central idea was, as he says, "that pedagogy should take notice of the child's distinctive needs." Their aim—"the aim of all education," as they proclaimed— was "the full development of individual potential." But that very idea and that very aim betrayed the ambivalence at the heart of progressive educational thought. Though the reformers denounced the mass production model of education prevalent everywhere in the modern world, they could not escape its entanglements. Though they knew the child-centered words, they had trouble with the tune. They sang of a "scientific" study of "childhood." They trumpeted schools "based on the unique development every child goes through."

In this counterpoint of uniqueness and universality, reformers exposed the paradoxes that pervaded their pedagogy. Even educators who meant to dispute or deny the applicability of the industrial model to the schooling of the young ended up infected by it. They as much as their opponents in the mainstream came to conceive of schools appropriate to "every child." And Winter himself voices the same equivocal conception of the child, at once singular and universal, when he urges reforms that recognize "the unique properties of childhood."

For Winter as for his progressive predecessors, reform pedagogy eventuates in a quest for scientific generalities—"a 'child-worthy' anthropology of the child"—that are themselves expressive of industrial thought. By his very ordering of the vagrancies of childish variation, he too subverts emancipation of the young under the banner of emancipation. By seeking scientific study of development, he too obviates conceptual recognition of individuality even as he celebrates individuality. It is not easy to pry children and adults apart, in the century of the child any more than in any other.

Culture and Conduct

Even when adults do not engage youth, adults define youth. The very fantasies of the elders implicate their offspring. Just as Ariès insisted, the projections and displacements that parents impose on children reveal the preoccupations of the parents.

In one essay after another in this collection, our authors develop and deepen Ariès's insight. Calvert suggests that the discourse of adults about the young tells us less about the young than about the process by which adults adjust themselves to social change. Stearns remarks that Americans expressed a heightened fear for the lives of their little ones in the very years after 1880 when the actual danger of infant and child mortality plummeted.

Comparable disconnections of conduct and conceptions appear beyond America. Like Stearns, and for that matter like Ariès, Nylan notes that demographic change does not drive ideational change, though the particular pattern of misphasing is different in contemporary China than in early modern France or modern America. As child mortality falls, under the Communist regime, care for children gets worse. As each child becomes each family's only child, in the years since Mao, care gets worse still. And Kojima also discovers that culture can evolve autonomously. Though he affirms in theory that behavior cannot be dissociated from its historical context, he finds in fact that it can. For a millennium and more of massive social structural change, Japanese notions of childrearing and of the life cycle changed scarcely at all.

But neither Kojima nor any of our other authors postulate a rupture of culture and experience as explicitly, as elaborately, or as brazenly as John Gillis does. In his account of the images of children that emerged in the Victorian era, Gillis predicates his entire analysis on one tantalizing contradiction, between a growing cultural presence of the child and an advancing behavioral absence of children in adult life in the West.

From his very title, Gillis proclaims that our most promising business is with what he calls virtual children. From his opening epigraph, he holds that our most intriguing subject is the thought child, not the actual one. In the body of his essay, he argues that men and women valued children in the nineteenth and twentieth centuries as grownups never valued children before and that men and women lived apart from children in those years as they never had before.

Gillis declares, unequivocally, that the twentieth-century child does cultural work—as a symbol, ritual center, and source of identity for adults—that is almost entirely distinct from the real behavior of children and, for that matter, from the real behavior of adults in their dealings with children. On such an understanding of the matter, there is no end in sight to the century of the child. Childhood absorbs us, preoccupies us, and affords us our identities and our emotional centers, now more than ever.

Developmentalists may demur that these quagmires of cultural construction and virtuality that snare—or tempt—historians do not touch their own austere science. But such demurrals would be mistaken. Developmental psychology has never been as immaculately above the coloration of culture as its behavioral heralds would have it. On almost every account, the discipline evolved under the aegis of G. Stanley Hall. And, as almost every study of that coiner of the modern concept of adolescence admits, Hall was a laughably bad scientist. He put his religious convictions before his scientific commitments, and he routinely preferred his prophecies to his empirical evidence.

Indeed, the discipline cannot stand outside the coloration of culture. As Breeuwsma shows with scathing wit, and Kojima with gentle schematics, developmental psychologists can no more touch nature neat than historians can. They too gather their data through a myriad of mediations. They filter their findings through their own morality, through the morality of their cultural milieu, and through what Bower calls their blinding preconceptions of what infants and children can and cannot do. They conform their conclusions to prevailing political and social winds if they hope to have funding and achieve influence.

Even with the most scrupulous integrity, devoted empiricists cannot decontaminate their data. At one remove or another, their scientific ideas reach parents and influence parent behavior, in Breeuwsma's West and Kojima's East alike. And the parent beliefs and behavior that are touched by those ideas affect child assumptions and performance, which feed back upstream, confirming the parent beliefs and scientific theories. And those parents themselves, under observation, try to act in accordance with what they take to be the expectations of the psychologists who observe them, feeding further back upstream, making the theories self-fulfilling prophecies three times over, inextricably enmeshed in the conventions of their culture.

To developmentalists every bit as much as to historians, the child presents an ill-defined but irresistibly suggestive ink-blot on which we project our aspirations for and discontents with civilization. On just that account, the child is bound to be, as Gillis says, an object of ambivalence: a vessel of what we hold most holy and hopeful and what we presume most profane and problematic, of what seems to us divine and what disturbing.

If few of our authors would concede as much to culture as Gillis does, others of very different dispositions discover in their data a very similar ambivalence toward the child. What Gillis sees in the sphere of cultural imagination, in our projections onto our virtual children, Peter Stearns finds in the domain of behavior, in our observations of real children.

Stearns speaks of the same opposition of the civilized and the savage, the restrained and the released, the rational and the erotic. But he sets this agon in child experience rather than in the adult psyche. He sees in the lives of twentieth-century youth an imposition by their elders of a regime of increasingly demanding discipline and, at the same time, of a compensating consumerism that shelters the young in a market niche of their own.

But Stearns emphasizes as Gillis does not—and as, compatibly with his argument, he cannot—the growing disparities between rich and poor children, suburban and city children, white and black children. Stearns insists on the salience of these gaping divides precisely because the debasement of poor youngsters that Americans permit would be impossible if the idealization of virtual children were as powerfully pervasive as Gillis posits. In so doing, Stearns reminds us that reality cannot be virtualized so sublimely. No matter how much we adore children as symbols, we do not find it impossible to disdain them as living, breathing creatures if they are poor. We do not even find their plight very much a cultural embarrassment.

With regard to modern schooling too, Stearns counterposes to emphases on the cultural sacralization of childhood a closer look at the sociological situation of actual children in actual schools. He maintains that, in fact, schools are institutions of coercive incarceration. They are run by adults, and those adults inflict a deleterious discipline on their charges: a relentless round of work, competition, and precocious responsibility. Again, Stearns reminds us that we uncouple representation from performance at our peril.

Somehow, in ways we have not fully worked out, we have got to work both sides of this street. We must encompass the realistic and the reflexive. We must seek behavior, naively, and remain aware of our construction of it, self-consciously.

In this endeavor, all of us have come together because we are willing to run risks in our quest for a fuller understanding of our society and ourselves. Our collaboration is not endangered by disciplinary divides between history and developmental psychology any more than it is by temperamental divides within history—between Gillis and Stearns, say—and in developmental psychology as well. And none of those divides keep us very far apart.

Take the divergence between Gillis and Stearns. Despite it, they discern very similar tensions at the center of their notions of modern youth and they arrive at very similar resolutions of those tensions. Gillis sees children primarily as cultural continuations of their elders. He treats them as fictional figments of adult imaginations and displacements of adults anxieties. Stearns does not see twentieth-century children as imagined by adults, but he does say that their days have been designed by adults. Even the spheres in which they escape sustained adult surveillance—the spheres of recreation and consumption—are essentially provided and paid for by adults, presumably to serve adult purposes. Adults lead lives revolving around acquisition, spectatorship, and consumption, and they socialize their children for such lives. As Stearns says, both the repressing and the releasing aspects of child life "prepared children for the experience they would face as adults." The tension was "functional and oddly consistent."

Whether in fiction, as for Gillis, or in fact, as for Stearns, children of this past century have not inhabited a world of their own. Just as the youth of the Middle Ages were a little apart from but essentially a part of their society in Hanawalt's account of medieval life, just as juveniles of the Dutch golden age were cherished as children but chastened as little adults in Kloek's account of the early modern era, so children of our own time have been bound to their elders. Calvert and Koops too argue that, in the end, twentieth-century child life has been more continuous with adult life than cloistered from it.

Whistling Past the Graveyard

And yet, perhaps, we protest too much. It might be that our contributors seek to reassure themselves. It might be that I seek to reassure myself. For, surely, there *is* something deeply disturbed, and disturbing, in the relation of the generations in the modern world, as Winter says. Surely there *is* something that has come unhinged. Ellen Key saw it a century ago. Jean-Jacques Rousseau felt it a century before that, and Dr. Benjamin Spock a half-century after. They all wrote with a quiet desperation. We, in this volume, all whistle past the graveyard.

The new conception of the child mind that developmentalists have advanced in recent years is not just an ideological phantasm. It grows out of ingenious theorizing and brilliant experimentation. It rests on striking demonstrations that infants and toddlers have a host of cognitive capacities that Piaget and his followers did not believe possible in little ones. As Koops says, it provides powerful evidence of continuity in cognitive competence from birth to maturity, and it bids fair to dethrone Piagetian presumptions of discontinuous and qualitatively distinct stages of cognitive development.

The new conception of adolescence that developmentalists have elaborated also arises out of acute observation and a compelling interpretation of convincing data. It rests on the fascinating finding that a transforming interlude of storm and stress is the exception rather than the rule among teenagers. It suggests that persistence rather than rupture may be the norm in the growth of personality, and it augurs the abandonment of old assumptions of stage-specific derangements of development that set adolescence off in a psychic precinct all its own (Offer and Offer 1975; Petersen and Ebata 1987; Petersen 1988; Compas, Hinden, and Gerhardt 1995).

Nonetheless, it is inconceivable that all this painstaking investigation and inventive postulation has occurred in a vacuum. Science and scholarship proceed in a social context. Scientists and scholars can no more quarantine their activity than children can. If the theorization of children's cognition and adolescent development is taking a new turn, we might wonder why.

We cannot account for it adequately by cynical assertions that the overthrow of old paradigms serves to promote new careers. Nor can we explain it by appeals to the mystical truism that these things go round in cycles. But perhaps we can see in these new constructions a new need to affirm a connection between the generations. Perhaps we can make some sense of the impulse to conceptualize cognitive and personality development as continuous by supposing it driven by our very fears that we have drifted apart.

There may be no chasm between the young and their elders such as some of our contributors sometimes claim. Indeed, if we consider childhood capaciously enough, there may be no theoretical possibility of such a categorical separation of the generations. Notions of incommensurable cultural formations or psychic stages, differentiated according to age, may be neither conceptually coherent nor empirically credible.

But a disturbingly large company of our authors, leading figures all of them in their various fields, remain persuaded that something has gone awry in relations between the young and their elders. They do not speak merely of the discontinuities in cultural conditioning that Ruth Benedict long ago pronounced ineluctable in modern life (Benedict 1938). They sense, and struggle to speak of, something much deeper.

They deal with different subjects in different ways. They do their work in different disciplines. They were, for the most part, strangers before they came together in this endeavor. Yet many of them converge easily, almost eerily. Breeuwsma, Calvert, and Gillis all observe that we do not deal with real youngsters, only with our own fond or phobic fictions of them. Winter laments that we do not treat them as our fellow citizens. Nylan rages that too many of us love too few of them.

Conflict and Confusion

Could they be right? Is it possible that more than a few of us, individually, do not love our children and that all of us, collectively, do not love or cherish the children of the poor and of the racial out-castes?

Surely Ariès is not wrong in this regard. Surely we can follow him this far. An ever-widening cultural imperative to admire and to cherish children *has* marked the modern West (and, as Kojima and Nylan show, significant sectors of the East as well). But a cultural imperative is synonymous neither with behavior nor with inclination. We chafe at cultural imperatives. And in the worldwide decay of decorum since the 1960s we have not just honored them more in the breach than in the observance. We have also, often, willfully dishonored them.

Just as Stearns suggests, we are caught in contradictions and in the moral muddle they entail. We will not dispense with the way of life that affords us our economic well-being, a way of life that depends on the instinctual renunciations that inform what Weber called the spirit of capitalism (Weber 1958). In our expanding corporate bureaucracies, we are subject to ever more exaggerated demands for self-denial. The exigencies of modern work allow ever less place to spontaneity, indiscipline, and irresponsibility. And yet we yearn for the extravagant expressivity and headlong hedonism to which we are enticed by media that also hold cultural imperatives before us. We must have gratifications we cannot have. We want what we want when we want it.

In generations past, as Ariès saw so brilliantly, we secured such gratifications by consigning them to children. Defining adulthood by burdens of conscience and control, and childhood by exemption from such obligations, we kept in touch with our primitive nature by treasuring the children on whom we displaced it. But the solutions that served for the past two or three centuries no longer suffice.

Now we want more. We want the substance, not just the sublimated shadow, of the self-indulgence that we never really relinquished. We want to reclaim what we so long denied ourselves. We are no longer willing to treat children as the repositories of the uncivilized. In what amounts to a determined if still inchoate drive to redefine civilization itself, we want back what once we gave away. And we do not like those to whom we gave it, who now have what we desire.

The evidence of our animosity is all about us. It is manifest in a multitude of small things and in some very large ones as well, such as our social policies. Every American administration of recent decades has been willing to borrow from the future rather than require taxpayers to pay for present benefits. The immense deficits that attended Ronald Reagan's defense spending binge were merely the most blatant expressions of this blithe bequest to the young of the costs of the country's current consumption. And these evidences of malevolence toward children are not just abstract and economic. Bill Clinton's welfare reforms did more than just pander to middle-class parents at the expense of lower-class children. They imperiled the development of those innocent youngsters in order to assuage resentment of their parents and send a message of uncertain efficacy to those parents. They staked the development and indeed the very survival of those children on a dubious experiment in which only the most rabid ideologists of the free market could have any confidence. Despite declarations of devotion, Americans simply do not treat children as if they adored them.

In the United States, neglect of the young is as lethal as it is legendary. Latchkey children—children who let themselves in and out of the house because no adult is at home—are a national plague. So are deadbeat dads, who desert their families and do not even pay the modest child support the courts impose. So are the courts, which ignore their own mandates and allow the great majority of deadbeat dads to walk away from their obligations.

So is television. American children spend five or six hours a day in front of the set. They have done so for decades, and we have known it for decades. And the deleterious effects of that exposure have been demonstrated in hundreds if not thousands of studies. (For a summary of such research, see Putnam 2000, esp. chapter 13.) Few Americans doubt the damage done, but fewer think to do without it. Television is, for most parents (and for more than a few daycare providers), an indispensable babysitter. It is, for most children, the source of the most consistent stimulation they get.

Every month, every week, almost every day, the newspapers and the networks tell of another tragedy that comes of parents who are too busy to be with their children. Some, such as the shootings that took fourteen lives in Littleton, Colorado, make the national media. Most, like the "Texas heroin massacre," remain essentially local lore (Gray 1999). But whether they concern affluent suburbs of Denver, rife with neo-Nazism, or rich suburbs of Dallas, awash in teenage drug dealing and adult denial, these stories all evoke an agonized wringing of hands because they all touch a nerve. As Stearns says, Americans are now involved more with their spouses and less with their children. He might have added, they are involved more with their work than with either their spouses or their children.

Every day, every hour, almost every minute, the authorities avert their eyes from other traumas that come of parents who are all too sadistically engaged with their children. Even at the highest levels of cultural legitimacy, Americans ignore or tolerate the epidemic brutalization of the nation's young. It is, for example, settled doctrine among social workers that abusive parents are to be treated as victims of their own prior oppression rather than as assailants of their offspring. Professing to promote the interests of the little ones, child welfare workers actually privilege the claims of those parents over the safety of the children they batter. Above all, agencies seek to rehabilitate parents and preserve their pathological family units. They remove a youngster from these killing fields only as a last resort (Gelles 1996).

And the churches and courts that are complicitous in these policies and priorities are, for the most part, unmoved by the most harrowing accounts of youthful suffering. Over and over again, ministers have exhorted their congregants to be mindful of the biblical injunction to chasten their children. Over and over again, judges and justices have upheld the prerogatives of parents and teachers alike to administer corporal punishment. The Supreme Court itself declared, in a 1977 decision that controls the law to this day, that American schoolchildren can claim no constitutional protection against physical assaults inflicted by teachers and administrators in the name of discipline (Greven 1991, esp. 98–107).

Our conflicted feelings about children are evident in the way we live our own lives as well as in the way we treat our youth. As Winter demonstrates, every one of the problems that lead to the infantilization of children is a problem that afflicts adults too. Industrialization, democratization, the loss of faith in progress, and the acceleration of scientific and technological change are all social issues as much as pedagogic problems. Mature men and women flee from intractable dilemmas into escapism, irresponsibility, and hedonism just as children do.

Ariès asked of the Middle Ages and the early modern era where the children were. Plessner and van den Berg ask of our own time where the adults are. A generation ago, we worried that adolescence might be vanishing and that children might never have a chance to be childish. Today, we might wonder whether any of us will ever reach adulthood.

Plessner and van den Berg, and Dasberg and Winter, all sense that feeling useful in the community is an essential condition of the attainment of adulthood. But all of them sense as well that the conditions of modern life militate against such a feeling. All of them fear that few people, young or old, have much chance of coming to a conviction of competence. And their anxiety echoes in the official and popular culture alike. It rings in proclamations by Western governments everywhere of policies of "permanent education" predicated on conceptions of maturity and adulthood as something sought over the entire life course rather than achieved at a certain age or status. It sounds in songs such as The Who's "Talkin' 'Bout My Generation," with its wistful "hope I grow up before I grow old."

Where do these developments leave us? Does youthland vanish, as pundits from the 1950s to our own time have warned (Friedenberg 1959; Postman 1982; Kotlowitz 1991)? Or does it metastasize, cancerously, to encompass us all? Do we shrink the sphere of childhood incompetence, or do we extend it to adults? If the pedagogic province is breaking up, as Winter muses it may be, is that because children are rising to a precocious maturity or because adults are descending to an unprecedented childishness?

Or are these questions very nearly meaningless? Can they be answered in any intelligible way? Or might their significance be that they can now be asked, if only incoherently? Might that very fact reveal that we are all in it together?

Certainly it is striking that, at the commencement of a new millennium, we can neither distinguish youth from adulthood nor define either one with any confidence. From a very early age, almost all of us are anxious, acquisitive, escapist consumers. Grown-ups are as irresponsible, sexually and familially, as adolescents. Parents no more prize citizenship for themselves than they permit it to their children.

A New Childhood?

The tension in our academic disciplines is the tension in our psyches, which is in turn the tension in our society and our culture. We sense, dimly but disturbingly, that we have conceded too much to our children. They become increasingly the bearers of our civilized discontents, because we have allotted to them what we now think we want, which isn't civilization after all. They embody more and more the return of our repressions, as we grow less and less disposed to pay the price of our maturity.

Where will it all end? History has a way of humbling those of us who study it. It makes us loath to predict the next morning, let alone the next decade or century. Who, a hundred years ago, could have foreseen that the twentieth century would be the century of Adolf Hitler and Joseph Stalin? Who could have imagined the thousand-year Reich? Who, even among Marxists, could have conceived socialism in one country, and such a socialism at that? Who could have dreamed that these mighty powers would fall, finally, before the juggernaut of soft drinks and sneakers and denims emanating from America? Who could have guessed that Coca-Cola and Nike and Levi's would win the globe that weapons could not conquer? And who could have conceived that an old man in Afghanistan and a handful of hijackers could cause that colossus to tremble?

But if we allow ourselves the imbecilic indulgence of taking the present writ larger for the future, we seem to stand now at the threshold of a new childhood. That childhood would appall Key, as in other ways it would appall Piaget and Ariès and Rousseau. But it is a childhood nonetheless, and its prospect seems as expansive—indeed, as infinite—as our consumer cravings.

As we enter the twenty-first century, as we recalculate the costs of modern life, we are necessarily renegotiating the compact that connects the generations. A millennium of childhood stretches before us.

Notes

Preface

1. The contributions to the conference by Dubas, Miller, and Petersen; Kett; and Vinovskis appear as a special section in *History of the Family: An International Quarterly* (2003). The introduction to that section, "An Historical Developmental Approach to Adolescence," frames the three papers on the history of adolescence and connects them to the present volume.

Chapter 1. Imaging Childhood

1. This concept rouses a pejorative meaning because of its root "infantile." The children's writer Guus Kuijer has been the most radical author in the Dutch language area in pointing out how our society has given every word that has to do with children a pejorative connotation: "Humanity is becoming infantile, some say (and note the connotation of inferiority that the word infantile has acquired), but the converse is also true: humanity is losing touch with children" (1980, 25). My definition of infantilization clearly shows that I use the term as a straightforward professional and descriptive term, without any pejorative association. This technical meaning is also shared by Kuijer, as the above quotation shows: in fact he wants to say, and that is what his whole collection of essays is about, that children in the recent history of Western culture have been so far removed from the world of adults that the world has lost its touch with childhood. This development is precisely what I mean when I use the term infantilization.

2. This patient inventory was performed by Dr. B. R. Hamel (1998).

3. The work of widely cited and explicit critics of Ariès such as Pollock (1983, 1987), Peeters (1966), Dasberg (1975), and Dekker (1995) is also open to much criticism. An important point here is that frequently the discontinuity and change hypotheses are not distinguished. A very important argument (against both Pollock and Peeters) is that the period studied is not sufficiently long to be able to test the change hypothesis reasonably (see Koops 1998).

4. The names Montaigne, Locke, and Rousseau are often proposed as milestones in the progressive modernization of our approach to children. Pointers to such a progressive interpretation can be found in textbooks such as Boyd (1968), Snyders (1971), and van der Velde (1975).

5. A pedagogic discretion that turned into the complete pedagogic resignation

of Piaget and the developmental psychology stimulated by Piaget's work (see Koops 1992, 1998).

6. "Pädagogik als Wissenschaft hängt ab von der praktischen Philosophie und Psychologie. Jene zeigt das Ziel der Bildung, diese den Weg, die Mittel und die Hindernisse." This citation can be found in Herbart's last, greatest, and most important pedagogic work, the *Umriss pädagogischer Vorlesungen* of 1835 (although the formulation given here is a more refined one from 1841; see Oelkers 1989, 61). This book can be found in part X of the *Sämtliche Werke* (19 volumes) edited by Kehrbach, Flügel, and Fritzsch in 1887–1912. Here the translations of the most important citations by Strasser and Monshouwer (1967) are used. Strasser and Monshouwer's book is still very relevant and provides a balanced evaluation of Herbart's work; data on the original publications by Herbart and the most important secondary literature about Herbart up to 1967 can be found in their publication. A professional and balanced summary of Herbart's attempts to introduce a scientifically based pedagogy and of the work of his most important followers can be found in Oelkers (1989).

7. Depaepe based his evaluation on thorough historical research, particularly that of Jäger and Tenorth in the 1987 *Handbuch der deutschen Bildungsgeschichte, dl. III*. See Depaepe (1998, 182 n. 28).

8. Thus is the strange, paradoxical expression "traditional renewal schools" possible (see Imelman and Meijer 1986; Kohnstamm, Koops, Peters, and Sixma 1987).

9. I want to emphasize here that Oelkers was certainly not the only one, or even the first, who saw that the reform pedagogues' antagonistic image of Herbart was not justified in as far as it concerned Herbart's own work. For example, Strasser and Monshouwer make it clear that Herbart has unfortunately for many decades "succumbed to the interpretation of the so-called Neo-Herbartians" (1967, 6). They show that Herbart "certainly did not go to work as rigidly as the later neo-Herbartians' interpretations . . . would imply" (17). The authors were able to call on historic research by Caselman (1962, 7 n. 1).

10. Depaepe (1986, 10) used the term "pedagogizing" instead of "infantilization," meaning "the increased (and still increasing) influence of 'the pedagogical' on the daily life of children and adolescents—a process that, although it started (much) earlier, secured its place particularly since the second half of the 18th century."

11. This swinging has of course everything to do with what Depaepe called the "subtle paradox of pedagogy," the "paradox of compulsion and freedom" (1998, 35).

12. Earlier (Koops 1992) I thought of Ellen Key simply as a late adept of Rousseau. That is not untrue, but it illustrates insufficiently the reactive character of Key's work. Like Rousseau, Key wanted to improve the world via the child. On the one hand she wanted to achieve this by means of eugenics (unlike Rousseau, she could employ evolutionary and genetic insights); on the other hand she wanted to achieve it by liberating the child from pedagogic and scholastic oppression. Rousseau wanted to give the child its own niche so that it could develop undisturbed; Key wanted adults to put the child on such a high pedestal that a special niche was unnecessary: devotion to the child was to happen all the time and everywhere.

13. Dasberg's publication runs along the same lines as Ariès and van den

Berg in many respects. She herself, however, hardly refers to Ariès and cites van den Berg only in passing (and then only to oppose him). In general, Dutch pedagogues prefer to cite Dasberg, normally without the link with van den Berg and Ariès. Developmental psychologists refer relatively more often to van den Berg and Ariès and more rarely to Dasberg. This underscores the provincial separatism of the Dutch academic disciplines of pedagogics and developmental psychology, a separation to be found in the universities of many European countries..

14. In a recent and excellent article, Arnett (1999) gives an overview of the available empirical evidence on "Storm and Stress." The author reaches the conclusion that there is evidence for a "modified storm and stress view," but we must realize that hormones and genes play only a very small role in this, that there is no universal phenomenon of adolescence, and that there are large individual differences. In addition he strongly emphasizes cross-cultural differences. It is remarkable that the author discusses a hundred-year-old hypothesis but does not use any historical data in his argument. It seems that he assumes that Hall's hypotheses can be tested on American data from 95 years later. The idea that Hall was right in 1904 concerning adolescents of his own time but that his hypotheses no longer apply to today's adolescents does not seem to have occurred to Arnett.

15. In this connection it should be considered significant that in the past twenty years a large number of books have appeared that ideologically wish to free children from the chains of their lack of adulthood. As illustrations I would point to Illich (1973), which calls for society to be *free of schools*—to abolish compulsory learning because it hinders children from participating in the adult world; Holt (1974), which pleads for liberating children from the chains of a 300-year tradition of subordination; and Farson (1974), which demands the vote for children, among other things, "because adults do not represent their interests and cannot vote for them" (1974, 179).

16. One of the first and internationally influential publications was the pioneering thesis by G. A. Kohnstamm, grandson of Philip Kohnstamm, the famous Dutch pedagogue and a student of Martinus Langeveld, the other influential Dutch pedagogue of the period. In his studies Kohnstamm (1967) showed that so-called inclusion tasks can be taught to children two years younger than the age that marked the start of the concrete operational phase according to Piaget. Following on from Kohnstamm and Langeveld—but now for the first time using experimental studies—he refuted Piaget's phase structure and the way Piaget used all sorts of logical and quasi-logical structural models as descriptive categories for psychological and developmental processes. The third statement accompanying Kohnstamm's thesis was "The structures of logical operations, as observed and determined by Piaget, do only exist on paper and in the minds of some psychologists."

17. I use the term neo-Piagetian to refer to the worldwide research arising from the American cognitive shift at the end of the 1950s on the tenability of Piaget's insights. The term post-neo-Piagetian refers to the "Child's Theory of Mind" tradition.

18. See, e.g., the already classic overview by Wellman (1990), the review paper by Rieffe et al. (1996), and the thesis by Rieffe (1998).

Chapter 4. Patterns of Childrearing in America

1. For studies of the process of acculturation of children see Greven (1977) and A. MacLeod (1976).

2. In the passage quoted, Buchan was describing attitudes common in his youth in the 1740s.

3. For further information on childhood and family in the seventeenth and eighteenth centuries, see Ariès (1962); Greven (1970); Beales (1975); Scholten (1985); Hoffer and Hull (1981); Morgan (1966); de Mause(1974); Calvert (1992); Hawes and Hiner (1985).

4. Fithian (1900); Flaherty (1972). For further information on childhood and family in the era of the new Republic see D. Smith (1980); Kett (1977); Hitchcock (1790).

5. Perhaps the leading authority was Bushnell (1847).

6. "Babies," *Appleton's* 1 (April 1899, 12); Panton (1893, 130); "Good Night Papa," *Nursery* 25 (March 1879): 86–87.

7. For further information on children's toys, see McClinton (1970); King (1977); Webster (1899, 57); McClintock and McClintock (1961); Sutton-Smith (1980). For information on the development of children's literature, see Avery (1954); Muir (1960); Kiefer (1958); A. MacLeod (1976).

Chapter 11. Developmental Psychology in a World of Designed Institutions

1. In his *Education of Man*, Froebel wrote, "Play is the purest, the most spiritual, product of man at this stage, and is at once the prefiguration and imitation of the total human life,—of the inner, secret, natural life in man and in all things. It produces, therefore, joy, freedom, satisfaction, repose within and without, peace with the world. The springs of all good rest within it and go out from it" (quoted in Brosterman 1997, 33).

2. Froebel's educational toys are usually described as being made up of ten gifts and ten occupations. But this appears to be a simplification and not all sources agree with those numbers. The most detailed and complete description of Froebel's inventions I have seen is to be found in Brosterman (1997).

3. Froebel died not long after the Prussian decree of August 7, 1851, banning kindergartens, on June 21 1852, without hope for a resumption of kindergartening. But followers of his—notably, the formidable Baroness Bertha von Marenholtz-Bulow—made kindergartens into a worldwide movement and before long got them restored in Prussia. Froebel's followers inevitably mixed their own educational purposes and designs together with his. In recent years, a number of writers have argued that kindergarten experiences may have taught children to see complex forms in a new way, and thus have had a substantial impact on both the producers and the consumers of twentieth-century art and architecture (Miller 1991; Brosterman 1997; Rubin 1999). If true, this would represent a remarkable long-term effect of early education, an effect drawing on Froebel's unique background as a crystallographer.

4. In 1898, Harris wrote a Hegelian educational psychology, *Psychologic Foundations of Education: An Attempt to Show the Genesis of the Higher Faculties of the Mind*, that was little noticed among American psychologists, committed as

they were to a different philosophical approach to learning and schooling. In today's post-Vygotskian era, Harris's book is well worth a reexamination.

5. As one might expect from his philosophical interests, Harris had a theoretical point of view about what might be accomplished using kindergartens. Blow and Harris advocated a theory of childhood education they called symbolic education. The principle was Hegelian. The child's thoughts exist as feelings and emotions. Through training of the intellectual faculties, a process that leads to reflection, the childhood feelings are given general form or "universality," thus allowing them to become ideas. The difficulty is that the ideas of children are hard to reach during the years between ages four and six, a period in which Hegelians believe the child lives in a world of outer and inner symbols (embryonic ideas). Before age four, the child has an understanding of the material world around him through sense impressions alone and is able to recall and analyze past sense impressions through memory, though he or she is still unable to form abstract thoughts. This psychological and educational transition period—between sense learning and abstract learning—was called the *symbolic stage* because Hegelians postulate that during this brief period the child perceives the world entirely through symbols.

6. In 1903 a magazine editor recognized the kindergarten as "our earliest opportunity to catch the little Russian, the little Italian, the little German, Pole, Syrian and the rest and begin to make American citizens of them."

7. Church and Sedlak (1976) describe the shift toward poor children in these terms:

> Kindergartens for the affluent concentrated on making the child's transition from being the egotistical center of the home to being one of many children in the classroom as easy and as flexible as possible. The kindergarten was ultimately supposed to socialize the rich child, to instill self-discipline and order, but it was to do so gradually and gently. . . . Goals for the slum child were far different. Their kindergarten was supposed to accelerate the socialization process, to get these difficult clients into school (and away from the unfortunate influence of their improper home lives and the ghetto street) as soon as possible. . . . The kindergarten was an alternative to the slum where the child could begin to learn the moral habits that, the kindergartners assumed, he could not learn at home. (323–24)

8. A table given by Hall (1911, 74–75). lists 81 different kinds of agencies and institutions for children in American society. Theodate Smith (1910), working in Hall's Children's Institute at Clark University, had conducted voluminous correspondence, compiled information about institutions and agencies for children, and categorized them. Hall's table is a reproduction of Smith's, with slight editings.

9. I am discussing what most developmental psychologists take to be the main line of historical work leading toward their present program. Although it is common to refer to the work of these three eras by different names—"child study," "the child development movement," "developmental psychology"— I believe there is sufficient continuity that the name of the contemporary era can be applied to the several eras of the tradition. A complete description of psychologists' research on children in the past would have to recognize some non-main-line programs such as work in early comparative psychology, educational psychology, the psychoanalytic study of the child, and research programs associated with several of the "whole-child professions."

10. The twelve steps, in Wilson's words, were

1. We admitted we were powerless over alcohol—that our lives had become unmanageable.
2. Came to believe that God could restore us to sanity.
3. Made a decision to turn our wills and our lives over to the care of God.
4. Made a searching and fearless moral inventory of ourselves.
5. Admitted to God, to ourselves, and to another human being the exact nature of our wrongs.
6. Were entirely ready to have God remove all these defects of character.
7. Humbly on our knees asked Him to remove our shortcomings.
8. Made a list of all persons we had harmed, and became willing to make amends to them all.
9. Made direct amends to such people wherever possible, except when to do so would injure them or others.
10. Continued to take personal inventory and when we were wrong promptly admitted it.
11. Sought through prayer and meditation to improve our conscious contact with God, praying only for knowledge of His will for us and the power to carry that out.
12. Having had a spiritual experience as the result of these steps, we tried to carry this message to alcoholics, and to practice these principles in all our affairs. (1942, 71–72).

Bibliography

Alberti, Leon Battista. 1969. *The Family in Renaissance Florence*. Trans. R. N. Watkins. Columbia: University of South Carolina Press.

Alcott, William. 1839. *The Young Mother or Management of Children in Regard to Health*. Boston: George W. Light.

Alexandre-Bidon, Danièle and Monique Closson. 1985. *L'enfant à l'ombre des cathédrales*. Lyon: Presses Universitaires de Lyon.

Alexandre-Bidon, Danièle and Didier Lett. 1997. *Les enfants au Moyen Age, Ve–XVe siècles*. Paris: Hachette.

Algemeene opvoedinge der hedendaagse kinderen of mal moertje mal kindje. 1690. Amsterdam: Adriaan Jansz. Van Wezel.

Allen, A. T. 1982. "Spiritual Motherhood: German Feminists and the Kindergarten Movement, 1848–1911." *History of Education Quarterly* 22: 319–39.

Amaya, U. 2003. "Questions Toward 'I': Ego-Experience as Assessed by a Semi-Structured Interview." *Japanese Journal of Developmental Psychology* (in Japanese).

Appleton, William W. 1951. *The Cycle of Cathay: The Chinese Vogue in England During the Seventeenth and Eighteenth Centuries*. New York: Columbia University Press.

Ariès, Philippe. 1960. *L'enfant et la vie familiale sous l'ancien régime*. Paris: Libraire Plon.

———. 1962. *Centuries of Childhood: A Social History of Family Life*. New York: Vintage Books.

Arnett, Jeffrey J. 1999. "Adolescent Storm and Stress, Reconsidered." *American Psychologist* 54: 317–26.

Arnold, Klaus. 1980. *Kind und Gesellschaft im Mittelalter und Renaissance*. Paderborn: Schöningh.

Avery, Gillian. 1954. *Nineteenth-Century Children's Heroes and Heroines in English Children's Stories, 1780–1900*. London: B.T. Batsford.

Barker, Roger G. and Herbert F. Wright. 1954. *Midwest and Its Children: The Psychological Study of an American Town*. Evanston, Ill.: Row, Peterson.

Barus, A. H. 1894. "Report on the Study of Child Development of the Association of Collegiate Alumnae." In *National Education Association: Journal of Proceedings and Addresses of the Year 1894*: 996–99.

Bary, William Theodore de and John W. Chaffee, eds. 1989. *Neo-Confucian Education: The Formative Stage*. Berkeley: University of California Press.

Beales, Ross W., Jr. 1975. "In Search of the Historical Child: Miniature Adulthood and Youth in Colonial New England." *American Quarterly* 27: 379–98.

Beatty, Barbara. 1995. *Preschool Education in America: The Culture of Young Children from the Colonial Era to the Present*. New Haven, Conn.: Yale University Press.

Beck, Ulrich and Elisabeth Beck-Gernshim. 1995. *The Normal Chaos of Love*. Trans. Mark Ritter and Jane Wiebel. Cambridge: Polity Press.

Bedaux, J. B. 1990. "Discipline for Innocence: Metaphors for Education in Seventeenth-Century Dutch Painting." In Bedaux, *The Reality of Symbols: Studies in the Iconology of Netherlandish Art, 1400–1800*. 's-Gravenhage: Gary Schwartz/SDU. 109–70

Beecher, Catherine E. 1848. *A Treatise on Domestic Economy*. New York: Harper and Bros.

Bell, Richard Q. and Lawrence V. Harper. 1977. *Child Effects on Adults*. Hillsdale, N.J.: Lawrence Erlbaum.

Benedict, Ruth. 1938. "Continuities and Discontinuities in Cultural Conditioning." *Psychiatry* 1: 161–67.

Bennett, Gary, ed. 1996. *China Facts and Figures Annual*. Gulf Breeze, Fla.: Academic International Press.

Berg, Jan Hendrik van den. 1956. *Metabletica: Of leer der veranderingen: Beginselen van een historische psychologie*. Nijkerk: Callenbach.

———. 1961. *The Changing Nature of Man: Introduction to Historical Psychology*. (English edition of *Metabletica*). New York: W.W. Norton.

———. 1971. *'s Morgens jagen, 's middags vissen*. Nijkerk: Callenbach.

———. 1977. *Gedane zaken: Twee omwentelingen in de westerse geestesgeschiedenis (Metabletica van de materie, deel 2)*. Nijkerk: Callenbach.

Beugelsdijk, Fons, C. R. M. Souverein, and Bas Levering. 1997. "Geesteswetenschappelijke pedagogiek." In Siebren Miedema, ed., *Pedagogiek in Meervoud*. 5th ed. Houten/Diegem: Bohn, Stafleu Van Loghum. 23–72.

Bientjes, Julia. 1967. *Holland und der Holländer im Urteil Deutscher Reisender (1400–1800)*. Groningen: J.B. Wolters.

Biesta, Gert J. J. 1995. "Opvoeding en intersubjectiviteit: Over de structuur en identiteit van de pedagogiek van John Dewey." *Comenius* 15: 21–36.

Biesta, Gert J. J., Siebren Miedema, and Joop W. A. Berding. 1997. "Pragmatische pedagogiek." In Siebren Miedema, ed., *Pedagogiek in Meervoud*. 5th ed. Houten/Diegem: Bohn, Stafleu Van Loghum. 313–53.

Biggs, John B. 1996. "Learning, Schooling, and Socialization: A Chinese Solution to a Western Problem." In Lau Sing, ed., *Growing Up the Chinese Way: Chinese Child and Adolescent Development*. Hong Kong: Chinese University of Hong Kong. 147–67.

Black, Alison Harley. 1986. "Gender and Cosmology in Chinese Correlative Thinking." In Caroline Walker Bynum, Stevan Harrell, and Paula Richman, eds., *Gender and Religion: On the Complexity of Symbols*. Boston: Beacon Press. 165–95.

Blankaart, Stephanus. 1684. *Verhandelinge van de opvoedinge en ziekten der kinderen vertoonende op wat wyse de kinderen gezond konnen blyven*. Amsterdam: Hyronymus Sweerts.

Blow, Susan E., ed. 1895. *The Mottoes and Commentaries of Friedrich Froebel's Mother Play*. Trans. Henrietta R. Eliot and Blow. New York: Appleton.

Boas, George. 1966. *The Cult of Childhood*. London: Warburg Institute.

Boring, Edwin G. 1950. *A History of Experimental Psychology*. 2nd ed. New York: Appleton-Century-Crofts.

Borthwick, Sally. 1983. *Education and Social Changes in China: The Beginnings of the Modern Era*. Stanford, Calif.: Hoover Institution.

Boswell, John. 1988. *The Kindness of Strangers: The Abandonment of Children in Western Europe from Antiquity to the Renaissance*. New York: Pantheon Books.

Bower, T. G. R. 1989. *The Rational Infant: Learning in Infancy*. San Francisco: Freeman.

Boyd, William. 1968. *The History of Western Education*. London: Adam and Charles Black.

Bradley, Ben S. 1989. *Visions of Infancy: A Critical Introduction to Child Psychology*. Cambridge: Polity Press.

Bradsher, Keith. 1995. "More on the Wealth of Nations." *New York Times Week in Review*, August 10: E6.

Braverman, Harry. 1974. *Labor and Monopoly Capital: The Degradation of Work in the Twentieth Century*. New York: Monthly Review Press.

Bray, Francesca. 1997. *Technology and Gender: Fabrics of Power in Late Imperial China*. Berkeley: University of California Press.

Breeuwsma, Gerrit. 1993. *Alles over ontwikkeling. Over de grondslagen van de ontwikkelingspsychologie*. Amsterdam: Boom.

Bremner, Robert Hamlett, ed. 1971. *Children and Youth in America: A Documentary History*. Cambridge, Mass.: Harvard University Press.

Brezinka, Wolfgang. 1978. *Metatheorie der Erziehung: Eine Einführung in die Grundlagen der Erziehungswissenschaft, der Philosophie der Erziehung, und der Praktischen Pädagogik*. München/Basel: Reinhardt.

———. 1981. *Erziehungsziele Erziehungsmittel Erziehungserfolg. Beitrage zu einem System der Erziehungswissenschaft*. München/Basel: Reinhardt.

Bronfenbrenner, Urie. 1958. "Socialization and Social Class Through Time and Space." in Eleanor E. Maccoby, Theodore M. Newcomb, and Eugene L. Hartley, eds., *Readings in Social Psychology*. New York: Holt. 400–425.

———. 1979. *The Ecology of Human Development: Experiments by Nature and Design*. Cambridge, Mass.: Harvard University Press.

———. 1989. "Ecological Systems Theory." In Ross Vasta, ed., *Six Theories of Child Development: Revised Formulations and Current Issues*. Annals of Child Development: 6. Greenwich, Conn.: JAI Press. 187–251.

Brosterman, Norman. 1997. *Inventing Kindergarten*. New York: Harry N. Abrams.

Bruner, Jerome S., Rose R. Olver, and Patricia Greenfield Marks. 1966. *Studies in Cognitive Growth: A Collaboration at the Center for Cognitive Studies*. New York: Wiley.

Bryant, Peter. 1974. *Perception and Understanding in Young Children: An Experimental Approach*. London: Methuen.

Buchan, William. 1809. *Advice to Mothers, on the Subject of Their Own Health; and of the Means of Promoting the Health, Strength, and Beauty of Their Offspring*. Philadelphia: Joseph Bumstead.

Burman, Erica. 1994. *Deconstructing Developmental Psychology*. London: Routledge.

Burnham, John. 1996. "Why Did the Infants and Toddlers Die? Shifts in Americans' Ideas of Responsibility for Accidents—from Blaming Mom to Engineering." *Journal of Social History* 29: 817–37.

Burns, Stanley. 1990. *Sleeping Beauty: Memorial Photography in America*. Altadena, Calif.: Twelve Trees Press.

Burrow, J. A. 1988. *The Ages of Man: A Study in Medieval Writing and Thought*. Oxford: Oxford University Press.

Burton, A. 1989. "Looking Forward from Ariès? Pictorial and Material Evidence for the History of Childhood and Family Life." *Continuity and Change* 4: 203–29.

Busfield, Joan and Michael Paddon. 1977. *Thinking About Children: Sociology and Fertility in Post-War England*. Cambridge: Cambridge University Press.

Bushnell, Horace. 1847. *Christian Nurture*. Hartford, Conn.: E. Hunt.

Cadogan, William. 1769. *An Essay ipon Nursing and the Management of Children, from their Birth to Three Years of Age*. London: Robert Horsfield.

Cahan, Emily D., Jay Mechling, Brian Sutton-Smith, and Sheldon H. White. 1993. "The Elusive Historical Child: Ways of Knowing the Child of History and Psychology." In Glen H. Elder, Jr., John Modell, and Ross D. Parke, eds., *Children in Time and Place: Developmental and Historical Insights*. Cambridge: Cambridge University Press. 192–223.

Cahan, Emily D. and Sheldon H. White. 1992. "Proposals for a Second Psychology." *American Psychologist* 47: 224–35.

Calvert, Karin. 1992. *Children in the House: The Material Culture of Early Childhood, 1600–1900*. Boston: Northeastern University Press.

Campbell, Donald T. 1988. *Methodology and Epistemology for Social Science: Selected Papers*. Ed. E. Samuel Overman. Chicago: University of Chicago Press.

Cao Xueqin. 1973. *The Story of the Stone: A Novel in Five Volumes*. Trans. David Hawkes. Harmondsworth: Penguin.

Carmichael, Ann. 1986. *Plague and the Poor in Renaissance Florence*. New York: Cambridge University Press.

Cats, Jacob. 1976 [1712]. *Alle de wercken*. Amsterdam: Jan van Heekeren e.a. Boekverkoopers.

Cavallo, Dominick. 1981. *Muscles and Morals: Organized Playgrounds and Urban Reform, 1880–1920*. Philadelphia: University of Pennsylvania Press.

Chafe, William H. 1991. *The Paradox of Change: American Women in the Twentieth Century*. New York: Oxford University Press.

Chance, Norman A. 1991. *China's Urban Villagers: Changing Life in a Beijing Suburb*. Fort Worth: Harcourt Brace.

Chandler, Alfred D., Jr. 1977. *The Visible Hand: The Managerial Revolution in American Business*. Cambridge, Mass.: Belknap Press.

Chen, Chuan-sheng, Shin-ying Lee, and Harold W. Stevenson. 1996. "Academic Achievement and Motivation of Chinese Students: A Cross-National Perspective." In Sing Lau, ed., *Growing Up the Chinese Way: Chinese Child and Adolescent Development*. Hong Kong: Chinese University of Hong Kong. 69–92.

Chen, S. J. 1996. "Positive Childishness: Images of Childhood in Japan." In C. Philip Hwang, Michael E. Lamb, and Irving E. Sigel, eds., *Images of Childhood*. Mahwah, N.J.: Lawrence Erlbaum. 113–27.

Church, Robert L. and Michael W. Sedlak. 1976. "Progressivism and the Kindergarten, 1870–1925." In Church and Sedlak, *Education in the United States: An Interpretive History*. New York: Free Press. 316–42.

Clarke-Stewart, Alison. 1982. *Day Care*. London: Fontana.

Cofer, Charles N. 1986. "Human Nature and Social Policy." In Lynette Friedrich-Cofer, ed., *Human Nature and Public Policy: Scientific Views of Women, Children, and Families*. New York: Praeger. 39–96.

Cole, Thomas. 1992. *The Journey of Life: A Cultural History of Aging in America*. Cambridge: Cambridge University Press.

Compas, Bruce E., B. R. Hinden, and Cynthia A. Gerhardt. 1995. "Adolescent Development: Pathways and Processes of Risk and Resilience." *Annual Review of Psychology* 46: 265–93.

Confucius. 1938. *The Analects of Confucius*. Ed. and trans. Arthur Waley. London: Allen and Unwin.

Corsaro, William A. 1997. *The Sociology of Childhood*. Thousand Oaks, Calif.: Pine Forge Press.

Corsini, Carlo A. and Pier Pablo Viazzo. 1997. *The Decline of Infant and Child Mortality: The European Experience, 1750–1990*. The Hague: Martinus Nijhoff/UNICEF.

Coumou, Hiskia and Willemina van Stegeren. 1987. "Sociale Pedagogiek in historisch perspectief." In Jan Hazekamp and I. van der Zande, eds., *Jongeren: Nieuwe wegen in de sociale pedagogiek*. Meppel: Boom. 35–49.

Cravens, Hamilton. 1987. "Recent Controversy in Human Development: A Historical View." *Human Development* 30: 325–35.

Cross, Gary. 1997. *Kid's Stuff: Toys and the Changing World of American Childhood*. Cambridge, Mass.: Harvard University Press.

Cruts, Augustinus A. N. 1991. "Folk Developmental Psychology: An Empirical Inquiry into Social Construction." Ph.D. dissertation, University of Utrecht.

Cumings, Bruce. 1999. *Parallax Visions: Making Sense of American-East Asian Relations at the End of the Century*. Durham, N.C.: Duke University Press.

Cunningham, Hugh. 1991. *The Children of the Poor: Representations of Childhood since the Seventeenth Century*. Oxford: Blackwell.

———. 1995. *Children and Childhood in Western Society Since 1500*. London: Longman.

Daalen, Rineke van and Ali de Regt. 1997. "Participatie, zelfdiscipline en formele controle." *0–25* 9: 10–13.

Daelemans, F. 1975. "Leiden 1581: Een socio-demografisch onderzoek." *AAG Bijdragen* 14: 137–215.

Darwin, Charles A. 1871. *The Descent of Man and Selection in Relation to Sex*. London: John Murray.

———. 1872. *The Expression of the Emotions in Man and Animals*. London: John Murray.

———. 1877. "A Biographical Sketch of an Infant." *Mind* 2: 285–94.

Dasberg, Lea. 1975. *Grootbrengen door kleinhouden als historisch verschijnsel*. Meppel: Boom.

Davids, Karel and Jan Lucassen. 1995. "Introduction." In Davids and Lucassen, eds., *A Miracle Mirrored: The Dutch Republic in European Perspective*. Cambridge: Cambridge University Press. 1–25.

Davin, Delia D. 1991. "The Early Childhood Education of the Only Child Generation in Urban China." In Irving Epstein, ed., *Chinese Education: Problems, Policies, and Prospects*. New York: Garland. 42–65.

Degler, Carl. 1980. *At Odds: Women and the Family in America from the Revolution to the Present*. New York: Oxford University Press.

Deininger, Klaus and Lyn Squire. 1996. *New Ways of Looking at Old Issues: Inequality and Growth*. Washington, D.C.: World Bank.

Dekker, J. J. H. 1996. "A Republic of Educators: Educational Messages in Seventeenth-Century Dutch Genre Painting." *History of Education Quarterly* 36: 155–83.

Dekker, Rudolf. 1995. *Uit de schaduw in 't groote licht: Kinderen in egodocumenten van de Gouden Eeuw tot de Romantiek*. Amsterdam: Wereldbibliotheek.

D'Emilio, John and Estelle Freedman. 1988. *Intimate Matters: A History of Sexuality in America*. New York: Harper and Row.

Demos, John. 1986. *Past, Present, and Personal: The Family And the Life Course in America*. New York: Oxford University Press.

Deng, Peng. 1997. *Private Education in Modern China*. Westport, Conn.: Praeger.

Depaepe, Marc. 1998. *De pedagogisering achterna: Aanzet tot een genealogie van de pedagogische mentaliteit in de voorbije 250 jaar*. Leuven/Amersfoort: Acco.

Dewees, William P. 1832. *A Treatise on the Physical and Medical Treatment of Children*. Philadelphia: Carey and Lea.

Dewey, John. 1923. *Democracy and Education: An Introduction to the Philosophy of Education*. New York: Macmillan.

———. 1938. *Experience and Education*. New York: MacMillan.

———. 1950 [1920]. *Reconstruction in Philosophy*. New York: Mentor.

———. 1967 [1887]. *Psychology*. Carbondale: Southern Illinois University Press.

———. 1976. "The School and Society." In *The Middle Works, 1899–1924*, ed. Jo Ann Boydston. Vol. 1, *Essays on School and Society, 1899–1901*. Carbondale: Southern Illinois University Press. 5–109.

Dewing. Mrs. T. W. 1882. *Beauty in the Household*. New York: Harper Brothers.

Dirlik, Arif. 1975. "The Ideological Foundations of the New Life Movement: A Study in Counterrevolution." *Journal of Asian Studies* 34: 945–80.

Dore, Ronald P. 1965. *Education in Tokugawa Japan*. Berkeley: University of California Press.

Douglas, Ann. 1977. *The Feminization of American Culture*. New York: Knopf.

Duncan, David. 1908. *The Life and Letters of Herbert Spencer*. London: Methuen.

Durantini, Mary Frances. 1983. *The Child in Seventeenth-Century Dutch Painting*. Ann Arbor, Mich.: UMI Research Press.

Easterlin, Richard A. 1980. *Birth and Fortune: the Impact of Numbers on Personal Fortune*. New York: Basic Books.

Eerenbeemt, B. C. J. M. van den. 1935. *Het kind in onze middeleeuwsche literatuur*. Amsterdam: Van Munster.

Eichorn, Dorothy H., J. A. Clausen, Norma Haan, Marjorie P. Honzik, and Paul H. Mussen, eds. 1981. *Present and Past in Middle Life*. New York: Academic Press.

Elder, Glen H., Jr. 1973. *Children of the Great Depression: Social Change in Life Experience*. Chicago: University of Chicago Press.

Elder, Glen H., Jr., John Modell, and Ross D. Parke, eds. 1993. *Children in Time and Place: Developmental and Historical Insights*. Cambridge: Cambridge University Press.

Elias, Norbert. 1939. *Über den Prozess der Zivilisation: Soziogenetische und psychogenetische Untersuchungen*. Basel: Haus zum Falken.

———. 1982. *The Civilizing Process*. Oxford: Blackwell.

Elkind, David. 1981. *The Hurried Child: Growing Up Too Fast, Too Soon*. Reading, Mass.: Addison-Wesley.

Elman, Benjamin. 2001. *A Cultural History of Civil Service Examinations in Late Imperial China*. Berkeley: University of California Press.

Epstein, Irving, ed. 1991. *Chinese Education: Problems, Policies, and Prospects*. New York: Garland.

———. 1990. "Chinese Women Face Increased Discrimination." *Off Our Backs* 3: 15.

Erbaugh, Mary Susan. Forthcoming. "Western Manners in Chinese Child-hood: The Decline of the Clan, the Training of Urban Individuals."

Erikson, Erik H. 1962. *Young Man Luther: A Study in Psychoanalysis and History*. New York: W. W. Norton.

Evans, Harriet. 1997. *Women and Sexuality in China: Dominant Discourses of Female Sexuality and Gender Since 1949*. Cambridge: Polity Press.

Farson, Richard Evans. 1974. *Birthrights*. New York: Macmillan.

Fass, Paula. 1997. *Kidnapped: Child Abduction in America*. New York: Oxford University Press.

FBIS. 1996. "White Paper on Child Welfare: The Situation of Children in China." Issued by the Information Office of the State Council, Beijing, Xinhua News Agency (FBIS-CHI-96-065).

Finkbeiner, Ann K. 1996. *After the Death of a Child: Living with Loss Through the Years*. New York: Free Press.

Finucane, Ronald C. 1997. *The Rescue of the Innocents: Endangered Children in Medieval Miracles*. New York: St. Martin's Press.

Fithian, Philip Vickers. 1900. *Philip Vickers Fithian: Journal and Letters, 1767–1774*. Ed. John Rogers Williams. Princeton, N.J.: University Library Press.

Flaherty, David Harris. 1972. *Privacy in Colonial New England*. Charlottesville: University Press of Virginia.

Fossier, Robert, ed. 1997. *La petite enfance dans l'Europe médiéval et moderne*. Paris: Presses Universitaires du Mirail.

Fowler, Orson. 1853. *A Home for All, or The Gravel Wall and Octagon Mode of Building*. New York: Fowler Wells.

———. 1870. *Creative and Sexual Science*. Philadelphia: National Publishing Company.

Franits, Wayne E. 1990. " 'Betemt de jueghd/Soo doet sy deugd': A Pedagogical Metaphor in Seventeenth-Century Dutch Art." *Leids Kunsthistorisch Jaarboek* 8: 217–27.

Friedenberg, Edgar. 1959. *The Vanishing Adolescent*. Boston: Beacon Press.

Froebel, Friedrich. 1889. *Autobiography of Friedrich Froebel*. Trans. E. Michaelis and H. K. Moore. Syracuse, N.Y.: C. W. Bardeen.

Furstenberg, Frank and Andrew Cherlin. 1986. *The New American Grandparenthood: A Place in the Family, a Life Apart*. New York: Basic Books.

Gamble, Sidney F. 1954. *Ting Hsien: A North China Rural Community*. New York: Institute of Pacific Relations.

Garrer, Anton Hedrik 1889. *Schonaeus: Bijdrage tot de geschiedenis der Latijnsche school te Haarlem*. Haarlem: De erven F. Bohn.

Gelber, Steven M. 1991. "A Job You Can't Lose: Work and Hobbies in the Great Depression." *Journal of Social History* 24: 741–66.

Gelles, Richard. 1996. *The Book of David: How Preserving Families Can Cost Children's Lives*. New York: Basic Books.

Gernet, Jacques G. 1996. *Daily Life in China on the Eve of the Mongol Invasion, 1250–1276*. Stanford, Calif.: Stanford University Press.

Gielis, A. 1995. "Kleine dienaren tussen gelijkheid en geloof. Metabletische en antropologische beschouwingen over gezag in de opvoeding." In Walter Vandereycken and Jacques de Visscher, eds., *Metabletische perspectieven: Beschouwingen rond het werk van J. H. van den Berg*. Leuven/Amersfoort: Acco. 85–113.

Giles, H. A., trans. 1910. *San tzu ching: Elementary Chinese*. Shanghai: Kelly and Walsh.

Gillis, John R. 1981. *Youth and History: Tradition and Change in European Age Relations, 1770–Present*. New York: Academic Press.

———. 1992. "Gender and Fertility Decline Among the British Middle Classes." In Gillis, L. Tilly, and D. Levine, eds., *The European Experience of Declining Fertility, 1850–1970*. Oxford: Blackwell.

———. 1996. *A World of Their Own Making: Myth, Ritual, and the Quest for Family Values*. New York: Basic Books.

Gläser, J. 1920. *Vom Kinde aus*. Hamburg: n.p.

Gluck, Carol G. 1985. *Japan's Modern Myths: Ideology in the Late Meiji Period*. Princeton, N.J.: Princeton University Press.

Goodman, W. L. 1949. *Anton Simeonovitch Makarenko, Russian Teacher*. London: Routledge and Kegan Paul.

Goossens, Frits A. 1987. *Quality of Attachment in Children of Working and Non-Working Mothers*. Leuven/Amersfoort: Acco.

Görzen, René. 1984. *Weg met de opvoeding*. Meppel: Boom.

Graham, A. C. 1989. *Disputers of the Tao: Philosophical Argument in Ancient China*. La Salle, Ill.: Open Court.

Grant, James P. 1995. *State of the World's Children: 1995*. Oxford: Oxford University Press for UNICEF.

Gray, Mike. 1999. "Texas Heroin Massacre." *Rolling Stone* 813 (May 27): 32–36.

Greenleaf, Barbara Kaye. 1979. *Children Through the Ages: A History of Childhood*. New York: Barnes and Noble.

Greven, Philip. 1977. *The Protestant Temperament: Patterns of Childrearing, Religious Experience, and the Self in Early America*. New York: Knopf.

———. 1991. *Spare the Child: The Religious Roots of Punishment and the Psychological Impact of Physical Abuse*. New York: Knopf.

Griswold, Robert. 1993. *Fatherhood in America: A History*. New York: Basic Books.

Groenendijk, Leendert F. 1984. *De nadere reformatie van het gezin: De visie van petrus Wittewrongel op de christelijke huishouding*. Dordrecht: uitgeverij J. P. van den Tol.

Guangdong Provincial Editorial Committee (Huang Huahua, et al.), ed. 1995. *Xin Sanzijing*. Canton. Foreign edition Hong Kong: Joint Publishing Committee.

Gulik, Robert Hans van. 1974. *Sexual Life in Ancient China: A Preliminary Survey of Chinese Sex and Society from ca. 1500 B.C. till 1644 A.D.* Leiden: Brill.

Haas, Louis. 1998. *The Renaissance Man and His Children: Childbirth and Early Childhood in Florence, 1300–1600*. New York: St. Martin's Press.

Habermas, Jürgen. 1981. *Theorie des kommunikatieven Handelns*. Frankfurt am Main: Suhrkamp Verlag.

Haks, Donald. 1982. *Huwelijk en gezin in Holland in de 17de en 18de eeuw*. Assen: Van Gorcum.

Hall, G. Stanley. 1904. *Adolescence: Its Psychology and Its Relations to Physiology, Anthropology, Sociology, Sex, Crime, Religion, and Education*. New York: Appleton.

———. 1911. *Educational Problems*. 2 vols. New York: Appleton.

Han Sung-Joo. 1999. *Changing Values in Asia: Their Impact on Governance and Development*. Tokyo: Japan Center for International Exchange, distributed outside Japan by Brookings Institution Press.

Hanawalt, Barbara A. 1977. "Childrearing Among the Lower Classes of Late Medieval England." *Journal of Interdisciplinary History* 8: 1–22.

———. 1986. *The Ties That Bound: Peasant Families in Medieval England*. New York: Oxford University Press.

———. 1993. *Growing Up in Medieval London: The Experience of Childhood in History*. New York: Oxford University Press.

———. 1998. *"Of Good and Ill Repute": Gender and Social Control in Medieval England*. New York: Oxford University Press.

Handlin, Johanna F. H. 1975. "Lu K'un's New Audience: The Influence of Women's Literacy on Sixteenth-Century Thought." In Margery Wolf and Roxane Witke, eds., *Women in Chinese Society*. Stanford, Calif.: Stanford University Press. 13–38.

Hara, H. and E. Minagawa. 1986. "Japanische Kindheit seit 1600." In Jochen Martin and August Nitschke, eds., *Zur Sozialgeschichte der Kindheit*. Freiburg: Verlag Karl Alber. 113–89.

Harbin, Henry T. and Denis J. Madden. 1979. "Battered Parents: A New Syndrome." *American Journal of Psychiatry* 136: 1288–91.

Harcourt, Mrs. C. 1907. *Good Form for Women*. Philadelphia: John C. Winston.

Harkness, Sara and Charles M. Super, eds. 1996. *Parents' Cultural Belief Systems: Their Origins, Expressions, and Consequences*. New York: Guilford Press.

Harris, William T. 1898. *Psychologic Foundations of Education: An Attempt to Show the Genesis of the Higher Faculties of the Mind*. New York: Appleton.

Hart, Roger A. 1992. *Children's Participation: From Tokenism to Citizenship*. Innocenti Essays 4. Florence: UNICEF.

Hawes, Joseph M. and N. Ray Hiner. 1985. *American Childhood: A Research Guide and Historical Handbook*. Westport, Conn.: Greenwood Press.

He Bochuan. 1991. *China on the Edge: The Crisis of Ecology and Development*. San Francisco: China Books.

Headland, Isaac Taylor. 1914. *Home Life in China*. London: Methuen.

Heijboer-Barbas, M. E. 1956. *Een nieuwe visie op de jeugd uit vroeger eeuwen*. Nijkerk: Callenbach.

Helmer, Frederic F. 1925. *China Chats: Talks with Children About Things of China*. Philadelphia: Sunday School Times Company.

Helmholz, Richard. 1975. "Infanticide in the Province of Canterbury During the Fifteenth Century." *History of Childhood Quarterly* 2: 379–90.

Herlihy, David. 1965. "Population, Plague, and Social Change in Rural Pistoia, 1201–1430." *Economic History Review* 18: 235–44.

Herlihy, David and Christiane Klapisch-Zuber. 1985. *Tuscans and Their Families: A Study of the Florentine Catasto of 1427*. New Haven, Conn.: Yale University Press.

Heyting, G. Frieda. 1997. *Het vanzelfsprekende en het discutabele: Een schets van opvoedkundig grondslagenonderzoek*. Utrecht: SWP.

Hill, Patty and Grace Brown. 1914. "Avoid the Gifts That Over-Stimulate." *Delineator* 85: 22–23.

Hinton, Carma and Richard Gordon. 1977. *Small Happiness: Women of a Chinese Village*. Film produced and directed by C. Hinton and R. Gordon. Distributed by Long Bow Group.

Hitchcock, D. D. 1790. *Memoirs of the Bloomsgrove Family*. Boston: Thomas and Andrews.

Ho Ping-ti. 1980. *The Ladder of Success in Imperial China: Aspects of Social Mobility, 1368–1911*. New York: Columbia University Press.

Hoare, Mrs. 1826. *Hints for the Improvement of Early Education and Nursery Discipline*. Philadelphia: John H. Putnam.

Hoffer, Peter C. and N. E. H. Hull. 1981. *Murdering Mothers: Infanticide in England and New England*. New York: New York University Press.

Holland, Patricia. 1992. *What Is a Child? Popular Images of Childhood*. London: Virago.

Hollingshead, August de Belmont. 1949. *Elmtown's Youth: The Impact of Social Classes on Adolescents*. New York: John Wiley.

Holmgren, Jennifer. 1981. "Myth, Fantasy, or Scholarship: Images of the Status of Women in Traditional China." *Australian Journal of Chinese Affairs* 6: 147–70.

Holt, John C. 1974. *Escape from Childhood*. New York: Dutton.

Holt, L. Emmett. *The Care and Feeding of Children: A Catechism for the Use of Mothers and Children's Nurses*. New York: Appleton, 1897.

Hooper, Beverley. 1985. *Youth in China*. New York: Penguin.

———. 1991. "Gender and Education." In Irving Epstein, ed., *Chinese Education: Problems, Policies, and Prospects*. New York: Garland. 352–74.

Horn, Margo. 1989. *Before It's Too Late: The Child Guidance Movement in the United States*. Philadelphia: Temple University Press.

Horowitz, Frances Degan. 1994. "John B. Watson's Legacy: Learning and Environment." In Ross D. Parke, P. A. Ornstein, J. J. Rieser, and C. Zahn-Waxler, eds., *A Century of Developmental Psychology*. Washington, D.C.: American Psychological Association. 233–50.

Houghton, Walter R. 1883. *American Etiquette and Rules of Politeness*. New York: Standard Publishing Co.

Hu Rui-wen, Jian Minghe, and Mao Hongxiang, eds. 1991. *Basic Education and National Development: Forty Years of Chinese Experience*. Shanghai: Institute of Human Resource Development, UNICEF/PEP.

Hughes, D. O. 1988. "Representing the Family: Portraits and Purposes in Early Modern Italy." In Robert I. Rotberg and Theodore K. Rabb, eds., *Art and History: Images and Their Meaning*. Cambridge: Cambridge University Press. 7–38.

Hulbert, Ann. 1996. "Doctor Spock's Baby: Fifty Years in the Life of a Book and the American Family." *New Yorker* 72 (May 20).

Hunnisett, R. F., ed. 1961. *Bedfordshire Coroners' Rolls*. Bedford Historical Record Society 41.

Hunt, David. 1972. *Parents and Children in History: The Psychology of Family Life in Early Modern France*. New York: Harper and Row.

Ida, S. 1999. "Un exemple de mise en practique des théories éducatives de l'Emile: Le cas de Nakae Chômin et de son Ecole d'Etudes françaises." *Annales de la Société franco-japonaise des sciences de l'éducation* 27: 102–10.

Illich, Ivan. 1973. *Deschooling Society*. Harmondsworth: Penguin.

Imelman, Jan Dirk and Wilna A. J. Meijer. 1986. *De nieuwe school gisteren en vandaag*. Amsterdam/Brussels: Elsevier.

Isaacs, Harold Robert. 1958. *Scratches on Our Minds: American Images of China and India*. Westport, Conn.: Greenwood Press.

Israel, Jonathan I. 1995. *The Dutch Republic: Its Rise, Greatness, and Fall, 1477–1806*. Oxford: Clarendon Press.

Jacobson, L. 1997. "Revitalizing the American Home: Children's Leisure and the Revolution of Play, 1920–1940." *Journal of Social History* 30: 581–96.

James, William. 1890. *The Principles of Psychology*. 2 vols. New York: Holt.

———. 1902. *The Varieties of Religious Experience: A Study in Human Nature*. New York: Modern Library.

Jia Shen. 1925. *Zhonghua funü chanzu kao*. Beijing: Ci xiang gong chang.

Jochim, Christian. 1995. "The Contemporary Confucian-Christian Encounter: Interreligious or Intrareligious Dialogue." *Journal of Ecumenical Studies* 32: 35–62.

Johnson, Thomas Wayne. 1975. *Shonendan: Adolescent Peer Group Socialization in Rural Japan*. Taipei: Orient Cultural Service.

Joselit, Jenna W. 1994. *The Wonders of America: Reinventing Jewish Culture, 1880–1950*. New York: Hill and Wang.

Kagan, Jerome. 1984. *The Nature of the Child*. New York: Basic Books.

Kagesato, Tetsuro, ed. 1978. *Hizo ukiyoe* (Treasured ukiyoe from von Siebolt collection, Rijksmuseum voor Volkenkunde, Leiden). Vol. 3. Tokyo: Kodan-sha.

Kaibara, E. 1976 [1710]. "Wazoku doji-kun" (Precepts on Childrearing and Education). In Masami Yamazumi and Kazue Nakae, eds., *Kosodate no sho* (*Documents on Childrearing*). Tokyo: Heibon-sha. 2: 3–57.

Kelso, William A. 1994. *Poverty and the Underclass: Changing Perceptions of the Poor in America*. New York: New York University Press.

Kerschensteiner, Georg. 1917. *Staatsbürgerliche Erziehung der deutschen Jugend*. Erfurt: Villaret.

Kessen, William. 1979. "The American Child and Other Cultural Inventions." *American Psychologist* 34: 815–20.

Kett, Joseph F. 1977. *Rites of Passage: Adolescence in America, 1790 to the Present*. New York: Basic Books.

Key, Ellen. 1900. *The Century of the Child*. New York: Putnam's.

Kiefer, Monica Mary. 1958. *American Children Through Their Books, 1700–1835*. Philadelphia: University of Pennsylvania Press.

Kildegaard, Bjarne. 1985. "Unlimited Memory: Photography and the Differentiation of Familial Intimacy." *Ethnologia Scandinavica*: 71–89.

Kincaid, James. 1992. *Child-Loving: The Erotic Child and Victorian Culture*. New York: Routledge.

King, Constance Eileen. 1977. *The Collector's History of Dolls*. New York: Bonanza Books.

King, Margaret L. 1994. *The Death of the Child Valerio Marcello*. Chicago: University of Chicago Press.

Kinney, Anne Behnke. 1993. "Infant Abandonment in Early China." *Early China* 18: 107–38.

———, ed. 1995. *Chinese Views of Childhood*. Honolulu: University of Hawai'i Press.

Kirkby, Richard J. R. 1985. *Urbanization in China: Town and Country in a Developing Economy, 1949–2000 A.D.* New York: Columbia University Press.

Kito, Hiroshi. 1983. *Nihon nisen-nen no jinko-shi* (*Demographical History of Japan over Two Thousand Years*). Kyoto: PHP Kenkyujo.

Klafki, Wolfgang. 1976. *Aspekte kritisch-konstruktiver Erziehungswissenschaft*. Weinheim/Basel: Beltz.

Klapisch-Zuber, Christiane. 1985. *Women, Family, and Ritual in Renaissance Italy*. Trans. Lydia Cochrane. Chicago: University of Chicago Press.

Kline, Stephen. 1995. *Out of the Garden: Toys, TV, and Children's Culture in the Age of Marketing*. London: Verso.

Know, Ronald and Shane Leslie, eds. 1923. *Miracles of Henry VI: Being an*

Account and Translation of Twenty-Three Miracles Taken from the Manuscript in the British Museum. Cambridge: Cambridge University Press.

Knuttel-Fabius, E. 1906. *Paedagogie en moraal in oude Nederlandsche kinderboeken.* 's-Gravenhage: Nijhoff.

Ko, Dorothy. 1994. *Teachers of the Inner Chambers: Women and Culture in Seventeenth-Century China.* Stanford, Calif.: Stanford University Press.

Koelman, Jacobus. 1679. *De pligten der ouders, in kinderen voor Godt op te voeden.* Amsterdam: J. Wastelier.

Kohn, Alfie 1989. "Suffer the Restless Children." *Atlantic* 264: 5.

Kohnstamm, Geldolph A. 1967. *Teaching Children to Solve a Piagetian Problem of Class Inclusion.* 's-Gravenhage: Mouton.

Kohnstamm, Geldolph A., Willem Koops, A. Peters, and J. Sixma, eds. 1987. *Scholenstrijd.* Lisse: Swets and Zeitlinger.

Kojima, Hideo. 1986a. "Child Development and Family Life Appearing in Two Sets of Family Diaries Written by Low-Ranking Warriors: Kuwana Nikki and Kashiwazaki Nikki, 1839–1848, I." *Bulletin of the Faculty of Education, Nagoya University (Educational Psychology)* 33: 1–24. (in Japanese)

———. 1986b. "Japanese Concepts of Child Development from the Mid-Seventeenth to Mid-Nineteenth Century." *International Journal of Behavioral Development* 9: 315–29.

———. 1987. "Child Development and Family Life Appearing in Two Sets of Family Diaries Written by Low-Ranking Warriors: Kuwana Nikki and Kashiwazaki Nikki, 1839–1848, II." *Bulletin of the Faculty of Education, Nagoya University (Educational Psychology)* 34: 189–217. (in Japanese)

———. 1989a. *Kosodate no dento o tazunete* (*Inquiry into the Tradition of Japanese Childrearing*). Tokyo: Shin'yosha.

———. 1989b. "Meiji shoki no hon'yaku ikujsho" (Translations of Western Child Care Books in the Early Meiji Period (1870s). *Journal of the Japan Society of Medical History* 35: 27–44.

———. 1996a. "Japanese Childrearing Advice in Its Cultural, Social, and Economic Contexts." *International Journal of Behavioral Development* 19: 373–91.

———. 1996b. "Zwei japanische Erziehungstagebücher aus dem 19. Jahrhundert." In Donata Elschenbroich, ed., *Anleitung zur Neugier: Grundlagen japanischer Erziehung.* Frankfurt am Main: Suhrkamp Verlag. 162–72.

———. 1997. "Problems of Comparison: Methodology, the Art of Storytelling, and Implicit Models." In Jonathan Tudge, Michael J. Shanahan, and Jaan Valsiner, eds., *Comparisons in Human Development: Understanding Time and Development.* New York: Cambridge University Press. 318–33.

———. 1999. "Ethnothéorie des soins et de l'éducation des enfants au Japon: Une perspective historique." Trans. R. Blin et H. Norimatsu. In Blandine Bril, Pierre Dasen, C. Sabatier, and B. Krewer, eds., *Propos sur l'enfant et l'adolescent: Quels enfants, pour quelles cultures?* Paris: L'Harmattan. 185–206.

Kojima, Hideo and Kazuo Miyake, eds. *Hattatsu shinre-gaku* (*Developmental Psychology*). Tokyo: Hoso Daigaku Kyoiku Shinkokai.

Koops, Willem. 1990a. "Adolescentie als thema in de ontwikkelingspsychologie." *Nederlands Tijdschrift voor de Psychologie* 45: 241–49.

———. 1990b. "Waarom historische ontwikkelingspsychologie?" *Tijdschrift voor ontwikkelingspsychologie* 17: 87–91.

———. 1992. "Is de eeuw van het kind eindelijk voorbij?" *Nederlands Tijdschrift voor de Psychologie* 47: 264–77.

———. 1996a. "Historical Developmental Psychology of Adolescence." In Lenie Verhofstadt-Denève, Ineke Kienhorst, and Carolien Braet, eds., *Conflict and Development in Adolescence*. Leiden: DSWO Press.

———. 1996b. "Historical Developmental Psychology: The Sample Case of Paintings." *International Journal of Behavioral Development* 19: 393–413.

———. 1996c. "Historische ontwikkelingspsychologie: een samenwerkings-project voor historici en ontwikkelingspsychologen." *Kind en Adolescent* 17: 207–12.

———. 1996d. Review of Glen H. Elder, Jr., John Modell, and Ross D. Parke, eds., *Children in Time and Place: Developmental and Historical Insights*. *International Journal of Behavioral Development* 19: 457–60.

———. 1998. "Infantilisatie bij kinderen, jeugdigen en volwassenen." In Nico Verloop, ed., *75 jaar onderwijs en opvoeding, 75 jaar Pedagogische Studiën*. Groningen: Wolters-Noordhoff. 131–61.

———. 2000. *Gemankeerde volwassenheid: Over eindpunten van de ontwikkeling en doelen van de pedagogiek*. Houten/Diegem: Bohn Stafleu Van Loghum.

Koops, Willem and Glen H. Elder, Jr. 1996. "Historical Developmental Psychology: Some Introductory Remarks." *International Journal of Behavioral Development* 19: 369–72.

Koops, Willem and B. R. Hamel. 1986. "Cognitieve ontwikkeling." In Jakobus F. Orlebeke, Pieter J. D. Drenth, Rob H. C. Janssen, and Cees Sanders, eds., *Compendium van de psychologie*. Muiderberg: Dick Coutinho. 6: 49–88.

Koops, Willem and Mark Meerum Terwogt. 1994. "Vroegkinderlijke psychologische theorieën: Een overzicht van actueel onderzoek." In Pim Steerneman and Huub Pelzer, eds., *Sociale cognitie en sociale competentie bij kinderen en jeugdigen*. Leuven: Garant. 25–46.

Korczak, Janus. 1986 [1920]. *Jak Kochac Dzieco*. Dutch edition: *Hoe houd je van een kind*. Utrecht: Bijleveld.

Kotlowitz, Alex. 1991. *There Are No Children Here: The Story of Two Boys Growing Up in the Other America*. New York: Doubleday.

Kruithof, Bernard. 1990. *Zonde en deugd in domineesland: Nederlandse protestanten en problemen van opvoeding, zeventiende tot twintigste eeuw*. Groningen: Wolters-Noordhoff.

Kuijer, Guus. 1980. *Het geminachte kind: Acht stukken*. Amsterdam: De Arbeiderspers.

Kuipers, Hans-Jan. 1992. *De wereld als werkplaats. Over de vorming van Kees Boeke en Beatrice Cadbury*. Amsterdam: IISG.

Kulander, Greg. 1995. "The Chinese Filter: Assimilation of Western Educational Theories in the Early 1980s." In Søren Clausen, Roy Starrs, and Anna Wedell-Wedellsborg, eds., *Cultural Encounters: China, Japan, and the West. Essays Commemorating 25 years of East Asian Studies at the University of Aarhus*. Aarhus: Aarhus University Press. 289–325.

Kurtz, Ernest. 1979. *Not-God: A History of Alcoholics Anonymous*. Center City, Minn.: Hazelden Educational Services.

Lamb, Michael E. 1981. *The Role of the Father in Child Development*. New York: John Wiley.

Langeveld, Martinus J. 1950. *Over het wezen der paedagogische psychologie en de verhouding der psychologie tot de paedagogiek*. Groningen/Djakarta: Wolters.

———. 1979. *Beknopte theoretische pedagogiek*. Groningen: Wolters Noordhof.

Lasch, Christopher. 1977. *Haven in a Heartless World: The Family Besieged*. New York: Basic Books.

Laurence, Anne. 1994. "How Free Were English Women in the Seventeenth

Century?" In Els Kloek, Nicole Teeuwen, and Marijke Huisman, eds., *Women of the Golden Age: An International Debate on Women in Seventeenth-Century Holland, England, and Italy*. Hilversum: Uitgeverij Verloren. 127–36.

Lempert, Wolfgang. 1971. *Leistungsprinzip und Emancipation: Studien z. Realität, Reform u. Erforschung d. berufl. Bildungswesens*. Frankfurt am Main: Suhrkamp Verlag.

Lerner, Richard M. and Nancy A. Busch-Rossnagel. 1981. *Individuals as Producers of Their Development: A Life-Span Perspective*. New York: Academic Press.

Lett, Didier. 1997. *L'enfant des miracles: Enfance et société au Moyen Age, XIIe–XIIIe siècle*. Paris: Aubier.

Leung, Angela Ki Che. 1995. "Relief Institutions for Children in Nineteenth-Century China." In Anne B. Kinney, ed., *Chinese Views of Childhood*. Honolulu: University of Hawai'i Press. 251–79.

Levy, Barry. 1988. *Quakers and the American Family: British Settlement in the Delaware Valley*. New York: Oxford University Press.

Levy, Howard S. 1966. *Chinese Footbinding: The History of a Curious Erotic Custom*. New York: Walton Rawls.

Lewin, Keith, A. Little, H. Xu, and J. Zheng. 1994. *Educational Innovation in China: Tracing the Impact of the 1985 Reforms*. Harlow: Longman.

Lewis, C. 1982. "The Observation of Father-Infant Relationships: An 'Attachment' to Outmoded Concepts." In Lorna McKee and Margaret O'Brian, eds., *The Father Figure*. London: Tavistock.

Lewis, Mark Edward. 1999. *Writing and Authority in Early China*. Albany: State University of New York Press.

Liang Qichao. 1896 *Shi Wu Bao*. Shanghai: Shi Wu Bao Guan.

Little, Daniel. 1989. *Understanding Peasant China: Case Studies in the Philosophy of Social Science*. New Haven, Conn.: Yale University Press.

Locke, John. 1693. *Some Thoughts Concerning Education*. London: Churchill. 1894

Lorenz, Konrad. 1971. *Studies in Animal and Human Behaviour*. Vol. 2. London: Methuen.

Loudon, John C. 1839. *An Encyclopaedia of Cottage, Farm, and Villa Architecture*. London: A. Spottiswoode.

Louie, Kam. 1980. *Critiques of Confucius in Contemporary China*. New York: St. Martin's Press.

Lourenço, Orlando and Armando Machado. 1996. "In Defense of Piaget's Theory: A Reply to 10 Common Criticisms." *Psychological Review* 103, 1: 143–64.

Lowe, H. Y. 1983 [1940]. *The Adventures of Wu: The Life Cycle of a Peking Man*. Princeton, N.J.: Princeton University Press.

Lundin, Susanne and Lynn Akesson. 1996. "Creating Life and Explaining Death." *Ethnologia Europea* 26.

Ma Duanlin. 1936. *Wenxian tongkao*. Shanghai: Commercial Press.

Maccoby, Eleanor E. 1994. "The Role of Parents in the Socialization of Children: An Historical Overview." In Ross D. Parke, P. A. Ornstein, J. J. Rieser and C. Zahn-Waxler, eds., *A Century of Developmental Psychology*. Washington, D.C.: American Psychological Association. 589–615.

MacLeod, Anne Scott. 1976. *A Moral Tale: Children's Fiction and American Culture, 1820–1880*. Hamden, Conn.: Archon Books.

Macleod, David. 1983. *Building Character in the American Boy: The Boy Scouts,*

YMCA and Their Forerunners, 1870–1920. Madison: University of Wisconsin Press.

―――. 1998. *The Age of the Child: Children in America, 1890–1920*. New York: Twayne.

Makita, S. 1990. *Nihon-jin no issho (Lifetime of the Japanese)*. Tokyo: Kodansha.

Mann, Susan. 1997. *Precious Records: Women in China's Long Eighteenth Century*. Stanford, Calif.: Stanford University Press.

March, Andrew L. 1974. *The Idea of China: Myth and Theory in Geographic Thought*. New York: Praeger.

Marsh, Margret. 1990. *Suburban Lives*. New Brunswick, N.J.: Rutgers University Press.

Martin-Fugier, Anne. 1990. "Bourgeois Rituals." In Michelle Perrot, ed., *From the Fires of Revolution to the Great War*. Vol. 4 of Philippe Ariès and Georges Duby, eds., *A History of Private Life*. Cambridge, Mass.: Harvard University Press.

Mass-Observation. *Britain and Her Birth-Rate*. 1945. London: Published for the Advertising Service Guild by J. Murray.

Matignon, Jean Jacques. 1936. *La Chine hermétique: Superstitions, crime, et misère*. Paris: Librairie orientaliste Paul Geuthner.

Matsuno, Y. 1980. "Kindai nihon ni okeru shugakuritsu no josho katei no set-sumei ni tsuite 1" (Explanation of the Process of Rising School Attendance in Modern Japan). *Toyo Daigaku Bungakubu Kiyo (Kyoikugakka and Kyoshoku Katei hen)* 34: 91–103.

Matsuzaki, K., ed. 1993. *Higashi Asia no shirei kekkon (Marriage of the Souls of the Dead in East Asia)*. Tokyo: Iwata Shoin.

Mauriceau, François. 1675. *Traité des maladies des femmes grosses, et de celles qui sont nouvellement accouchées*. Paris: Gerard.

Mause, Lloyd de. 1974a. "The Evolution of Childhood." In de Mause, ed., *The History of Childhood*. New York: Psychohistory Press. 1–73.

―――, ed. 1974b. *The History of Childhood*. New York: Psychohistory Press.

―――. 1974c. Introduction to Barbara A. Kellum, "Infanticide in England in the Later Middle Ages," *History of Childhood Quarterly* 1: 367.

May, Elaine Tyler. 1995. *Barren in the Promised Land: Childless Americans and the Pursuit of Happiness*. New York: Basic Books.

McClintock, Inez B. and Marshall McClintock. 1961. *Toys in America*. Washington, D.C.: Public Affairs Press.

McClinton, Katharine Morrison. 1970. *Antiques of American Childhood*. New York: Clarkson Potter.

McGraw, Myrtle B. 1943. *The Neuromuscular Maturation of the Human Infant*. New York: Columbia University Press.

McLaughlin, Mary Martin. 1974. "Survivors and Surrogates: Children and Parents from the Ninth to the Thirteenth Centuries." In Lloyd de Mause, ed., *The History of Childhood*. New York: Psychohistory Press. 101–81.

Meijer, Wilna A. J. 1996. *Stromingen in de pedagogiek*. Nijkerk: Intro.

Mennicke, C. A. 1933. *Sociale Pedagogie: Grondslagen, vormen en middelen der gemeenschapsopvoeding*. Utrecht: Erven J. Bijleveld.

Miedema, Siebrened. 1997. *Pedagogiek in Meervoud*. 5th ed. Houten/Diegem: Bohn, Stafleu Van Loghum.

Miles, A. Clement. 1912. *Christmas in Ritual and Tradition, Christian and Pagan*. London: T. Fisher Unwin.

Miller, Alice. 1984. *Am Anfang war Erziehung*. Frankfurt am Main: Suhrkamp Verlag.

Miller, J. Abbott. 1991. "Elementary School." In Ellen Lupton and J. Abbott Miller, eds., *The ABC's of [yellow triangle, red square, blue circle]: The Bauhaus and Design Theory*. New York: Cooper Union for the Advancement of Science and Art. 4–21.

Mitchell, B. R. 1980. *European Historical Statistics, 1750–1975*. 2nd ed. London: Macmillan.

Moerman, A. K. H. 1974. *Daniel Heinsius: zijn "Spiegel" en spiegeling in de literatuurgeschiedschrijving*. Leiden: New Rhine Publishers.

Mollenhauer, Klaus. 1968. *Erziehung und Emancipation: Polemische Skizzen*. München: Juventa.

———. 1986. *Vergeten samenhang: Over cultuur en opvoeding*. Meppel: Boom.

Morgan, Edmund S. 1966. *The Puritan Family: Religion and Domestic Relations in the Seventeenth Century*. New York: Harper.

Morss, John R. 1996. *Growing Critical: Alternatives to Developmental Psychology*. London: Routledge.

Mote, Frederick W. 1973. "China's Past in the Study of China Today." *Journal of Asian Studies* 32, 1: 107–20.

Muir, Percy H. 1960. *English Children's Books, 1600 to 1900*. Cambridge: Cambridge University Press.

Murchison, Carl A. 1933. Preface. In Murchison, ed., *A Handbook of Child Psychology*. Worcester, Mass.: Clark University Press.

Murchison, Carl A. and S. Langer. 1927. "Tiedemann's Observations on the Development of the Mental Faculties of Children." *Pedagogical Seminary and Journal of Genetic Psychology* 34: 204–30.

Murris, Roelof. 1925. *La Hollande et les Hollandais au XVIIe et XVIIIe siècles vus par les français*. Paris: Libraire Honoré Champion.

Naban, Gary Paul and Stephen Trimble. 1994. *The Geography of Childhood: Why Children Need Wild Places*. Boston: Beacon Press.

Nakauchi, T. 1998. Shigakko no shakai katei (The Social Process of the History of "New Schools"). In Nakauchi, *Nakauchi Tosho chosakushu (Selected Works of Nakauchi Toshio)*. Tokyo: Fujiwara Shoten. 2: 135–93.

Natorp, Paul. 1899. *Sozialpädagogik: Theorie der Willenserziehung auf der Grundlage der Gemeinschaft*. Stuttgart: Frogman.

Nehru, Vikram, Aart Kraay, and Xiaoqing Yu 1997. *China 2020: Developmental Challenges in the New Century*. Washington, D.C.: World Bank.

Nicholas, David. 1983. *The Domestic Life of a Medieval City: Women, Children, and the Family in Fourteenth-Century Ghent*. Lincoln: University of Nebraska Press.

Nissenbaum, Stephen. 1996. *The Battle for Christmas: A Social and Cultural History*. New York: Knopf.

Niu Xiaodong. 1992. *Policy, Education, and Inequalities in Communist China Since 1949*. New York: New York University Press.

Noordman, Jan. 1989. *Om de kwaliteit van het nageslacht: Eugenetica in Nederland, 1900–1950*. Nijmegen: SUN.

Nossent, S. 1994. "De competente baby: ontdekt of geconstrueerd?" *Psychologie and Maatschappij* 67: 85–96.

Nylan, Michael. 2000. "Golden Spindles and Axes: Elite Women in the Achaemenid and Han Empires." In Chenyang Li, ed., *The Sage and the Second Sex: Confucianism, Ethics, and Gender*. 199–222. La Salle, Ill.: Open Court.

————. 2001. "Claiming the Canon in Modern China." In *The Five "Confucian" Classics*. New Haven, Conn.: Yale University Press.

Oden, M. H. 1968. "The Fulfillment of Promise: 40-Year Follow-Up of the Terman Gifted Group." *Genetic Psychological Monograph* 77: 3–93.

Oelkers, Jürgen. 1989. *Die grosse Aspiration: Zur Herausbildung der Erziehungswissenschaft im 19. Jahrhundert*. Darmstadt: Wissenschaftliche Buchgesellschaft.

————. 1996. *Reformpädagogik: Eine kritische Dogmengeschichte*. Weinhein: Juventa.

Offer, Daniel and Judith Baskin Offer. 1975. *From Teenage to Manhood: A Psychological Study*. New York: Basic Books.

Ohta, M. 1994. *Edo no oyako (Parents and Children in the Edo Period)*. Tokyo: Chuo-koron-sha.

Ong, Aihwa. 1997. "Chinese Modernities: Narratives of Nation and of Capitalism." In Ong and Donald Macon Nonini, eds., *Ungrounded Empires: The Cultural Products of Modern Chinese Transnationalism*. New York: Routledge. 171–202.

OPIN. 1996. "Opinions of the State Education Commission in Regard to Further Strengthening the Work of Moral Education in the Middle and Primary Schools, April 13, 1990." Document excerpted from the Political Report of the State Education Commission, no. 6, 1990. Trans. in *Chinese Education and Society* 29, 4: 89–100.

Palmore, Erdman B. and Daisaku Maeda. 1985. *The Honorable Elders Revisited: A Revised Cross-Cultural Analysis of Aging in Japan*. Durham, N.C.: Duke University Press.

Panton, J. E. 1893. *From Kitchen to Garret*. London: Ward and Downey.

Parke, Ross D. 1981. *Fathers*. Cambridge, Mass.: Harvard University Press.

————. 1995. "Fathers and Families." In Marc H. Bornstein, ed., *Handbook of Parenting*. Hillsdale, N.J.: Lawrence Erlbaum. 3: 27–63.

Pease, Catherine E. 1995. "Remembering the Taste of Melons: Modern Chinese Stories of Childhood." In Anne B. Kinney, ed., *Chinese Views of Childhood*. Honolulu: University of Hawai'i Press. 279–320.

Peeters, Harry F. M. 1966. *Kind en jeugdige in het begin van de Moderne Tijd (1500–1900)*. Meppel: Boom.

Pepper, Suzanne. 1990. *China's Education Reform in the 1980s: Policies, Issues, and Historical Perspectives*. Berkeley, Calif.: Institute for East Asian Studies.

Petersen, Anne. 1988. "Adolescent Development." *Annual Review of Psychology* 39: 583–607.

Petersen, Anne and A. T. Ebata. 1987. "Developmental Transitions and Adolescent Problem Behavior: Implications for Prevention and Intervention." In Klaus Hurrelmann, Frans-Xaver Kaufmann, and Friedrich Lösel, eds., *Social Intervention: Potential and Constraints, Prevention and Intervention in Childhood and Adolescence*. New York: de Gruyter. 167–84.

Piaget, Jean. 1926. *The Language and Thought of the Child*. New York: Harcourt Brace.

————. 1928. *Judgment and Reasoning in the Child*. New York: Harcourt Brace.

————. 1929. *The Child's Conception of the World*. New York: Harcourt Brace.

————. 1930. *The Child's Conception of Physical Causality*. London: Kegan Paul.

————. 1932. *The Moral Judgment of the Child*. London: Kegan Paul.

Pine, J. M. 1992. "Maternal Style at the Early One-Word Stage: Re-evaluating the Stereotype of the Directive Mother." *First Language* 12: 169–86.

Platt, Anthony. 1969. *The Child Savers: The Invention of Delinquency*. Chicago: University of Chicago Press.

Plessner, Helmuth. 1946. "Over de infantilserende invloed van de moderne maatschappij op de jeugd." *Paedagogische Studiën* 23: 193–202.

Pollock, Linda A. 1983. *Forgotten Children: Parent-Child Relations from 1500 to 1900*. Cambridge: Cambridge University Press.

———. 1987. *A Lasting Relationship: Parents and Children over Three Centuries*. Hanover, N.H.: University Press of New England.

Polman, P. 1965. "Heyman Jacobsz: En zijn 'sondaechs-schole.' " *Archief voor de Geschiedenis van de Katholieke Kerk in Nederland* 7: 162–90.

Pols, Wouter. 1997. "De opvoedingswetenschappen in Frankrijk." In Siebren Miedema, ed., *Pedagogiek in Meervoud*. 5th ed. Houten/Diegem: Bohn, Stafleu Van Loghum. 263–308.

Pomes, Hendrikus. 1908. *Van Alphen's kindergedichtjes: Bijdrage tot de kennis van de opveeding hier te lande in de 18e eeuw*. Rotterdam: W. L. and J. Brusse.

Porter, Roy and Dorothy Porter. 1988. *In Sickness and in Health: The British Experience, 1650–1850*. Oxford: Blackwell.

Postman, Neil. 1992. *The Disappearance of Childhood*. 2nd ed. New York: Vintage.

Preyer, Wilhelm T. 1882. *Die Seele des Kindes: Beobachtungen über die geistige Entwicklung des Menschen in den ersten Lebensjahren* (*The Mind of the Child*). Leipzig: Fernau.

Prins, Franciscus W. 1963. *Verleden en heden: Beknopte geschiedenis van opvoeding en onderwijs*. Groningen: Wolters.

Putnam, Robert D. 2000. *Bowling Alone: The Collapse and Revival of American Community*. New York: Simon and Schuster.

Qian Jiaju. 1985. *Gaodeng jiaoyu xuebao* (*Journal of Higher Education*) 1: 64.

Radding, Charles M. 1985. *A World Made by Men: Cognition and Society, 400–1200*. Chapel Hill: University of North Carolina Press.

Raleigh, Sir Walter. 1694. *The History of the World in Five Books*. London: T. Basset.

Rang, Brita. 1990. " 'Geeft mijn kindeken dog sijn willeken': Discussies over opvoeding in het begin van de Gouden Eeuw." In J. D. Imelman et al., eds., *Cultuurpedagogiek*. Leiden: Martinus Nijhoff Uitgevers.

Raphals, Lisa Ann. 1998. *Sharing the Light: Representations of Women and Virtue in Early China*. Albany: State University of New York Press.

Rapoport, Rhona, Robert N. Rapoport, and Ziona Strelitz. 1977. *Fathers, Mothers, and Others: Perspectives on Parenting*. London: Routledge and Kegan Paul.

Rawski, Evelyn Sakakida. 1979. *Education and Popular Literacy in Ch'ing China*. Ann Arbor: University of Michigan Press.

Razi, Zvi. 1980. *Life, Marriage, and Death in the Medieval Parish: Economy, Society, and Demography in Halesowen, 1270–1400*. Cambridge: Cambridge University Press.

Riché, Pierre and Danièle Alexandre-Bidon. 1994. *L'enfance au Moyen Age*. Paris: Editions du Seuil.

Riddy, Felicity. 1996. "Mother Knows Best: Reading Social Change in a Courtesy Text." *Speculum* 71: 66–86.

Rieffe, Carolien. 1998. "The Child's Theory of Mind: Understanding Desires, Beliefs, and Emotions." Ph.D. dissertation, Vrije Universiteit, Amsterdam.

Rieffe, Carolien, Willem Koops, and Mark Meerum Terwogt. 1996. "Vroegkinderlijk begrip van mentale processen: de Child's Theory of Mind." In Joop D. Bosch et al., eds., *Jaarboek ontwikkelingspsychologie, orthopedagogiek, en kinderpsychiatrie* 2: 216–35. Houten/Diegem: Bohn Stafleu van Loghum.

Riemens, Johanna R., R. Reurslag, and R. Yzer. 1930. "Desiderius Erasmus." In Riemens, Reurslag, and Yzer, *De ontwikkeling van opvoedkundige denkbeelden*. Utrecht: Kemink en Zoon. 2, 39–68.

Rijksmuseum voor Volkenkunde. 1987. *Kawahara Keiga: Photographer Without a Camera*. Leiden: Rijksmuseum voor Volkenkunde.

Rijt, Hetty van de and Frans X. Plooij. 1992. *Oei, ik groei! De acht sprongen in de mentale ontwikkeling van je baby*. Ede: Zomer and Keuning.

Roberts, Benjamin. 1998. *Through the Keyhole: Dutch Child-Rearing Practices in the Seventeenth and Eighteenth Century. Three Urban Elite Families*. Hilversum: Uitgeverij Verloren.

Robson, Catherine. 2001. *Men in Wonderland: The Lost Gilrhood of Victorian Gentlemen*. Princeton, N.J.: Princeton University Press.

Romanes, George J. 1883. *Animal Intelligence*. New York: Appleton.

———. 1884. *Mental Evolution in Animals*. New York: Appleton.

———. 1889. *Mental Evolution in Man: Origin of Human Faculty*. New York: Appleton.

Rosenblum, Robert. 1988. *The Romantic Child: From Runge to Sendak*. New York: Thames and Hudson.

Ross, Dorothy. 1972. *G. Stanley Hall: The Psychologist as Prophet*. Chicago: University of Chicago Press.

Ross, Heidi. 1991. "The 'Crisis' in Chinese Secondary Schooling." In Irving Epstein, ed., *Chinese Education: Problems, Policies, and Prospects*. New York: Garland. 66–108.

Ross, James Bruce. 1974. "The Middle-Class Child in Urban Italy, Fourteenth to Early Sixteenth Century." In Lloyd de Mause, ed., *The History of Childhood*. New York: Psychohistory Press. 183–228.

Rothman, Barbara Katz. 1989. *Recreating Motherhood: Ideology and Technology in Patriarchal Society*. New York: W.W. Norton.

Rotundo, E. Anthony. 1993. *American Manhood: Transformations in Masculinity from the Revolution to the Modern Era*. New York: Basic Books.

Rousseau, Jean-Jacques. 1763. *Emile, or on Education*. London: Nousse and Vaillant.

Rubin, Jeanne Spielman. 1999. "Frank Lloyd Wright and the Froebel Kindergarten." Manuscript.

Ruby, Jay. 1995. *Secure the Shadow: Death and Photography in America*. Cambridge, Mass.: MIT Press.

Ruhräh, John, ed. 1925. *Pediatrics of the Past: An Anthology*. New York: Paul B. Hoeber.

Saari, Jon L. 1990. *Legacies of Childhood: Growing up Chinese in a Time of Crisis, 1890–1920*. Cambridge, Mass.: Harvard University Press.

Scarr, Sandra. 1984. *Mother Care/Other Care*. New York: Basic Books.

Schaffer, H. Rudolph. 1992. "Joint Involvement Episodes as Context for Development." In Harry McGurk, ed., *Childhood Social Development: Contemporary Perspectives*. Hillsdale, N.J.: Lawrence Erlbaum. 99–129.

Schama, Simon. 1987. *The Embarrassment of Riches: An Interpretation of Dutch Culture in the Golden Age*. New York: Knopf.

Scheper-Hughes, Nancy. 1987. "Culture, Scarcity, and Maternal Thinking:

Mother Love and Child Death in Northeast Brazil." In Scheper-Hughes, ed., *Child Survival: Anthropological Perspectives on the Treatment and Maltreatment of Children*. Dordrecht:Reidel. 187–208.

Schlossman Stephen and Brian Gill. 1996. "A Sin Against Childhood: Progressive Education and the Crusade Against Homework, 1897–1941." *American Journal of Education* 105, 1: 27–66.

Schnabel, Paul. 1992. "Het kostbare kind: Reflecties bij de eeuw van het kind." *Tijdschrift voor Kindergeneeskunde* 60, 4: 91–97.

Scholten, Catherine A. 1985. *Childbearing in American Society, 1650–1850*. New York: New York University Press.

Schultz, James A. 1991. "Medieval Adolescence: The Claims of History and the Silence of German Narrative." *Speculum* 66: 519–39.

———. 1995. *The Knowledge of Childhood in the German Middle Ages, 1100–1350*. Philadelphia: University of Pennsylvania Press.

Schutz, Alfred. 1964 [1946]. "The Well-Informed Citizen: An Essay on the Social Distribution of Knowledge." In *Collected Papers*, vol.2, *Studies in Social Theory*. Ed. Arvid Broderson. The Hague: Martinus Nijhoff. 120–34.

Sears, Robert R., Eleanor E. Maccoby, and Harry Levin. 1957. *Patterns of Child Rearing*. Evanston, Ill.: Row, Peterson.

Sebald, Hans. 1976. *Momism: The Silent Disease of America*. Chicago: Nelson-Hall.

Senn, Milton J. E. 1975. *Insights on the Child Development Movement in the United States*. Monographs of the Society for Research in Child Development 40, 3–4 (Serial No. 161). Chicago: University of Chicago Press.

Sennett, Richard. 1970. *Families Against the City: Middle Class Homes of Industrial Chicago, 1872–1910*. Cambridge, Mass.: Harvard University Press.

Shapiro, Michael S. 1983. *Child's Garden: The Kindergarten Movement from Froebel to Dewey*. University Park: Pennsylvania State University Press.

Sharpe, Reginald R., ed. 1913. *Calendar of Coroners' Rolls of the City of London, A. D. 1300–1378*. London: Richard Clay and Sons.

Shek, Daniel T. L. 1996. "Mental Health of Chinese Adolescents: A Critical Review." In Lau Sing, ed., *Growing Up the Chinese Way: Chinese Child and Adolescent Development*.. 169–99.

Shiho-sho (Ministry of Justice), ed. 1877. *Minji kanreiruishu* (Collection of Civil Customs). Tokyo: Shiho-sho (2nd ed., 1880).

Shorter, Edward. 1975. *The Making of the Modern Family*. New York: Basic Books.

Siegel, A. W. and S. H. White. 1982. "The Child Study Movement: Early Growth and Development of the Symbolized Child." *Advances in Child Behavior and Development* 17: 233–85.

Sigel, Irving E., ed. 1985. *Parental Belief Systems: The Psychological Consequences for Children*. Hillsdale, N.J.: Lawrence Erlbaum.

Sing Lau, ed. 1996. *Growing Up the Chinese Way: Chinese Child and Adolescent Development*. Hong Kong: Chinese University of Hong Kong.

Sing Lau and Patricia P. W. Yeung. 1996. "Understanding Chinese Child Development: The Role of Culture in Socialization." In Lau Sing, ed., *Growing Up the Chinese Way: Chinese Child and Adolescent Development*. Hong Kong: Chinese University of Hong Kong. 29–44. Hong Kong: Chinese University of Hong Kong.

Smith, Daniel Blake. 1980. *Inside the Great House: Planter Life in Eighteenth-Century Chesapeake Society*. Ithaca, N.Y.: Cornell University Press.

Smith, Theodate L. 1910. "Correspondence Department of the Children's Institute." *Pedagogical Seminary* 17: 176–82.

Snyders, G. 1971. *Die grosse Wende der Pädagogik*. Paderborn: Ferdinand Schöningh.

Sommerville, John. 1982. *The Rise and Fall of Childhood*. Beverly Hills, Calif.: Sage.

Song Jian et al. 1991. "Quantitative Research and Analysis for the Optimal Population Target for China." In *Selected Essays on Population Geography (Renkou dili lunwen xuan)*. Huadong: Population Studies Group of Huadong Normal University.

Sontag, Susan. 1972. *On Photography*. New York: Delta.

Spence, Jo and Patricia Holland. 1991. *Family Snaps: The Messages of Domestic Photography*. London: Virago.

Spencer, Herbert. 1904. *An Autobiography*. New York: Appleton.

Spock, Benjamin. 1946. *The Common Sense Book of Baby and Child Care*. New York: Duell, Sloan, and Pearce.

Stafford, Charles. 1995. *The Roads of Chinese Childhood: Learning and Identification in Angang*. Cambridge: Cambridge University Press.

Stafford, Laura and Cherie L. Bayer. 1993. *Interaction Between Parents and Children*. Newbury Park, Calif.: Sage.

Starbuck, Edwin D. 1897. "Some Aspects of Religious Growth." *American Journal of Psychology* 9: 70–124.

———. 1898. "A Study of Conversion." *American Journal of Psychology* 10: 268–308.

———. 1899. *The Psychology of Religion*. New York: Charles Scribner's Sons.

Stearns, Peter N. 1989. *Jealousy: The Evolution of an Emotion in American History*. New York: New York University Press.

———. 1994. *American Cool: Constructing a Twentieth-Century Emotional Style*. New York: New York University Press.

———. 1996. "Children's Sleep: Sketching Historical Change." *Journal of Social History* 30: 345–66.

———. 1998. "Consumerism and Childhood: New Targets for American Emotions." In Jan Lewis and Stearns, eds., *An Emotional History of the United States*. New York: New York University Press. 396–416.

Steedman, Carolyn. 1995. *Strange Dislocations: Childhood and the Idea of Human Interiority*. London: Virago.

Stephens, Sharon. 1995. "Introduction: Children and the Politics of Culture in Late Capitalism." In Stephens, ed., *Children and the Politics of Culture*. Princeton, N.J.: Princeton University Press.

Stolberg, Sheryl Gay. 1998. "Shifting Certainties in the Abortion War." *New York Times*, January 11.

Stone, Lawrence. 1977. *The Family, Sex, and Marriage in England, 1500–1800*. New York: Harper and Row.

Strasser, Stephan and Anton Monshouwer. 1967. *Herbart als opvoedkundig denker*. 's-Hertogenbosch: Malmberg.

Strien, C. D. van. 1989. "British Travellers in Holland During the Stuart Period: Edward Browne and John Locke as Tourists in the United Provinces." Ph.D. dissertation, Vrije Universiteit, Amsterdam.

Suh-ho. 1915. "In Praise of Footbinding." *New Republic*, December 18, 170–72. (in Chinese)

Sully, J. 1881. "Extracts from a Father's Diary: Babies and Science." *Cornhill Magazine* 43: 539–54.

Sutton-Smith, Brian. 1980. "Toys for Object Role and Mastery." In Karen Hewitt and Lorine Roomet, eds., *Educational Toys in America: 1800 to the Present.* Burlington, Vt.: University Press of New England.

Swaef, Joannes de. 1740 [1621]. *De geestelycke queeckerye van de jonge planten des Heeren . . . ofte tractaet van de christelycke opvoedinghe der kinderen.* Middelburg: M. En A. Callenfels.

Takeda, Akira. 1990. *Sorei saishi to shirei kekkon* (Festivals for Ancestor Souls and Marriage of the Souls of the Dead). Kyoto: Jinbun Shoin.

Takeuchi, Toshimi, Tomohiko Harada, and Toshijiro Hirayama, eds. 1969. *Nihon shomin seikatsu shiryo shusei* (Collection of Historical Documents on Common Lives in Japan). Tokyo: San'ichi Shobo. 9: 453–843.

Tarr, Joel and Mark Tebeau. 1996. "Managing Danger in the Home Environment, 1900–1940." *Journal of Social History* 29: 797–816.

Teiser, Stephen F. 1994. *The Scripture on the Ten Kings and the Making of Purgatory in Medieval Chinese Buddhism.* Honolulu: University of Hawai'i Press.

Terman, Lewis M. 1925. *Genetic Studies of Genius.* Vol. 1, *Mental and Physical Traits of a Thousand Gifted Children.* Stanford, Calif.: Stanford University Press.

Thiel, P. J. J. van. 1987. "Poor Parents, Rich Children, and Family Saying Grace: Two Related Aspects of the Iconography of Late Sixteenth- and Seventeenth-Century Dutch Domestic Morality." *Simiolus* 17: 90–149.

Thøgersen, Stig. 1990. *Secondary Education in China After Mao: Reform and Conflict.* Aarhus: Aarhus University Press.

Tiedemann, Dietrich. 1787. "Beobachtungen über die Entwicklung der Seelenfähigkeiten bei Kindern." *Hessische Beiträge zur Gelehrsamkeit und Kunst* 2: 313–15; 3: 486–88.

Tobin, Joseph J., David Y. H. Wu, and Dana H. Davidson. 1989. *Preschool in Three Cultures: Japan, China, and the United States.* New Haven, Conn.: Yale University Press.

Tocqueville, Alexis de. 1981 [1835, 1840]. *Democracy in America.* Trans. Henry Reeve, Francis Bowen, and Phillips Bradley. New York: Modern Library.

Trabasso, Tom. 1977. "The Role of Memory as a System in Making Transitive Inferences." In Robert V. Kail and John W. Hagen, eds., *Perspectives on the Development of Memory and Cognition.* New York: John Wiley. 333–66.

Trexler, Richard. 1973a. "The Foundlings of Florence, 1395–1455." *History of Childhood Quarterly* 1: 159–84.

———. 1973b. "Infanticide in Florence: New Sources and First Results." *History of Childhood Quarterly* 1: 98–116.

Tyack, David and Elisabeth Hansot. 1990. *Learning Together: A History of Coeducation in American Public Schools.* New Haven, Conn.: Yale University Press.

UNICEF. 1992. *Statistics on Children in UNICEF Assisted Countries.* New York: UNICEF.

Valsiner, Jaan and G. Litvinovic. 1996. "Processes of Generalization in Parental Reasoning." In Sara Harkness and Charles M. Super, eds., *Parents' Cultural Belief Systems: Their Origins, Expressions, and Consequences.* New York: Guilford Press. 56–82.

Van Dale. 1995. *Groot woordenboek der Nederlandse taal.* Utrecht/Antwerpen: Van Dale lexicografie.

Van Horn, Susan H. 1988. *Women, Work, and Fertility, 1900–1986.* New York: New York University Press.

Veblen, Thorstein B. 1973 [1899]. *The Theory of the Leisure Class*. Boston: Houghton Mifflin.

Veerman, Philip E. 1992. *The Rights of the Child and the Changing Image of Childhood*. Dordrecht: Nijhoff.

Velde, Isaac van der. 1967. *Jean-Jacques Rousseau Pedagoog*. Amsterdam/ Brussels: Agon Elsevier.

———. 1974. "Johann Bernard Basedow." In Alphons de Block et al., eds., *Standaard Encyclopedie voor opvoeding en onderwijs*. Antwerpen: Standaard Uitgeverij. 143–44.

———, ed. 1975. *Grote denkers over opvoeding*. Amsterdam: Meulenhof.

Veroff, Joseph, Elizabeth Douvan, and Richard A. Kulka. 1986. *The Inner American: A Self-Portrait from 1957 to 1976*. New York: Basic Books.

Verwey, Anton C., Klaas Sijtsma, and Willem Koops. 1999. "An Ordinal Scale for Transitive Reasoning by Means of a Deductive Strategy." *International Journal of Behavioral Development* 22: 61–85.

Vinikas, Vincent. 1992. *Soft Soap, Hard Sell: American Hygiene in an Age of Advertisement*. Ames: Iowa State University Press.

Vletter, Antonie de. 1915. *De opvoedkundige denkbeelden van Betje Wolff en Aagje Deken: bijdrage tot de kennis van de opvoeding hier te lande in de achttiende eeuw*. Groningen : Wolters.

Vries, Jan de and A. M.van der Woude. 1995. *Nederland 1500–1815: De eerste ronde van moderne economische groei*. Amsterdam: Uitgeverij Balans.

Vygotsky, Lev Semyonovitch. 1978. *Mind in Society: The Development of Higher Psychological Processes*. Cambridge, Mass.: Harvard University Press.

Walker, Alexander. 1839. *Intermarriage, or the Mode in which, and the Causes Why, Beauty, Health, and Intellect, Result from Certain Unions, and Deformity, Disease, and Insanity from Others*. New York: J and H. G. Nangley.

Wallace, D. B., M. B. Franklin, and R. T. Keegan. 1994. "The Observing Eye: A Century of Baby Diaries." *Human Development* 37: 1–29.

Waltner, Ann. 1995. "Infanticide and Dowry in Ming and Early Qing China." In Anne B. Kinney, ed., *Chinese Views of Childhood*. Honolulu: University of Hawai'i Press. 157–92.

Walzer, John F. 1974. "A Period of Ambivalence: Eighteenth-Century American Childhood." In Lloyd de Mause, ed., *The History of Childhood*. New York: Psychohistory Press.

Wang, Jing. 1996. *High Culture Fever: Politics, Aesthetics, and Ideology in Deng's China*. Berkeley: University of California Press.

Wang, Y. C. 1960. "Western Impact and Social Mobility in China." *American Sociological Review* 25: 835–67.

Warner, Marina. 1995. *Six Myths of Our Time: Little Angels, Little Monsters, Beautiful Beasts, and More*. New York: Vintage.

Waterink, J. 1926. *Berekening of constructie*. Wageningen: Zomer and Keuning.

———. 1956. *De schooljaren onzer kinderen: Samenspel van school en gezin*. Kampen: Kok.

Watson, John B. 1928. *The Psychological Care of the Infant and Child*. New York: W. W. Norton.

———. 1970 [1924]. *Behaviorism*. Rev. ed. New York: W.W. Norton.

Weber, Max. 1958. *The Protestant Ethic and the Spirit of Capitalism*. New York: Scribners.

Webster, E. 1899. "Teaching Children to Play." *Ladies Home Journal* 16: 57.

Wei, H. 1995. "Authoritative Comments on China's Educational Law." *Beijing Review* 38 (May 22): 12–15.

Weinstein, Donald and Rudolph M. Bell. 1982. *Saints and Society: The Two Worlds of Western Christendom, 1000–1700*. Chicago: University of Chicago Press.

Wellman, Henry M. 1990. *The Child's Theory of Mind*. Cambridge, Mass.: MIT Press.

Wells, Richard A. 1890. *Manners, Culture, and Dress of the Best American Society*. Springfield, Mass.: King, Richardson.

Werner, Heinz. 1961. *The Comparative Psychology of Mental Development*. New York: Science Editions.

West, Elliott and Paula Petrick, eds. 1992. *Small Worlds: Children and Adolescence in America, 1850–1950*. Lawrence: University of Kansas Press.

White, Merry I. 1993. *The Material Child: Coming of Age in Japan and America*. New York: Free Press.

White, Sheldon H. 1976. "Developmental Psychology and Vico's Concept of Universal History." *Social Research* 43: 659–71.

———. 1978. "Psychology in All Sorts of Places." In Richard A. Kasschau and Frank S. Kessel, eds., *Psychology and Society: In Search of Symbiosis*. New York: Holt, Rinehart, and Winston. 105–31.

———. 1983. "The Idea of Development in Developmental Psychology." In Richard M. Lerner, ed., *Developmental Psychology: Historical and Philosophical Perspectives*. Hillsdale, N.J.: Lawrence Erlbaum. 55–77.

———. 1990. "Child Study at Clark University: 1894–1904." *Journal of the History of the Behavioral Sciences* 26: 131–50.

———. 1991a. "The Rise of Developmental Psychology: Retrospective Review of *Cognitive Development in Children: Five Monographs of the Society for Research in Child Development*." *Contemporary Psychology* 36: 469–73.

———. 1991b. "Three Visions of Educational Psychology." In Liliana Tolchinsky-Landsmann, ed., *Culture, Schooling, and Psychological Development*. Norwood, N.J.: Ablex. 1–38.

———. 1992. "G. Stanley Hall: From Philosophy to Developmental Psychology." *Developmental Psychology* 28: 25–34. Reprint in Ross D. Parke, P. A. Ornstein, J. J. Rieser and C. Zahn-Waxlerc eds., *A Century of Developmental Psychology*. Washington D.C.: American Psychological Association,1994. 103–25.

———. 1995. "Child Development, 1930–1934: Organizing a Research Program." Paper presented at "The Children's Cause: Some Early Organizations," Society for Research in Child Development, Indianapolis, March.

———. 1996. "Developmental Psychopathology: From Attribution Towards Information." In Steven Matthysse, Deborah L. Levy, Jerome Kagan, and Francine M. Benes, eds., *Psychopathology: The Evolving Science of Mental Disorder*. 161–97. New York: Cambridge University Press.

White, Sheldon H. and Stephen L. Buka. 1987. "Early Education: Programs, Traditions, and Policies." *Review of Research in Education* 14: 43–91.

White, Sheldon H. and Deborah A. Phillips. 2001. "Designing Head Start: Roles Played by Developmental Psychologists." In David L. Featherman and Maris Vinovskis, eds., *Social Science and Policy Making: A Search for Relevance in the Twentieth Century*. 83–118. Ann Arbor: University of Michigan Press.

Wiebe, Robert H. 1967. *The Search for Order, 1877–1920*. New York: Hill and Wang.

Wielenga, Geert. 1975. "Dewey." In Isaac van der Velde, ed., *Grote denkers over opvoeding*. Amsterdam: Meulenhof. 311–36.

Wilson, Bill. 1942. *Acoholics Anonymous: The Story of How More Than Six Thousand Men and Women Have Recovered from Alcoholism*. New York: Works Publishing Company.

Wilson, Louis N. 1975. *Bibliography of Child Study: 1898–1912*. New York: Arno.

Winn, Marie. 1984. *Children Without Childhood*. Harmondsworth: Penguin.

Winter, Micha de. 1997. *Children as Fellow Citizens: Participation and Commitment*. Oxford: Radcliffe Medical Press.

Winter, Micha de and Marieke Kroneman. 1998. *Jeugdig gezinsbeleid: Visies van jongeren op het gezin, de opvoeding en het gezinsbeleid, en wat de overheid daarmee zou kunnen doen*. Rijswijk: Ministerie van Volksgezondheid, Welzijn en Sport.

Wolf, Arthur P. 1985. "Chinese Family Size: A Myth Revitalized." In Hsieh Jih-chang and Chuang Ying-chang, eds., *The Chinese Family and Its Ritual Behavior*. Nankang: Institute of Ethnology, Academia Sinica. 30–49.

Wortis, R. P. 1974. "The Parental Mystique." In Arlene Skolnick and Jerome H. Skolnick, eds., *Intimacy, Family, and Society*. Boston: Little, Brown.

Woude, A. M. van der. 1972a. *Het Noorderkwartier*. 3 vols. AAG Bijdragen 16. Utrecht: HES.

———. 1972b. "Variations in the Size and Structure of the Household in the United Porvinces of the Netherlands in the Seventeenth and Eighteenth Centuries." In Peter Laslett and Richard Wall, eds., *Household and Family in Past Time*. Cambridge: Cambridge University Press. 299–318.

———. 1991. "De schilderijproduktie in Holland tijdens de Republiek: Een poging tot kwantificatie." In J. C. Dagevos et al., eds., *Kunst-zaken: Particulier initiatief en overheidsbeleid in de wereld van de beeldende kunst*. Kampen: Kok Agora. 18–50.

Wright, Peter. 1987. "The Social Construction of Babyhood: The Definition of Infant Care as a Medical Problem." In Alan Bryman et al., eds., *Rethinking the Life Cycle*. London: Macmillan.

Wu, David Y. H. 1996. "Parental Control: Psychocultural Interpretations of Chinese Patterns of Socialization." In Lau Sing, ed., *Growing Up the Chinese Way: Chinese Child and Adolescent Development*. Hong Kong: Chinese University of Hong Kong. 1–28.

Wu, Wen and Luo Daming. 1995 [1994]. *Heavy Laden Wings: Sad Contemplations on China's Education*. Chapters 5–7 reprint, special issue, *Chinese Education and Society* 28, 1.

Wu Yü. 1921. "Shuo hsiao." In *Wu Yü wen lu*. Shanghai: Ya-tung. 14–23.

Wurtz, Felix. 1856. *An Experimental Treatise of Surgerie in Four Parts*. London: Gertrude Dawson.

Xu, Ben. 1998. "From Modernity to 'Chineseness': The Rise of Nativist Cultural Theory." *Post-1989 China* 6: 203–28.

Yamada, Y. and Y. Kato. 1998. "What Kind of Images Do Japanese Youth Have of Their World and the Next World? The Spatial Relationships Between the Two Worlds Represented in Their Drawings." *Kyoto Daigaku Kyoiku-gakubu Kiyo* 44: 86–111. (in Japanese)

Yanagita, K. 1946. *Senzo no hanashi (On Ancestors)*. Tokyo: Chikuma Shobo.

Yang, Mayfair Mei-hui. 1994. *Gifts, Favors, and Banquets: The Art of Social Relationships in China*. Ithaca, N.Y.: Cornell University Press.

Yokoyama, Gennosuke. 1985 [1898]. *Nihon no kaso shakai* (*The Lower Strata of Japan*). English trans. E. Yutani. Ann Arbor, Mich.: UMI Research Press.

Young, K. T. 1990. "American Conceptions of Infant Development from 1955 to 1984: What the Experts Are Telling Parents." *Child Development* 61: 17–28.

Zelizer, Viviana. 1985. *Pricing the Priceless Child: The Changing Social Value of Children*. New York: Basic Books.

Zuckerman, Michael. 1993a. *Almost Chosen People: Oblique Biographies in the American Grain*. Berkeley: University of California Press.

———. 1993b. "History and Developmental Psychology, a Dangerous Liaison: A Historian's Perspective." In Glen H. Elder, Jr., John Modell, and Ross D. Parke, eds., *Children in Time and Place: Developmental and Historical Insights*. Cambridge: Cambridge University Press. 230–41.

Contributors

GERRIT BREEUWSMA teaches developmental psychology at the University of Groningen in the Netherlands. His work focuses on continuities and changes in developmental thinking. He has written a number of articles and several books on life-span developmental psychology, on the history and foundations of developmental psychology, and on art, imagination, and psychology.

KARIN CALVERT is an independent consultant and lecturer. She received her M.A. from the Winterthur Program in Early American Culture and her Ph.D. from the University of Delaware in conjunction with Winterthur. She served as Assistant Professor of American Civilization and Director of the Museum Curatorial Program at the University of Pennsylvania and as Director of the National Faculty's Delta Teachers Academy based in New Orleans. Among her publications is *Children in the House: The Material Culture of Childhood in America, 1600–1900*.

JOHN R. GILLIS is a Professor of History at Rutgers University. He has written books on Prussian bureaucracy, European age relations, British marriage, memory, and the cultures of European and American family life. He is currently writing about Atlantic islands and the prominent place they have held in the Western imagination since the time of the ancients.

BARBARA A. HANAWALT, George III Professor of History at Ohio State University, has received a host of honors for her work in medieval British history and the history of the family. She has written books on gender and social control, on the experience of childhood, on peasant families, and on crime and conflict in medieval England, as well as a textbook on Western civilization and, most recently, *The Middle Ages: An Illustrated History*.

ELS KLOEK, Senior Lecturer in History at Utrecht University in the Netherlands, writes on Dutch women and family life in the early modern era. Her most recent work is on Kenau, the widow of Haarlem who fought against the Spanish siege and remains to this day the symbolic virago of the Dutch. She edited *Women of the Golden Age*, and she is currently working on a dictionary of women in Dutch history from 1550 to 1850.

HIDEO KOJIMA is Professor of Psychology at Kyoto Gakuen University and professor emeritus at Nagoya University in Japan, His research focuses on human development in cultural and historical contexts. Though most of his works have appeared in Japanese, he has also published three dozen journal articles and book chapters in English, German, and French. Among his most recent publications is *Development of Mind and Culture* (in Japanese).

WILLEM KOOPS is Dean of Social Sciences and Professor of Developmental Psychology at Utrecht University in the Netherlands, where he directs a research program on the development of aggression. He is also president of the European Society of Developmental Psychology. He has written textbooks on developmental psychology and published over 150 research papers on cognitive and social development. Among his books are *Development of Interaction and Attachment* and the forthcoming *A Developmental Approach to Antisocial Behavior*.

MICHAEL NYLAN teaches early and modern Chinese history at the University of California at Berkeley, where she is a professor of history. She has written a multitude of articles—on Han dynasty art, on historiography, on political philosophy and education, on Confucian piety, on calligraphy, on elite women, and on the body and the body politic—as well as three books. The most recent is *The Five "Confucian" Classics*.

PETER STEARNS, Professor of History and Provost at George Mason University, is a prolific author in U.S., European, and world social and cultural history. His recent works include books on the struggle for self-control in modern America, on bodies and beauty in Western society, on gender in world history, and on patterns of change and continuity in world history. He is also editor of the *Journal of Social History* and of the six-volume *Encyclopedia of European Social History from 1350 to 2000*.

SHELDON H. WHITE is John Lindsley Professor of Psychology Emeritus at Harvard University. His research interests in children's learning, attention, and memory involved him in designing and evaluating programs such as Sesame Street, Head Start, Follow Through, and the Title I projects of the Elementary and Secondary Education Act. In recent years, he has chaired a series of committees for Head Start and has been chair of the Board on Children and Families of the National Research Council.

MICHA DE WINTER is Professor of Social Education in the Department of Child and Adolescent Studies at Utrecht University in the Netherlands. He has written widely on child health care, on the changing relationship between parents and health professionals, and on youth participation as a model of civic education. Recently he has been developing "peer research" as a new way to study the development of marginalized youth. Among his publications is *Children as Fellow Citizens: Participation and Commitment*.

MICHAEL ZUCKERMAN, Professor of History at the University of Pennsylvania, studies American character and popular culture. His first book, *Peaceable Kingdoms*, was an early community study. His collection of essays, *Almost Chosen People*, offers oblique biographies of such American icons as Thomas Jefferson, Ben Franklin, P. T. Barnum, Horatio Alger, and Dr. Spock.

Index